995

XINGU
The Indians, Their Myths

Edited by Kenneth S. Brecher
Institute of Social Anthropology
Oxford University

Translated by Susana Hertelendy Rudge

Drawings by Wacupiá

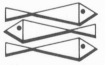

Orlando Villas Boas
Claudio Villas Boas

XINGU

THE INDIANS,
THEIR MYTHS

Farrar, Straus and Giroux
New York

Grateful acknowledgment is made
to the publishers of the Brazilian edition, Zahar Editores,
Rua México 31, Rio de Janeiro, Brazil

Assistance for the publication of this volume was
given by the Center for Inter-American Relations

CONTENTS

vi | CONTENTS

FOREWORD

In our modest opinion, the true defense of the Indian is to respect him and to guarantee his existence according to his own values. Until we, the "civilized" ones, create the proper conditions among ourselves for the future integration of the Indians, any attempt to integrate them is the same as introducing a plan for their destruction. *We* are not yet sufficiently prepared.

Orlando and Claudio Villas Boas

It is now almost thirty years since the Villas Boas brothers (Orlando, born 1916; Claudio, born 1918; Leonardo, born 1920, died 1961, the year that the Alto-Xingu became Brazil's first national Indian park) led the expedition known as "Brazil's March to the West," which was intended to open up the heart of the interior for colonization. They were overwhelmed by the beauty and cultural richness of the network of Xingu tribes which they discovered, and when the expedition disbanded they remained in the jungle to protect the Xinguanos from the land speculators, state senators, diamond prospectors, skin hunters, and rubber gatherers who had followed in their wake. The three brothers, who had posed as illiterates and joined a national military expedition looking for adventure, found themselves responsible for the survival of more than a dozen known or still-uncontacted tribes in an area larger than some of Brazil's smaller states. That the Xingu tribes continue to exist, in fact to thrive, is due largely to the extreme dedication, intelligence, cunning, and physical strength of these brothers.

Xingu: The Indians, Their Myths is drawn from the Villas Boas brothers' journals. These were begun on the day the expedition reached the Kuluene River—three years and three hundred miles of hand-cut path behind them. Little was known about the Xingu tribes, and the Indians knew even less about our civilization. Who were the three brothers who came slowly to visit their villages, share their fish, admire their skills in weaving and pottery, and learn their kinship structures?

The Indians observed that the brothers gave presents and medicines without asking anything in return; that they knew how to walk silently in the forest and how to protect themselves from the months of rain and the cold of the jungle night; that they did not fight among themselves. The Indians recognized their honesty and saw that their suspicious fascination with babies and children was not witchcraft or envy, only kindness. They were impressed that the brothers showed no fear in speaking with the great and revered chiefs of the Xingu tribes and that they respected the knowledge of the tribal shamans, even though they had medicines of their own to offer. "The brothers," the old Waurá chief told me, "appeared to be chiefs who for some unknown reason had left their own tribesmen, their lands, their women, and their way of life, to live among the tribes of the Xingu." How long they would stay, no one knew, but it became obvious to the perceptive Indian observers that the oldest brother (Orlando) seemed instinctively to know their secrets without even speaking their language; the youngest brother (Leonardo) seemed more at ease squatting with the men in the village plaza, or lying in a palm-fiber hammock in the house of the chief of the Kamaiurá, than sitting on the canvas stool or resting on the hard wooden bed of his own tribesmen; while the middle brother (Claudio) was unlike either of them. He carried books with him at all times and spent entire days staring at the mysterious paper. He spoke very quietly and seemed happiest when among the tribes of the north, who wore wooden disks in their lips and spoke Jê languages. All three of the brothers were remarkable in that they went alone among those unnamed tribes whom the rest of the Xinguanos dismissed as too wild, and too dangerous, to be considered men.

What it is that sustains two men in an inhospitable place (Claudio once did not leave the jungle for nine years) and allows them to endure more than two hundred malarial attacks, as well as extreme discomfort and loneliness, can only be a vision of a world that is made more acceptable by the presence of Indian tribes who are not themselves aware of the existence of another, dominant, society. When one attempts to analyze the motives of the Villas Boas brothers, one is met with a series of physical and ideological paradoxes: a fat man and a thin man, who have the faces of El Greco saints yet own one hundred firearms between them; spiritual men who have fought for more than two decades to keep missionaries of all religions away from the tribes; revolutionaries whose cause finds little support among the intelligentsia of Brazil and none at all among the masses; men who, twice nominated for the Nobel Peace Prize, treasure a nearly illegible thank-you letter from a backwoodsman's widow to whom they sent half a sack of rice; men who are opposed to the isolation and marginalization of minority groups but who argue that the integration of the Indian must wait until there is a place for him in the structure of Brazilian society: "What is more valuable to our country," they ask, "100,000 healthy, self-sufficient, dignified Indians, or another 100,000 illiterate, frustrated, marginalized peasants?"

Xingu: The Indians, Their Myths provides a privileged view into the history, ritual, myth, symbolism, material culture, and social structure of the tribes of the Alto-Xingu. The myths, to be fully appreciated, require that the reader redefine those categorical boundaries which separate mankind from animals, night from day, the natural from the supernatural. Once our own cultural categories are suspended, it is easier to understand how it is that in myth we find truths about ourselves and our own society, already half-suspected but now fully revealed from a unique perspective. From the myths of the Xingu, the Indians derive their material culture and the precedents and justification for their actions. They are the psychological basis, the common experience, the definitive kinship, and the higher authority of the Xingu culture. (When I told the Waurá tribesmen that my tribe had sent men to the moon, they were not particularly surprised and certainly not impressed.) All adult tribesmen, male and female, are more or less familiar with most of the myths of their tribe, but each tribe has a few individuals, often the shamans and the chiefs, who are especially skillful in the presentation and use of myth. The stimulus for the telling of a myth may be a seasonal or physiological change (birth and death, puberty and menstruation), a ritual event, or the need to acknowledge indirectly but publicly a source of friction or tribal tension. In the latter case the myths are told in such a way that the appropriate tribesmen are certain to recognize the validity of the myth for themselves.

When I left the Xingu after nearly two years of anthropological field work among the Waurá tribesmen on the Batoví River, I was accompanied by a man called Tawapuh, a son-in-law of the Waurá chief. He was suffering from a hernia. The Waurá's knowledge of curing is extensive and effective, but does not extend to surgery. Several months prior to leaving the Xingu, I had confided to Tawapuh that my tribe knew the cure for his ailment, so when I began my journey away from the Waurá village to the Villas Boas outpost, Tawapuh accompanied me in search of his cure.

With the help of Orlando Villas Boas, Tawapuh and I were squeezed onto the Brazilian Air Force cargo plane which, in principle, arrives each week with food, gasoline, and mail. The geographical isolation of the Xingu tribes is so extreme, and the country so vast, that this ancient airplane is virtually the only transport to the outside world. Wearing clothes for the first time, Tawapuh began his journey away from the six elliptical thatched houses which until that moment had comprised his world.

During the plane ride I became intensely worried about the psychological effect that our society might have on my companion. I knew the shock would be great, one to be assiduously avoided had Tawapuh not been badly in need of an operation. I feared that the plastic richness and visual abundance of our culture would appeal to him and produce a feeling of discontent and an alienation from the ways of the Waurá. In my months in the village I had carefully avoided offering much information about my own tribe, and the Waurá had eventually concluded that I was the son of a great chief who had been sent to them to learn how to make the clay pottery which they alone, of all the Xingu tribes, are able to produce. I decided that, since I would be the only one who could speak Tawapuh's language, I must always be at his side.

Just before our descent to the enormous São Paulo airport, Tawapuh asked me how many houses there were in the village below, and held up one hand, and then the other, to suggest the number of houses in the village plaza. I pointed to the endless rows of skyscrapers now in view, but just as when I had first shown the Waurá photographs of themselves I found them unable to conceive of men as tiny, flat, black-and-white designs reproduced on an unfamiliar surface (paper), so Tawapuh found it impossible to grasp the spatial boundaries of the city revealed below us.

The first few hours in São Paulo, one of the world's fastest-growing and most polluted cities, were spent in silence. As we sped by taxi to the house in which we would be staying before he went into the hospital, Tawapuh held my hand and watched everything and everyone with great concentration and interest. None of his dignity was lost as he strained to catch a familiar word in the language being spoken around him. Sleeping on a bed instead of the traditional Xingu hammock, using a flush toilet instead of the jungle behind the chief's house, drinking coffee instead of manioc soup were all novelties, but failed to stimulate a reaction. I remained with him and waited until he was ready to discuss my world.

After almost a week Tawapuh pulled my face close to his own and, looking sadly into my eyes, very quietly said: "How could you return to this world after seeing how we live? How can you breathe this foul air or sleep with these terrible noises [the traffic]? How can you eat this food made to. have tastes which are not its own? Why would you want to have intercourse with these women who seem afraid to be women and hide themselves and cover their eyes? And who are these men with guns who stand in the paths of the village [the ever-present Brazilian military police]?"

"They are the men of the chief," I replied, and without a moment's hesitation Tawapuh continued:

"Well, then, your chief is not a real chief or he would not need men with guns to guard his village. How can you return to this after having been with us?"

"Will you tell the tribe what you have seen?" I asked Tawapuh.

"No," he said, "they would not believe me, and they would be unhappy to think of you having to live here. The chief is an old man and it is better that he doesn't know. Perhaps one day I will tell my son about your tribe. Perhaps not."

Tawapuh's intuitive ability to perceive the problematic nature of our society is not unique to him. It is but one example of the Indian as an astute observer of the world around him—be it familiar or unfamiliar. The myths presented in this book show that same ability to recognize the telling nuances and common reality of our human, animal, and spiritual relationships. Unlike Tawapuh, the Villas Boas brothers are not reluctant to repeat what they have seen and heard in the other world. The significance and beauty of the culture revealed in their observations and the myths make Tawapuh's depressing comment seem even more profound.

The drawings which illustrate this book were done by a Waurá tribesman called Wacupiá, who, using pen and paper for the first time, produced a fascinating record of the animals, spirits, and material culture of the Alto-Xingu. The drawings were done over a period of several months and in secret, as Wacupiá feared that they might be interpreted as witchcraft by the rest of the tribe. The Xingu tribes paint their bodies and certain material objects in highly symbolic geometrical patterns, but they would have no interest in or occasion for drawing as a means of record or pleasure. The Waurá do frequently resort to witchcraft, and I believe that Wacupiá was very interested to see if he could, like the Sun in the Xingu myth ("Iamulumulu: The Formation of the Rivers"), employ drawing as a means of reviving the dead or gaining control over the spirit of the object in question.

Kenneth S. Brecher
Oxford
June 1973

Observations

In this work we have employed the word "*Xinguano*" when we were exclusively concerned with the ten tribal groups of the Upper Xingu. And, likewise, we have written "Alto-Xingu" when our intention was to refer strictly to the region crossed by the Kuluene, the Ronuro, the Batoví, and the Kurizêvo Rivers.

Most of the Indian words and expressions appearing in the text are in Kamaiurá, but they correspond in terminology with any of the other languages of the area.

And finally, to simplify and abbreviate, we have often used the expressions "Karib" and "Aruak," rather than enumerating, one by one, the groups coming out of these two linguistic branches.

O.V.B.

C.V.B.

Editor's Note

The Indian and Portuguese words appearing in the text will be found in the Glossary at the end of the book. In the Introduction and in Part One, brief descriptions of some species have been given in brackets and footnotes to aid the reader, while in the myths footnotes have been omitted and very brief definitions given in brackets, in the hope of allowing the reader to appreciate the myths uninterrupted.

K.S.B.

XINGU
The Indians, Their Myths

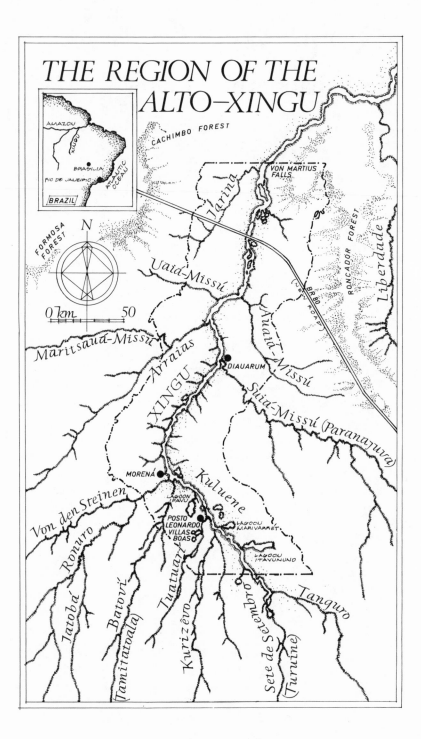

THE REGION OF THE ALTO–XINGU

INTRODUCTION

The Xingu National Park is a federal reservation created by the Brazilian government in 1961 and enlarged in 1968 to its present area of approximately thirty thousand square kilometers, or about eleven thousand five hundred square miles. The park is situated in the north of the state of Mato Grosso, in a zone of floral transition between the Planalto Central and the Amazon. This entirely flat region, where tall-treed forests predominate, interspersed with *cerrados*,[1] is traversed by the rivers that make up the Xingu and by its first tributaries from right and left. The larger streams forming the Xingu are the Kuluene, the Ronuro, and the Batoví. Tributaries are the Suiá-Missú, the Maritsauá-Missú, the Uaiá-Missú, the Auaiá-Missú, and the Jarina Rivers.

In creating the Xingu National Park, the Brazilian government had two important goals: to build a natural reservation where fauna and flora would be safeguarded for the distant future of the country, as evidence of Brazil at the time of its discovery; and, even more important, to extend protection immediately to the indigenous tribes of the region, offering them assistance and defending them from premature and harmful contact with the occupying fronts of the national society.

The region of the Alto-Xingu has an approximate area of two hundred thousand square kilometers, or about seventy-seven thousand square miles, extending between the Tenth and Fourteenth Parallels. It is traversed in the south by the streams that make up the Xingu River and in the north by that river and its tributaries, the Suiá-Missú and the Maritsauá-Missú. In its physical-phytogeographic configuration, the region is a large plain almost entirely Amazonian in appearance.

The forests covering the region are not as lush as the Hylean,[2] since the trees are smaller in size, but they correspond to the general Amazonian type in density, in the perennial dark-green color, and, above all, in the texture of the forest that extends indefinitely in all directions.

[1] Sections of land scattered with small trees and shrubs; bush country or scrublands.
[2] Denomination given by Humboldt to the great botanic region occupying the major part of the Amazon and bordering regions.

Open fields rarely occur along the middle and lower courses of the rivers in the south; when they are not simple clearings, they are never more than alluvial flats, sometimes fairly large but always limited by the dominating high forests.

Toward the south, southeast, and southwest the plain gradually loses these characteristics and new topographic formations appear, including cerrados and fields, and the land becomes a transitional zone—mainly floral—between the Amazon and the Planalto Central.

The Kuluene, the Ronuro, and the Batoví Rivers, which flow in the southern half of the plain, have their source in numerous ridges and tablelands of the midwestern portion of the Planalto Central. From all directions and corners of the immense barren region an infinite number of rivulets flow and join waters along the way, their courses diverting to various valleys where rivers begin to form and swell; after running for a distance across fields, these enter the forest and finally converge at a point in the north and form the Xingu River.

In the southern part of the Alto-Xingu, a series of beautiful lagoons, relatively large in size, are situated in the lower courses of the streams comprising the Xingu. These lagoons, pluvial in origin, are fed by perennial outlets, flowing out of the nearby large groves of *buriti* palms that connect with the Xingu during floods by means of *igarapés*.[3] They abound in fish and their water is in most cases clean and potable. Surrounded by fields and arable land, they are preferred by some tribes of the region as the site for their villages.

The Alto-Xingu is rich in animal life and has almost all the species present in the Amazon, so that its little-explored forests and lagoons are a veritable paradise of fauna.

The region is densely inhabited—each species is represented in proportion to its characteristic occurrence—by *onças*,[4] tapirs, *porcos-do-mato* [wild pigs], deer, capybaras, otters, *ariranhas* [giant otters], *graxains* [wild dogs], tayras, monkeys, pacas, agoutis, coatis, sloths, coendous [prehensile-tailed porcupines], tamanduas [anteaters], to mention the most important of the hairy animals; the feathered ones are curassows and their relatives the *jacubins* and *mutums,* macaws, *jacamins, jaós*,[5] ducks, *marrecãos* [geese or ducks], jabiru storks, herons, *mangu-*

---

[3] Rivulet between narrow-set banks.

[4] Any of various wildcats, pumas, cougars, or, as translated in the myths, jaguars.

[5] A kind of tinamou; any of a number of South and Central American birds resembling the partridge and quail but belonging to the ostrich group.

Agouti

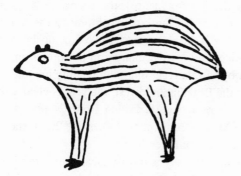

Paca

Tamandua

aris [American storks], *colhereiros* [roseate spoonbills], *socós* [herons], *biguás* [cormorants], white-faced glossy ibises, *anhumas* [horned screamers], eagles, and an incalculable number of smaller birds.

In the rivers, lakes, and lagoons the variety of fish is also great; outstanding for their quality and quantity are the *tucunaré,* the *pacu* [snapper], the *piau,* the *jaraguí,* the *curimatá,* the *matrinxã,* the *trairão,* the piranha, the *corvina,* the *surubi,* the *barbado,* the *piratinga,* the *jaú* [catfish], the *pirarara,* the *poraquê* [electric eel], and many others, smaller in size.

Among the reptiles, the commonest in the region are the *jacaretinga* [alligator or cayman], the *lagarto* [lizard], the *cágado-cabeça-torta* [a land tortoise], the *jabuti* [another land tortoise]; among the snakes, the *sucuri* [anaconda], the *jibóia* [boa], the rattlesnake, the bushmaster, the fer-de-lance, the *jararaca,* and a great many non-poisonous snakes.

The Alto-Xingu enjoys a relatively mild and healthy climate, and as in the other regions of the Brazilian midwest, the year is clearly divided into two seasons only: a rainy season lasting from October to April, and a dry season from May to September. In central Brazil the former is called winter and the latter summer.

Until the end of August, the sky is mostly clear, but often it will be blurred with mist and scatterings of smoke, which come mainly from the annual burning of the fields but also from great fires that break out every year and spread south through the barren border zones.

In September the first clouds appear in great white tufts (cumulus) and, propelled by currents high up, they generally move from north to south. The temperature rises considerably during windless hours, and the nebulosity or *bruma seca* [dry mist], as it is commonly known, clings to the ground, blurring and suffocating everything. From the middle of the month on, the clouds, once white, gradually darken; that is, change from cumulus to cumulo-nimbus. These heavy clouds are always accompanied by great heat, oppressive mugginess, and occasional thunder. Swarms of *piuns* and *borrachudos* [varieties of buffalo gnat], agitated by the weather conditions, become doubly aggressive, especially in open places such as the banks of rivers or lakes.

Almost every year, the second half of September is the same, and in spite of the threatening skies, there are usually no important rains.

Tesoura, a bird related to
the flycatcher and kingbird

Jacamin

Surucuá, a smaller bird

Urutau, a nocturnal bird
related to the bacurau

However, in the beginning of October, sometimes after strong winds the atmosphere releases its burden of moisture, heat, and electricity in a violent cloudburst. With these first rains of the season, generally preceded by great discharges of lightning, weather conditions improve markedly. The bruma seca disappears, the temperature descends, the pressure diminishes, and the days become clear and light. But this relief never lasts long. In a few days the weather turns ugly again, with even greater heat and pressure, until showers alleviate the oppressive atmosphere. After the October cloudbursts, which are accompanied by violent magnetic storms, it rains with increasing frequency throughout the month of November. The rivers rise, covering their shores and overtaking their lower banks.

At the end of December and the beginning of January, the increasing pace of "winter" is interrupted by a brief pause in the rains, which sometimes results in an appreciable lowering of the water level. Once this short drought is over, the sky becomes overcast again and real "winter" begins. For weeks on end, the sky remains covered with thick layers of cloud, rays of sunlight breaking through only briefly. And with brief respites of a day or so, the rains, with no wind or thunder, fall gently and steadily.

Thus the months of February and March pass; this is the great flood period. The rivers overflow, invading the woods on both banks. Certain species of fish leave the rivers in schools, heading for the flooded woods to eat fallen fruit. And in their slender bark canoes, the Indians glide stealthily between the trees with their arrows and wooden spears, making plentiful catches of their favorite fish.

In April the rains taper off and the waters recede. From the second half of this month on, the showers are practically over, the shores reappear, and the rivers recede to their original beds. The clouds turn white and vaporous and are propelled by cold gusts of wind coming from the south and the southeast. It is the beginning of "summer."

At this time of the year, it is common to see birds flying across the skies, beautiful formations of jabiru storks, flocks of white herons, and pairs of colhereiros in search of lagoons and *igapós*.[6]

As the waters recede from the shores, gulls, *bacuraus de coleira*

---

[6] Periodically inundated parts of riverine woodland; swampland.

branca,[7] ducks, and marrecãos fly in. The *tracajás* [fresh-water turtles] and small alligators, who at flood time had clung to floating tree trunks, search for sandy shores to enjoy the heat of the sun.

The smaller birds are the ones most excited by the arrival of "summer." As soon as the rains stop completely (at the end of April), real festivity begins in the bird kingdom. Enormous flocks of *araçaris* [toucans], *maracanãs* [macaws], various sorts of parrots including *tirivas, curicas,* and *tuins* [parakeets] of various kinds fly across the skies in every direction, in a real frenzy of sounds and movement. They alight on a tree, taking it over from all sides, and a second later, without noticeable provocation, they fly off in a wild racket. The *tucanos reais,* a variety of toucan with an enormous black-and-yellow beak, alight on the branches of the tallest trees and remain there, whistling and making half-turns in a single hop.

In May "summer" is at its hottest. The days are short, transparent, and agitated by fresh gusts of wind coming from the south. The nights are long and almost cold.

When the waters recede, the monkeys, curassows, *jacus* [guans], jaós, and other feathered and hairy animals, which had withdrawn into the woods during the floods, reappear and take over the river banks. In the cold early mornings of June, July, and August, one constantly hears the squawks of the curassows, the plaintive cries of the jacamins, the shrieks and whistles of monkeys, and, once in a while, the roar of a jaguar as it wanders along the shores.

September is the month when the tracajás lay their eggs. At night they go to the shores, where they dig their nests and lay their eggs without much hope of hatching them, not because they will rot but because of the many who greedily claim them. During that period of the year, the graxains, the eagles, and, most of all, the *urubus* [vultures] spend their days turning the sand over in search of brood.

It is also during this period of drought (August and September) that the Indians of the area carry out their great fishing expeditions with *timbó,* a poisonous liana that soaks in the motionless waters and drugs the fish. They choose this season for this method of fishing because of the low water level, which easily allows them to isolate small bays and

---

[7] Bacurau is the common name of the birds of the family Caprimulgidae. The bacurau de coleira branca is the white-collared bacurau.

igarapés from the rivers and lagoons, using weirs made of sticks, branches, and grass. All kinds of fish stream into them.

From mid-September on, as we have noted above, "summer" starts to give way to "winter," which makes its appearance with bruma seca, sullen clouds, and distant thunder.

Our experience has shown that the Alto-Xingu remains to this date an extraordinary field for anthropological research in general, not just because it still retains, without major alterations, all the characteristics that distinguished it at the time of its discovery but also because the blend of its cultures and intertribal relations presents aspects not yet properly studied.

Part One
THE INDIANS

Xingu digging sticks, used mainly in the planting and harvesting of manioc

I

THE INHABITANTS IN 1946
AND THOSE OF TODAY

In 1946, the year we arrived at the headwaters of the Xingu, the native inhabitants were, in their various practices and habits, strictly the same as those found in 1887 by the German ethnologist Karl von den Steinen on his ethnographic expedition. The distribution of the villages in the region was identical; the communication and the relations among them the same; the natives still displayed the same peaceful nature, the same hospitality and curiosity that is transformed on contact with strangers into the naïve and friendly attitudes that so impressed the German explorer and inspired him to make a highly detailed and expressive record of them.

Nothing appeared to have changed. The few metal instruments introduced before this time in the area, replacing primitive stone axes and greatly facilitating the Indians' production, in general did not, as we were able to confirm, have repercussions on the original system of organization and association of the elements constituting the group, so that the latter remains practically unaltered to date.

The only verifiable change that took place in the region between 1887 and our times was the great reduction in population to almost half the original number of inhabitants; if, as seems certain, the population estimate of von den Steinen is approximately correct. We attribute this significant decrease in the indigenous population of the Alto-Xingu to the first violent outbreaks of influenza, dysentery, and other infectious diseases that invaded the region about thirty years ago, when groups of Indians inhabiting the lower Kurizêvo began to travel upstream and made contact with civilized clusters along the Upper Paranatinga, at Posto Simões Lopes, and other places.

On some of these trips, the goal of which was to acquire tools, axes, and large knives, the Indians were contaminated by certain diseases that worsened on the way back to their villages. They were completely defenseless against these diseases, and practically all of them died. The few who managed to get back to their villages were carriers, and the devastation spread to an even larger number of defenseless people. The Indians relate that on one of these occasions—they are unable to give the exact date—the death rate was so high that entire "houses" disappeared between Meináco and Trumái.

Today fourteen tribes, divided into two concentrations, occupy the area of the park. The northern half of the reservation is inhabited by the Suiá, Txukarramãe, Caiabí, and Juruna Indians. The first two tribes are classified among the Jê, and the Caiabí among the Tupi. The last, the Juruna, are of uncertain affiliation and may belong to an isolated "Tupinized" linguistic family, together with their relatives from downstream, the Xipáia Indians, now extinct.

In the southern part of the park live the ten tribes of the Alto-Xingu, numbering approximately eight hundred, a figure that does not include the Txikão, Agavotoqueng, Suiá, Juruna, Auaicü, and Txukarramãe groups, of which we shall speak in other chapters; rather, it refers to the total population of culturally bound tribes on friendly terms with each other, who today are scattered throughout the region of the rivers forming the Xingu. Here in the Alto-Xingu three of the four main linguistic families of Brazil—Tupi, Karib, Aruak, and Jê—are represented among nine of these tribes. They are the Kamaiurá and Auetí (Tupi); the Kuikúru, Kalapalo, Matipú, and Nafuquá (Karib); the Waurá, Meináco, and Iaualapití (Aruak). The tenth tribe, the Trumái, belongs to an isolated linguistic family. The ten tribes live in separate villages named after them.

Not long ago the Txikão Indians (supposedly Karib), whose cultural and physical characteristics isolate them from the other tribes, were brought into the Upper Xingu.

Though they speak different languages, these ten tribes of the Upper Xingu, except for the Txikão, have merged to such an extent, through an intense secular exchange, that today they display a great cultural uniformity, especially in their magic practices and mythico-religious traditions.

The notes we are presenting in this book, taken and gathered over a long period, are about the many aspects of the life of this culturally

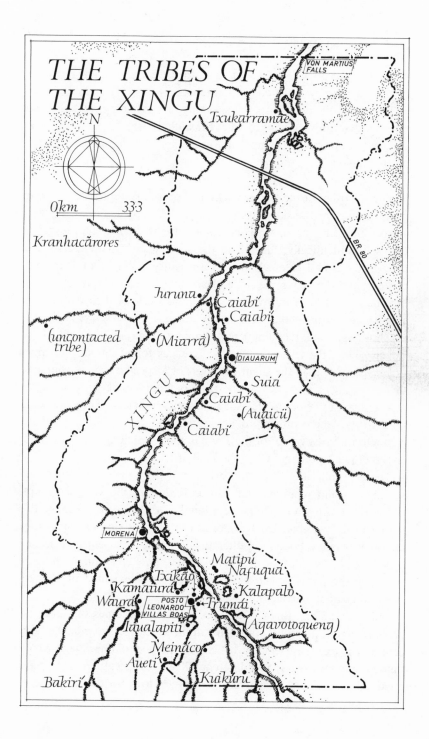

THE TRIBES OF
THE XINGU

N

0 km   33·3

VON MARTIUS FALLS

Txukarramãe

Kranhacãrores

Juruna

Caiabí
Caiabí

(uncontacted tribe)

(Miarrã)

DIAUARUM

Suiá

Caiabí

(Auaicü)

Caiabí

XINGU

MORENA

Matipú
Nafuquá

Txikão

Kamaiurá

Kalapalo

Waurá

POSTO
LEONARDO
VILLAS BOAS

Trumái

Iaualapiti

(Agavotoqueng)

Meináco

Aueti

Bakirí

Kuikúru

BR 80

merged group of Alto-Xingu Indians. In it we also present thirty-one myths narrated by the Indians themselves.

This book is not, properly speaking, an ethnological study but rather a descriptive record of what the authors were able to hear, see, and grasp during more than twenty-five years of living with the Indians of the region.

The ten tribes of the Upper Xingu live so intimately bound that they might almost be considered one "nation," except that most of them speak different languages. Their habits are the same; they organize themselves identically; they share the same beliefs and superstitions; their festivals and ceremonial rites are entirely similar in shape and content; and they have the same ideas about practically all aspects of life and the world. The rhythm, nature, and cycle of their activities in general are virtually the same in all villages. There is even a strong psychological and temperamental similarity among some members. Taken singly, the few behavioral differences found among the tribes are never more than the slight emphasis of a specific trait of character or temperament revealed by one tribe or another, never to a degree deep enough to be described as truly distinct in nature. Thus, we could refer to the "mercantilism" of the Auetí, the "premeditation" of the Kamaiurá, the "shyness" of the Trumái, the "simplicity" of the Waurá, or the crude "spontaneity" of the Kuikúru.

These peculiarities, however, are annulled by the numerous correspondences and relations that join and equalize the various groups, giving them as a whole the air of a family. All kinds of ties make this homogeneity possible. In their religious activities, for example, they are so intimately bound together that the participation of a second tribe is obligatory in some of the most important ceremonies of a single tribe. On the purely social plane, relations are cemented by the frequent intertribal marriages.

This interchange, this tightening of relations, becomes still more expressive and intentional through "apprenticeship," a practice very common among these Indians, by which a member of one village spends time (sometimes years) in a different village. "Apprentices" are almost invariably male, and their main objective is to learn the language of the friendly tribe.

As we shall see, another important factor in the establishment of intertribal bonds is commercial relations.

In times of war, the Xinguano villages on friendly terms with each other unite against hostile neighbors. The tribes called upon for this kind of assistance are rewarded, but as we can verify, the ambition for reward is never stronger than the spontaneous desire to help, a desire born naturally out of the instinctive need for a common defense.

It is evident from the above that the friendly tribes of the Alto-Xingu form a legitimate "society of nations," relatively more compatible than they had been in the past. That is because at the present, in the Xinguano society there is no preponderance of the stronger, no controlling superalliances, no subjection of the weaker. Since the human potential and productive capacity of each group are not taken into account, a perfect balance and respect prevail among its co-participants. They all live under a regime of mutual and beneficial dependency.

II
TRACES OF A REMOTE OCCUPATION

It is impossible to fix a date or period in the past when these Indians first entered the region of the Alto-Xingu, but it seems that this occurred a very long time ago. It is also hard to determine with absolute certainty which, among the groups existing today, is the oldest in the region. None of these groups—with the exception of the Trumái, who speak of the migratory movement that brought them here—refers with clarity to that point. And as a matter of fact, even the Trumái, who are perhaps the newest Xinguanos, have an extensive past in the Alto-Xingu, a conclusion that may be drawn from their narrative of the immigration, which has already taken the form of a myth.

The great areas surrounding the villages, either devastated or where the original vegetation has undergone transformations, are evidence of the long-established presence of the Indians in these places. How many years did they spend toiling with their stone tools to transform expanses of the forest into vast *mangabeira*[1] and *pequi*[2] orchards, and other, still larger areas into cerrados exhausted by successive cultivation?

On the other hand, in abandoned former villages there are places where the vegetation renewed itself so completely that it cannot be distinguished from the virgin forest.

Until recently, no archaeological research has been carried out in the Alto-Xingu. Only after such a study will it be possible to know more about some interesting signs found in the region that would seem to indicate an extremely old human occupation.

---

[1] Tree yielding latex, grown by the Indians for its sweet, apricot-shaped fruit.
[2] Tree yielding a large green fruit, which replaces manioc as the staple in the first months of the rainy season.

Mainly these traces consist of ditches present in almost all former and present village sites, having the following average dimensions: depth, 2.5 m.; width, 3 to 4 m.; length, 1,000 m. At the junction of the Kuluene and the Ronuro, there is a ditch of much larger dimensions. These earthworks must have been much deeper at one time, considering the natural process of accumulation over an indeterminate period of time. In plan the ditches take the shape of an arc running from a spot in the interior of the forest to the nearest waters. Nearby there are signs of excavations in the shape of circles 10 to 15 m. in diameter.

What could have been the purpose of these earthworks? The idea that first comes to mind on seeing them is that they were trenches dug for the protection of former villages. But that is positively not the case, since the ditches never completely enclose an area, nor do they evince any concern with strategic factors. It is more likely that they were dug to serve as shelter from weather during a long cold spell or from icy currents coming from the south, though for this we would have to admit the great antiquity of man in the region.

The creators of these earthworks, as we will show with corroborative data, were certainly not the "grandparents" of today's Indians, although the latter have occupied the region for a very long time. One has the impression of standing before the remains of something very distant in time, fading out in a millennial horizon. Other occupants of the region, today extinct, or perhaps transformed through cultural amalgamation with later immigrants, must have been responsible for the ditches.

This hypothesis is neither impossible nor improbable, once it is accepted that the presence of man in this part of the continent goes back thousands of years. Surely we cannot pretend that the race of men who left traces in Lagoa Santa[3] lived exclusively in that restricted area, inside caves, and that they became extinct there.

If the presence of humans in our territory eight to ten thousand years ago is a recorded fact, why, we may inquire, would it be impossible for the region of the Xingu to have been occupied long before it is imagined to have been? And in such remote times, could there not have

---

[3] Archaeological site in the state of Minas Gerais, which shows the presence of man in Brazil from 8000 B.C.

been, as we have supposed, a temporary and accentuated climatic alteration that would have made these shelter-ditches necessary?

In the section of myths there is one ["Viti-Vití," pp. 163–165] referring to the origin of these ditches. Myths always give a magical explanation of phenomena, but in this one there is a curious detail that confirms our idea. This coincidence leads us to imagine that no radical supplanting of population took place in the area but rather that there was a gradual taking over of one by another, with transmissions of traits and traditions. Consequently, although different peoples and cultures succeeded each other in the region, a real thread of Ariadne holds them together throughout time, so that the most ancient events may be transmitted to us today in mythical language.

III
EARLY HISTORY

The actual remote past of the Xinguanos, their historical past, is characterized by a turbulence created by the successive invasions of warring hordes and by inner clashes between some groups in phases of accommodation.

Judging from the innumerable stories we have heard, among the present Xinguanos the Indians with the strongest ties to this very ancient past of strife were the Auetí, the Kamaiurá, and, slightly later, the Trumái.

The early history of the Alto-Xingu may be divided into two periods: one very remote and another more recent. The first would take in the cycle of invasions by powerful tribes from the west that, with the exception of the Auetí and Bakirí, are almost completely extinct today. The second comprises the phase of accommodation of groups coming from the outside. The events that took place at this stage in the Alto-Xingu already clearly outline the region's present cultural features. The Indians of that period are the same as those of today, plus some others who disappeared in massacres, epidemics, or by assimilation.

The Auára, the Anumaniá, the Bakirí, the Auetí, and the Tonorí Indians were the first invaders of the region, unleashing their attacks on every tribe without making any distinctions. It is odd that the Bakirí and Auetí figure among these strangers to the Alto-Xingu, especially the latter, who are today so deeply integrated in the cultural area of the headwaters of the Xingu.

The route of access into the region used by these early invaders was, except in the case of the Tonorí, the Kurizêvo River, by which they reached the Kuluene, where the density of the population was greater. The majority of the Karib and Aruak groups were located there.

In these times, the Kamaiurá lived in the north, probably around the mouth of the Paranajuva River, or the Suiá-Missú, as it is called on maps.

After many attacks, the Bakirí, Auetí, and Anumaniá established themselves in the region. The Bakirí settled midway along the Kurizêvo and the Batoví Rivers, occupying them until some dozen years ago, when they returned to their ancient domain along the upper Paranatinga. The Anumaniá and the Auetí established roots along the Kurizêvo, near the junction of this river with the Kuluene. Some time later, the Anumaniá broke away from their allies, the Auetí, and occupied the Itavununo lagoon, located near the mouth of the Kurizêvo River, on the right bank of the Kuluene. Later they were almost completely wiped out by the Trumái.

After vague references to the Bakirí and to the Anumaniá, who seemingly waged wars against them, the Kamaiurá narrate their history more clearly, saying that in former days they lived at the source of the Paranajuva River, at a place which to this date carries the name Uavitsá. From there, they went up the Xingu River in stages, establishing villages along the way. The largest of these villages during this migratory phase was named Curuquiçá and was located about 40 kilometers, or 25 miles, below the junction of the rivers forming the Xingu.

After a long period of calm, Curuquiçá was menaced by a powerful nation called Tonorí, who came from the vicinity of the Ronuro River. Hoping to free themselves from these attacks, the Kamaiurá tried to hide in the woods, transferring their dwellings to the source of a stream far from the river bank. This new village was named Pitãhuatap, and in it they lived peacefully for many years, until the Tonorí found them again. For some time the Kamaiurá resisted the Tonorí's ferocious attacks, but finally they were forced to accept the invitation of the Waurá to move to the region they occupied, on the banks of the Ipavu lagoon above the junction of the Ronuro and Kuluene Rivers. Later, the Waurá moved to the vicinity of the Batoví River, and the Kamaiurá have remained to this date beside the Ipavu lagoon.

These last displacements probably occurred more than 150 years ago.

As we shall see later from the stories of the Indians, it is clear that in the past the Auetí, Kamaiurá, and Trumái moved about, joining forces at the headwaters of the Xingu, where they began to relate to each other and merge culturally with the Karib and Aruak tribes. The latter probably had occupied the region since time immemorial, because they never refer to former migrations, except for minor displacements within the area they occupy today.

As to the movements carried out by today's Indians to occupy the Alto-Xingu, the clearest and most complete history known to us is that of the Trumái.

Among the ten extant allied tribes, the Trumái are without a doubt the last to arrive in the region. They relate that their forefathers lived north of their present home on the banks of a vast lake that they call Pararrú. As a result of violent attacks unleashed on them by a nation called Aussumadí, who invaded their lands, the Trumái decided to move. Under the leadership of two great chieftains, Auaturí and Jaquanarí, they headed for "where the sun sets." After trekking through extensive forests, they arrived at the banks of a river that they said was the Kuluene (the Xingu, in our nomenclature).

Along the way, on account of an incident that arose over the unequal division of the meat of a rhea they had caught, Jaquanarí rebelled and went back to his villages, with all of the large group who had followed him.

Auaturí continued the journey up the river in a large number of canoes. After many days of traveling, he stopped and made a village, but shortly he was forced to abandon the place because it was infested with mosquitoes. Heading up the river, the Trumái finally set up their village on the right bank of the Kuluene, just above its junction with the Ronuro and the Batoví.

The place was named Anariá, and there the tribe greatly increased in numbers. A series of new villages appeared. The first village to break away from Anariá was Urucutú, followed by Vanivaní, Jacaré, Kranhãnhã, and Iupép. They all coexisted and were, according to the stories about them, heavily populated. They were founded along the right bank of the Kuluene, and until recently the Trumái continued to occupy that same bank of the river. The Trumái are a small tribe now, their population not exceeding thirty, but in the past they were very numerous and dominated the lands in the vicinity of the headwaters of the Xingu.

Not so long ago, we heard from an old Trumái woman another version—surely the closest to the truth—of the early migrations of her people. According to her, the Trumái did not come from the lower Xingu but from the headwaters of a left-bank tributary of the Kuluene. As for the cause of the displacement and other details (such as the incident that motivated the tribe's division), her version agrees with the first one.

The composite story seems accurate because of the series of coincidences and curious consonances between the two versions. In both stories, an allusion is made to a rhea, a bird that seems not to exist in the forests of the lower Xingu. The living conditions of the earlier Trumái, who did not cultivate manioc and corn, are probably more plausibly connected with the arid tablelands of the south, rather than with the northern regions dominated by the more advanced cultures of the Aruak, Tupi, and others.

This means that it is probable that the Trumái came not from the north but from the east or southeast of the Alto-Xingu; that is, from the area dominated today by the Xavante Indians.

Everything points to and reinforces this hypothesis, principally the access route to the region, which, according to traditional stories of the Kuikúru Indians, was the Tanguro River, which branches off from the Rio das Mortes and leads into the Kuluene.

The Kuikúru, with curious details, tell of the sudden appearance of the Trumái on the shores of the Kuluene and of the first contacts between the two tribes. The Kuikúru are said to have welcomed the invaders, offering them quantities of food and receiving arrows, bows, and feather ornaments in exchange. They also report that the Trumái, to express their contentment with the pleasant reception they had been given, performed a dance they called the *tauarauanã,* which the Kuikúru had never seen before.

It is interesting to note that this dance resembles, in essence and partly in form, the great Aruanã ceremony of the Karajá Indians of the Araguaia River region. This coincidence becomes even more significant when taken together with the fact—unquestionable according to our evidence—that the Trumái introduced spear throwers[4] in the

---

[4] These spear throwers, once weapons, now have only a ceremonial function.

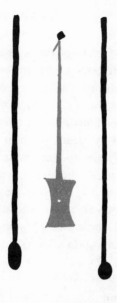

Spears and spear-thrower used in the Javarí festival

Alto-Xingu, where this important instrument is used, just as it is among the Karajá, in a great festival, entertaining and semi-religious in character.

If the Trumái, as we have just indicated, were actually the carriers of these traits, which clearly corroborate connections between the Araguaia and the Xingu regions, it would follow logically that, in their migratory movement, the Trumái must have come from some place between the two rivers, where they came into contact with the great eastern nation of the Karajá. This assumption of former relations between the two tribes is particularly reinforced by the curious similarity between the "Rãrã-resá" myth of the Karajá and the "Urxsku diquê" myth of the Trumái, both of which concern the origin of day. In both, a person pretends to be dead; first, the flies come; then, the *urubu-rei* [king vulture], who is trapped and called upon to bring the headdress made of red macaw feathers; he brings several headdresses before the correct one, with which comes the light of day. There is also some similarity of pronunciation between the words "Tehuú" (Karajá) and "Aterlá" (Trumái), both meaning Sun.

The Trumái relate that their villages used to be visited by a nation far to the east, who came to take part in the Javarí festival with them. Except for the Meináco tribe, all of the Xinguano Indians participate in this festival, which is entertaining and semi-religious in character.

In its general lines, the Javarí consists of a series of beautiful choral songs and dances that last for several days and end, when the guest tribe arrives, in a scene of individual skirmishes, using arrows with beeswax or resin tips shot by means of spear throwers. At the feast, particularly on the last day, the Indians paint their bodies with urucu and charcoal powder, and adorn themselves with handsome and varied feather ornaments, belts and arm bands made of jaguar leather. Using *tabatinga* [a chalklike powder], ashes, and crushed charcoal over a pequi oil base, the festival's host paints his body, imitating the design and colors of the feathers of a certain kind of eagle.

The mysterious tribe that brought them the Javarí in all its pomp is called Panhetá by the Trumái. According to them, the Panhetá were peaceful and very numerous. The purpose of their frequent visits was simply to perform this ceremony.

The fact that in the Alto-Xingu only the Trumái knew about the Panhetá Indians leads us to conclude that the contact between them must have taken place in another area, from which the Trumái were later displaced. It is not unlikely that the Indians who expelled the Trumái from their former domains east of the Alto-Xingu were the Xavante. The name given by the Trumái to their former aggressors, Assumadí, has a certain phonetic affinity to the Xavante tongue. The Xavante are likely to have come to the region of the Rio das Mortes[5] and the Roncador Mountains approximately a century and a half ago, probably at the same time as the Trumái immigration.

It has been mentioned earlier that the Trumái claim that their ancestors were not acquainted with manioc, corn, and most of the other plants they now cultivate, and that they lived exclusively on game, fish, fruits, and wild roots. Indian narratives make frequent reference to a past that lacked the habits, resources, and means of subsistence of today and for a number of reasons these stories seem to hold more

---

[5] The Xavante Indians (cannibals) killed all who tried to cross the river, before the Villas Boas brothers succeeded in passing over it; for this reason it is called the River of the Dead.

than a grain of truth. For aspects of the past conditions of the Trumái, we find confirmation in their language, namely in the persistence of names for things that have ceased to exist, and in the presence of words from other Xinguano languages for things that were new to them.

According to the Trumái, in early times their vegetable nutrition was based on the *patacat, cumanaú,* and *terreté* fruits, and the *tassit* root. The first is a round bean, very abundant in the region. The cumanaú is the fruit from the *mucanā* liana. The terreté is the fruit of the *jatobazeiro.*[6] The tassit, a water root shaped something like an onion, was their main vegetable food, being the tastiest and most abundant of all. After cooking, the tassit has a sweetish taste similar to that of the *inhame* [yam].

The Trumái supplemented their diet with almost all existing varieties of game. Today they are the only Indians of the area who eat the meat of hairy animals, except for the monkey.

In order to cook, they manufactured two types of pots: a large one, the *urumach,* and a smaller one, the *anitsucú,* a vessel later replaced by others made by the Waurá.

The Trumái males wore their hair long and wrapped a string of vegetal fiber around their penis, in the manner of the Karajá. This adornment, called *apí,* encased their member and was sometimes continued upward, circling the neck, then returning to its point of departure.

Instead of the *tameóp,*[7] the women used something called *dessiní,* made of the inner bark of lianas and consisting of a wide strap circling the waist and passing between the legs. In those days, the Trumái were not acquainted with the hammock. They slept on straw mats, in the manner of the Karajá.

Although today their habits and customs are practically the same as those of the other Xinguanos, they still remain in some respects quite different. One of their particularities, and a very important one, is their non-participation in the large ceremonies of the *kuarup* or ritual funeral, an important religious festival for the other groups of the area.

---

[6] The *jatobá* tree, also called *jataí;* the courbaril tree (*Hymenea courbaril*).
[7] The vaginal ornament made of the white inner bark of the tameóp tree, and more commonly called the *uluri.*

IV
EXTINCT TRIBES

A side from the Indians of today, several other tribes once lived in the Alto-Xingu. Some have disappeared completely in wars with neighboring groups, and all that remain of them are names and the sad stories of their final disasters. Others, more recently cut down by epidemics that broke out in the region some thirty or forty years ago, are presently reduced to a few individuals scattered throughout several villages.

The Anumaniá, Arupatí, Maritsauá, Iarumá, and Aualáta are among those completely extinct. The Tsúva, Naruvôt, Nafuquá, and Kutenábu (or Kustenau) have a few survivors; they were members of the cluster of allied tribes with roots near the headwaters of the Xingu.

Massacred and Extinct

T he Anumaniá, as we have mentioned before, were the Indians who, with the Auetí, were hostile invaders of the region and later came to occupy the Itavununo lagoon on the right bank of the Kuluene. Considered bad people, they never were welcomed in the area. Except for their former allies, the Auetí, no other group maintained friendly relations with them or carried out any other type of interchange.

On one occasion, all the males of this tribe decided to visit the Trumái at Kranhãnhã, a place relatively near the Itavununo lagoon. Like the other Indians of the area, the Trumái were not fond of this neighboring tribe, but they received the Anumaniá with apparent good will. It is said that when the Trumái noticed how many Anumaniá there were and that there were no women or children among them, it strongly contributed to their decision to liquidate their guests.

To do this, the Trumái feigned spontaneous friendship and invited their guests to bathe in a river some distance from the village. The Anumaniá, not suspecting the trap, accepted the invitation and headed for the river bank. As soon as they were out of the village, the women and some Trumái men who had deliberately stayed behind made imperceptible cuts in the strings of the Anumaniá's bows, rendering them completely useless. When the Anumaniá returned from their swim, they made themselves comfortable in the hammocks, unsuspecting. The Trumái prepared quietly, and at an opportune moment they threw themselves on their visitors in a sudden and violent act of aggression. After the first shock, the Anumaniá ran for their bows, the strings of which snapped as soon as they were drawn. Weaponless, they were all killed at arrow point or by clubbing.

When they heard what had happened, the Anumaniá women, old men, and children who had stayed home escaped to their friends the Auetí and remained among them.

These events, which we believe to have actually taken place, may explain certain peculiarities in the Auetí dialect. Possibly as a result of this Anumaniá intrusion, it sometimes sounds like badly pronounced Tupi; for example, the Auetí say *tajá, tombá,* and *cunhanha,* instead of the Tupi *tatá, tupá,* and *cunhã.*

The Arupatí Indians dominated the lower course of the Ronuro River. Their numbers were greatly reduced by continuous attacks from the Suiá; and afterward they were almost completely exterminated by the Kamaiurá, who took the few surviving women and children to their villages. From what we know, the Arupatí spoke Tupi.

The Maritsauá lived near the river named after them. They existed at the time of von den Steinen's expedition in 1884. The Suiá were also to blame for their disappearance. Apparently the Suiá were inspired to slaughter the Maritsauá because the Maritsauá had attacked and killed an entire group of Iaualapití, who were on their way home after a friendly visit to the Suiá. The complaints of the blind old chief of the Iaualapití are recorded in von den Steinen's second book about the Xingu, *Entre os Aborígines do Brasil Central [Among the Aborigines of Central Brazil],* and give us the opportunity of verifying the degree of truthfulness and fidelity of our narrators of today.

The Iarumá lived near the Tanguro, a right-bank tributary of the

Kuluene. Their contacts with the Xinguanos were limited mainly to the Kuikúru and the Kalapalo Indians. We have met a Iarumá woman, whose name is Quevêso; she was the wife of Iauaícuma, a Kalapalo chief. The Iarumá were almost totally wiped out by the Kuikúru a little more than half a century ago, during a visit they paid to the Kuikúru village.

Apparently, at the time of the visit, the Kuikúru were carrying on their usual warlike tournaments. At a certain point in the competition, the Kuikúru invited the Iarumá to participate in their tournament, to teach them the tricks of their violent sport. The Iarumá accepted and headed toward the center of the village, where they were attacked by the stronger Kuikúru wrestlers and beaten to death with *tacapes*.[8]

Weakened by the loss of so many men, the Iarumá joined the Suiá, whose village near the Paranajuva River was not far from their own, near the Tanguro River. A peculiarity of the Iarumá was the sound of their earrings, like small bells. Other information about the Iarumá is scarce and unclear.

The Aualáta, who lived among the Trumái, are an obscure and almost mysterious tribe. They also disappeared as a consequence of wars, though not so abruptly as those mentioned above. They died off gradually in the many bloody encounters between the Suiá and the Trumái. It is said that the Aualáta spoke the same language as the Trumái, but with a different, very slow intonation, as if they had difficulty pronouncing the words.

Although the information we have concerning them is vague, there is no doubt that they did exist at one time. The veil of obscurity surrounding them may result from their having always lived in the shadow of a more powerful and numerically larger tribe, the Trumái.

---

[8] Club, cudgel for human sacrifices among the Indians.

Victims of Diseases

Three or four Naruvôts, survivors of this Karib group, live among the Kalapalo. They speak the same language.

The Tsúva or Aipatse lived for a long time with the Kuikúru but are no longer with them today. Only two families remain, and they live with the Kalapalo and the Nafuquá.

Of the Kutenábu (or Kustenau), two individuals alone, mother and son, remain. They live with the Waurá and speak precisely the same language. Like the Waurá, they manufactured pottery. This woman is the most skillful molder of zoömorphic vases in the village where she lives.

V
HOSTILE AND ASOCIAL TRIBES

Hostile Tribes

We classify those Indians as hostile who, though they live in the region, are not allied with or related in a normal way to the *cultural area* of the headwaters of the Xingu. These are: the Suiá, inhabitants of the Paranajuva River; the Txukarramãe, occupants of the left bank of the Xingu, in the heights near the Von Martius waterfalls; the Juruna, who make their home at the mouth of the Maritsauá-Missú; and finally the Txikão Indians, who live along the Jatobá River, in the heart of the Alto-Xingu, and frequently attack the Xinguano villages closest to them. For the purposes of this study, the Suiá are the most important of these groups, given the close relations they maintained with the Indians of the Xinguano area, assimilating from them various customs and ways of living during the long periods of friendly contact.

The Suiá[9]

The Suiá are affiliated with the Jê ethnic-linguistic family, to this date preserving, despite other influences, those marked traits that characterize and distinguish their great nation so clearly.

The Kamaiurá say that the Suiá broke into the region through the Ronuro River long ago, beginning to fight almost immediately with the Trumái. Once they became hostile, they started to move down the Xingu and finally settled for a long time in the heights near the mouth of the Paranajuva River. The chosen spot, on the right bank, about two kilometers or one and a quarter miles below the mouth of the Paranajuva, was named Diauarum ("black jaguar"). It was there that

[9] The Suiá of the Paranajuva River were attracted in 1960 by Claudio and Orlando Villas Boas, as members of the Brazilian Indian Protection Service.

von den Steinen found them settled, when he went down the Xingu in 1887.

At the same place, Diauarum, the whole of a North American ethnographic expedition had a tragic end at the hands of the Suiá at the close of the last century. Their remains, in the form of shards of fine porcelain, can still be found buried at the site of the old village.

With the exception of the Trumái, their irreconcilable foes, the Suiá from the beginning maintained friendly relations with the Xinguanos. They exchanged visits, traded, and jointly carried out certain festivals and ceremonies. It was surely in the socio-economic atmosphere of friendly periods that the Suiá became acquainted with and assimilated a series of new traits and habits. Hammocks, Waurá pottery, the use of manioc to prepare *beijus*,[10] the structure of dwellings that are a visible fusion of different indigenous patterns, perhaps the canoe, and certain ceremonies that are typically Xinguano in social, magical, or recreative foundation are, among the Suiá, the most important manifestations of this influence.

When they talk about the history of the early movements of their tribe, the Suiá, with whom we are in contact today, say that their ancestors lived far to the east of the Xingu. When they migrated, their path was a great arc toward the north, and after many interruptions, they came to the mouth of the Maritsauá-Missú River. At this point, the tribe split in half: one branch went down the Xingu, the other went up the Maritsauá, settling in the lands far to the west. Later they were chased out by other Indians, and they returned to the Xingu by going down the Ronuro River.

Curiously, the Txukarramãe tell the same story about the Suiá, pointing to the east as their place of origin and to the west as the region known to their forefathers. They add that, in the west, their grandparents met a nation whose tribesmen wore a piece of bamboo in their nose. This doubtless refers to the Nhambiquara Indians, who settled on the Juruena River and who wear a piece of bamboo in a hole pierced through the septum. The Txukarramãe's name for these people encountered by the early migrators is *Kubeniacrecrãcruapú*, or "people who wear pieces of bamboo in their noses."

---

[10] A thin white bread or pancake made from manioc flour.

It is possible that, during their migration from the east, on reaching the Xingu, the Suiá and the Txukarramãe (Kaiapó) formed a single tribe, and that subsequently their relations with the Xinguanos impressed upon the Suiá group the traits that today isolate them from the other groups of their nation.

The Suiá remained for many years near the mouth of the Paranajuva, until new and dangerous enemies appeared in the region and forced them to move. For many generations, the Suiá had been in the habit of visiting the Von Martius waterfalls, nearly 200 kilometers or about 125 miles down the Xingu from their lands. They knew of the existence of inhabitants there but had never seen them up close. On their way back from one of these trips, they noticed a great number of Indians waving at them from the treetops along the river bank, inviting them to come ashore. Naturally the Suiá did not obey the calls; instead they headed their canoes for the middle of the river and paddled as fast as they could to get back to their village. They paddled without stopping for a day and a night. Long before landing, they had shouted to the village the whole story of their unpleasant encounter. The commotion among the Suiá was great when they learned of the dangerous meeting. Some immediately began to make arrows and cudgels, while others, perhaps more prudent, suggested that the village should be abandoned. In the end, the site was not abandoned, and as a safety measure, the Suiá would go no farther than a couple of hundred yards from their village to collect wood for their fires.

One morning, after several days of this arrangement, some men and women, doubtless tired of the confinement, ventured farther out. They went into the woods searching for pequi fruit, but moments later they ran back to the village terrified, shouting that there were strangers in the area. Naturally there was an uproar, but according to those who tell the story, at first the Suiá were not particularly frightened. Arming themselves with bows, arrows, and clubs, they prepared for what was to come, but the rest of the day passed without incident, as if nothing out of the ordinary had happened.

After the sun disappeared, they began to hear noises coming from the edge of the woods: the breaking of dry branches, the rustle of leaves being stepped on, pigs' grunts, jaguars' roars, jacamins' wails, monkeys' chatter, and other voices of animals. As the night progressed, the visitors became increasingly agitated, until finally they began a real outcry around the village, shrieking and calling to the Suiá by name. Then the Suiá began to be really afraid and thought that their enemies must be very numerous. All were terrified, with the exception of an old Indian named Cocoró, who at that time was the main chief of the tribe. Cocoró, taking up a bow and arrow, stayed outside his hut, dancing in the village clearing. The other Indians, who were inside their huts, kept warning him about the danger to which he was exposing himself, but the old chief paid no attention and was completely absorbed in his war chant.

As soon as day began to break, an Indian came out of the forest and, from afar, beckoned to Cocoró, calling him by name and offering him a stone hammer. He waved for the old man to come close, to take the gift from his hand. Cocoró, fearless and imprudent, came close and was laid out by a violent cudgel blow to the head. This was the signal for the attack. Wave after wave of Indians came out of the woods screaming. They invaded the village, storming the huts and attacking the people inside. The Suiá, though more numerous, were badly stricken. According to the story, more than half the population of the village was massacred, and only those who were able to reach their canoes and cross the river were saved. For three days they stayed on the opposite bank, waiting for their enemies to leave. There was nothing they could do, since they had almost no weapons. In the destroyed village, the invaders spent most of this time playing their flutes and dancing among the corpses.

When the strangers finally left, the Suiá hurried across the river to see what was left. There was nobody alive in what had once been their village. In the clearing, encircled now by ashes, the corpses were laid out in a row. The women, whom they thought would have been spared, lay face up, their lifeless bodies in an advanced state of putrefaction, their legs spread apart by wooden struts forced between the knees.

After the burials, the Suiá moved beside a small lagoon hidden on the left bank of the river, a little above the mouth of the Paranajuva. Decades later, the Suiá returned to Diauarum.

The Juruna[11]

It was about the same time in the history of the Alto-Xingu, that is, some fifty or sixty years ago, that the Juruna first appeared in the region. For some time they had been moving up the Xingu in stages, to get away from the *seringueiros* [rubber-plantation farmers] and the hordes of Kaiapó who dominated the middle reaches of the Xingu.

When they first came into contact with the Suiá, then settled near the mouth of the Paranajuva River, the Juruna still lived much further north.

At first the relations between the two tribes were exceptionally pleasant, and the Suiá, in this phase, gave many women in marriage to the Juruna. When we established contact with the Juruna in 1949, some of these women, though very old, were still alive.

This friendship, however, did not last long. For reasons that the Indians are unable to clarify even today, the Juruna, using .44 rifles, which they had brought from the lower course of the river, attacked the Suiá and forced them to abandon the Diauarum site and to move away along the Paranajuva. Their new village, located some forty kilometers or about twenty-five miles above the mouth of the Paranajuva, was named Iamuricumá. Some time later, another attack from the Juruna forced the Suiá to move again, this time toward the upper course of the Paranajuva, where for many years they remained withdrawn.

Since they already knew the Indians of the headwaters of the Xingu—the Trumái and especially the Kamaiurá—the Juruna decided to go upriver to renew their long-severed ties with them. The group was made up of twelve men led by Aumãma, general chief of the Juruna. Near the mouth of the Tuatuarí River, Aumãma and his people came across nearly the entire population of Kamaiurá who were in the midst of one of their major seasonal fishing expeditions. The Junaunas were apparently well received. But in reality the Kamaiurá, still resentful of the disaster at Anariá, in which the Juruna accidentally killed two Kamaiurás, and tempted by the large number of firearms in the possession of their visitors, decided to kill them. They managed to do so after separating them from one another, using many shrewd

---

[11] This Juruna group, as is stated in a report made in the days of the former Brazilian Indian Protection Service, was attracted by the forefront of the Roncador–Xingu Expedition headed by the Villas Boas brothers in 1950.

maneuvers. None of the Jurunas survived. Aumãma's entire group was massacred.

Months after this occurrence, two Juruna men, Chief Xibutê and a companion, arrived at the Kamaiurá village in search of their relatives. The Kamaiurá reported that Aumãma had gone up the Kurizêvo River to visit the Bakirí and that it would probably be a while before he came back. The Jurunas returned to their village, taking along a young woman named Canhanacu, who had left her husband. The Juruna were invited to come back in greater numbers to wait among the Kamaiurá for the others to return.

Back home, the Juruna made ready to go upriver in response to the Kamaiurá invitation, but a Kamaiurá named Aparrurú, who lived with the Juruna, got drunk on *caxiri,* a fermented drink, and warned them not to make the trip, saying that the Kamaiurá had lied and had already killed Aumãma and his companions.

Nhariacú, another Juruna chief, did not believe the confession, asserting that reparations had been made for the death of the two Kamaiurá in Anariá and that nothing could have happened to Aumãma.

Convinced of this, Nhariacú traveled upriver with eight companions, to wait for the return of his relatives to the Kamaiurá village. Once there, the Juruna chief was welcomed heartily by the Kamaiurá, who even lodged him in their own huts. After several days of waiting, the Juruna began to show impatience, creating a certain uneasiness in the village. The Kamaiurá, perceiving this, made haste to carry out their plan to eliminate their guests.

One afternoon, when the Jurunas had gathered in the village square, the Kamaiurá expressed a desire to see how they made arrows. Unsuspecting, the Jurunas made themselves comfortable on little stools provided for them and began to work under the attentive gaze of many onlookers. When it was apparent to the Kamaiurá that the Juruna were entirely absorbed, one by one they casually collected the rifles leaning against their Juruna owners, who were surrounded by many people and could not keep track of everything that was going on. As soon as the Kamaiurá had all the rifles, they tackled the Juruna, killing them after hitting them over the head with clubs.

The Indians today say that the Juruna, then living a little below the mouth of the Maritsauá-Missú River, learned of the disaster through the revelation of one of their *pajés* [witch doctor]. When they found out what had happened to their relatives at the hands of the Kamaiurá, the Juruna made ready and went upriver to avenge their deaths. A band of eight men was led by Maricauá, a brave Indian hardened by many wars. After ten days of traveling, starving and feverish, they reached the headwaters of the Xingu. And there were the Kamaiurá, in appreciable numbers, carrying out the collective fishing that, nearly every year, forms part of their religious festivities.

For a few moments the Juruna could not decide what to do and stayed behind some branches on the opposite bank. Maricauá, realizing that it would be impossible to attack in the normal way, given the numbers and position of the enemy, decided to show himself and to simulate a peaceful approach. He set out ahead of his companions and paddled his canoe slowly in the direction of the Kamaiurá campsite. The Kamaiurá had already spotted him and were watching from a clearing on the shore. To keep them in the clearing, Maricauá gesticulated for them to wait, giving them to understand that his motives were peaceful. But as soon as they were very close, Maricauá and his companions, giving them no time to escape, fired their guns in unison at the large group of Kamaiurás standing at the water's edge. Four men were killed: Teporá, Jiripá, Tavairã, and Taviraná. The first had lived for many years among the Juruna. The Jurunas also managed to capture a girl who was slow in escaping.[12]

The Txukarramãe[13]

Of all the Indians we have classified as hostile, the Txukarramãe are the most important.

Our first information about them was given to us by the Kalapalo in 1946, the year we reached the Kuluene River. The Kalapalo used to call them Aveotó or Suiá-Catí, adding that they were the most dangerous and the largest tribe of the entire region.

They also said that the Aveotó did not carry bows and arrows, only spears and clubs, and that they did not live in a specific place but

---

[12] This last encounter was related by a Juruna Indian named Xatuná. There is another version of the Juruna attack on the Kamaiurá. It will be transcribed in another work.
[13] This group, Mekrangnontí or Metotíre, was attracted in 1953 by the Villas Boas, as members of the Brazilian Indian Protection Service.

wandered through the forest. They also warned us at that time not to try to go down the Xingu.

Some time later, from the Kamaiurá and Trumái, we received new and more detailed information about the Indians living on the banks of the Xingu around the Von Martius falls. It was then that we heard for the first time the name Txukarramãe. Neither the Kamaiurá nor the Trumái had seen them, but from the Suiá and especially from the Juruna they knew a lot about them. They knew that the Txukarramãe, like the Suiá, wore a wooden disk in their lower lip; they did not travel in canoes; and their chief weapons were heavy wooden clubs, from which they would not be parted.

An old Kamaiurá named Karatsipá repeated to us several times the dramatic story of the massacre perpetrated long ago by the Txukarramãe against the Suiá. When, in 1949, we established contact with the Juruna, who were living at the mouth of the Maritsauá-Missú, we were able to gather new and more illuminating information about the Txukarramãe. With these new data, we began to identify them with the bellicose and savage Kaiapó hordes, who, in their resistance to the invasion of civilization, overran and terrorized the forests in the south of the state of Pará. We learned that Txukarramãe is a Juruna word meaning "having no bows."

This was the extent of our knowledge about these Indians when, in 1953, we came into direct contact with them. We verified nearly all the information we had collected about them since the Kalapalo's report. What they were was a large group belonging to a nation that calls itself Kaiapó.

Their real name is Mekrangnontí, or Metotíre, as some Indians prefer. In all, they number about a thousand. They are presently divided into two groups living close together. Their villages are situated near the headwaters of a left-bank tributary of the Jarina River, about 40 kilometers or 25 miles from the left bank of the Xingu, around the Von Martius waterfall.

Generally the Txukarramãe are tall and slender in build. The women are particularly strong. In the long trips that these Indians are perpetually undertaking, the women are responsible for carrying almost everything. Rare is the married woman who does not carry, suspended from a shoulder strap, a child not always very young. They paint themselves with the blue-black juice of the genipap fruit, covering most of the body. Otherwise they live completely nude. The single women wear something like a baldric made of cotton thread. They pierce their ears and shave the hair over the forehead as far as the crown; some cut all their hair off.

The men pierce their lower lips and put wooden disks in them. These are round in shape, and some are as much as 12 centimeters or about 5 inches in diameter. The men also pierce their ears. On their penis they wear a small funnel-shaped sheath made of palm leaf, to conceal and protect the glans. They too shave their heads above the forehead and let their hair grow long in back. They paint their bodies with a variety of designs, using charcoal and genipap.

Among the Txukarramãe there are Juruna, Tapirapé, Gorotire, and Brazilian settlers, all captured as children during their habitual raids along the Middle Xingu and the flatlands of the lower Araguaia.

The Txikão[14]

The Txikão have not yet been identified with a particular linguistic group. They inhabit the area around the Jatobá River, and periodically they would invade the lower courses of the Batoví and Kurizêvo Rivers, where they assaulted the villages of the Waurá, the Meináco, and the Nafuquá, situated along the river banks. Today the Txikão are pacified and have become part of the Xingu National Park, where they live on friendly terms with the other groups in the region. The Txikão are few in number, but they are very active and industrious. On the Jatobá, where we met them, we found them subsisting on hunting, fishing, and fruit-picking, rather than on agricultural activities.

The goods they manufacture are not varied. Their small and large baskets, sieves, *tipitis*,[15] and fans made of woven palm branches are noteworthy for their rough finish. On the other hand, the whimsical fashioning of their weapons (arrows, bows, and clubs), and their cotton work are both very impressive. The threads are so well twisted that they seem machine-made. The cloths made with this thread, in delicacy of weave and in appearance, reveal a refined technique that contrasts markedly with the coarse basketry mentioned earlier. Their hammocks,

---

[14] Brought into the Xingu National Park in 1966 by the Villas Boas brothers.
[15] A cylinder of the jacitara palm used to press the poisonous juice out of manioc.

made of cotton and buriti fiber, are identical to those of the Alto-Xingu, in that the longitudinal cords of buriti fiber are interwoven with cotton threads.

In physical constitution, male and female Txikão are both remarkably slender. Among them, there is not a single fat or overmuscular individual. Their height is frequently under five feet. But in spite of their apparent frailty, these Indians are strong and resistant, owing to their way of life as hunters and gatherers. Their skin, light in color, is smooth and entirely hairless, thanks to systematic depilation. The hair style is the same for both sexes. It is trimmed short. The upper layers of bangs fall in grades down the nape of the neck, where they are shaped into a rounded point that resembles an ynambu or tinamou bird's tail. The Txikão wear no clothes or protective pieces. They adorn themselves soberly with armlets, earrings, and collars. Armlets for men are made of little ribbons woven out of cotton and worn around the biceps. Collars, which are worn by women, are made of tiny cylindrical coconut beads strung on a long thread and wound several times around the neck. Earrings are worn by both sexes and are small rectangular blades made of shells and tied to the ear by a circlet of thread. Red urucu paint is used to protect or adorn by both men and women. Feather ornaments are rare. Perhaps they are used with more variety in ceremonies we have not yet witnessed.

In temperament, the Txikão are nervous and restless, reacting promptly to any novel stimulus or situation that crops up. This trait, very pronounced in them, may be a natural result of the isolation in which they live.

For sustenance, the Txikão do not rely heavily on agriculture. They cultivate five plants only: corn, manioc, cotton, urucu (or annatto), and calabash for gourds. The latter two are planted by preference around the huts. Manioc is eaten in the form of thick, hard beijus; corn is roasted in hot coals. Hunting, fishing, and fruit-picking provide their main source of sustenance. Daily they struggle, around their villages or on long and protracted trips, to obtain the major part of their food supply. They move around uninterruptedly, hunting, fishing, extracting honey, or picking fruit in the woods. Fish are caught either at arrow point or in bays and small lagoons by means of weirs and timbó.

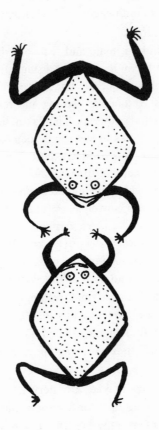

Pererecas

The Txikão have a special taste for the *pererecas* [tree toads] that live in the marshes. Women and children spend hours searching for them in the grass. Another of their characteristic hunting methods is to dig pits in their village to catch the mice and lizards that scurry around their huts. Larger pits for the capture of game—capybaras, pigs, and other animals—are dug at the river's edge and on animal trails in the forest.

As we have seen, the Txikão struggle arduously to assure their survival, which, in the last analysis, is a logical consequence of their isolation, their rudimentary agriculture, and, finally, of their hunting habits in a territory little favored by nature.

Asocial Tribes

We classify as asocial those Indians who inhabit the region but live completely withdrawn, without any kind of communication, present or previous, with the Xinguano tribes. Among the various tribes of this kind pointed out to us by the Indians, we will list only those whose actual existence is certain.

The most interesting are the Agavotoqueng, who live, according to the Matipú, between the Kuluene and Kurizêvo Rivers. The Matipú say that the Agavotoqueng speak the same language as the Iaualapití and seem in all other respects to be, like them, Xinguanos. Like the Iaualapití, they wear their hair short, use urucu abundantly, and adorn themselves with necklaces, armlets, and feather earrings. It is not unlikely that they are a part of the Iaualapití group, broken away from the main part of the tribe a long time ago. "Agavotoqueng" is made up of two separate words in the Matipú language, part of the Karib group: *agavoto* = Iaualapití; *queng* = another—meaning, therefore, "another Iaualapití."

Feather earrings

A little farther away live other Indians of whose existence we are certain: the Auaicü, on the upper Paranajuva River; the Miarrã, at the headwaters of the Arraias, a tributary of the Maritsauá; and some Indians whose names are not known and who leave traces every year at the mouth of the Maritsauá. The existence of the Auaicü is confirmed by all tribes of the region, especially by the Kuikúru, who habitually visit the Itavununo lagoon; there they always find traces of these Indians: footprints, remains of fires, or man-made trails. A few months ago, while visiting the Suiá, we had a confirmation of the existence of the Auaicü. Going up the Paranajuva in search of *taquari* [bamboo] to make arrows, the Suiá came upon a hunting camp, where they surprised the Indians, who were roasting a capybara. According to the Suiá, the Auaicü are very timid. Whenever they are discovered, they flee in terror.

The Caiabí, who live at the mouth of the Arraias River, have found many traces of the Miarrã on their hunting trips up this river. On one of these trips they found a recently extinguished campfire, as well as improvised wooden frames made by hand without using tools. However, it is possible that these Indians were not Miarrã but a surviving group of the Maritsauá, who had escaped upriver. Today we know that the Maritsauá, at the time of the Suiá attacks, were living at the mouth of the Arraias River, where we have found remains of the large clay pots they made.

And last, there are the Indians of unknown name who every summer "thrash around" in the forest along the banks of the Maritsauá. The Juruna say that these strange inhabitants of the forest often visit their plantations or approach their huts at night to steal manioc dough and other things stored on the racks in the clearing. Once the Juruna had made camp on a large sandbar that appears every year in the river in front of the village; one afternoon, when the sun was still high in the sky, they noticed a strange movement inside their huts. Moving closer to see what was going on, they had time to watch a group of Indians hastily clear out of the village, carrying off bunches of bananas and some tools.

There are other groups of Indians like these, but we lack enough evidence to confirm their actual existence. The most curious of these, of doubtful existence, almost legendary, are the pygmies mentioned by almost all Indians of the region. The Kamaiurá call them "Sapoins"; the Kuikúru, "Tavuglis"; the Waurá, "Camitsotsés"; the Suiá, "Cupémerrés"; the Juruna, "Ipimdáis." They all say that these pygmies live to the east of the Xingu, and are numerous and very aggressive. They say that a long time ago these Indians invaded the Suiá village, killing many men after immobilizing them with arrows aimed at their knees. It is understandably difficult to believe such a story, but the Indians talk about these pygmies as if they were quite real and not fantasies.

VI
The Mythical History

The present state of affairs among the various groups of Indians, and their histories and traditions, rather eloquently confirm what was suggested by the vestiges of ditches referred to earlier. That is, we must conclude that the cultural fusion observed among the many different tribes in the Alto-Xingu took a very long time. Particularly in their mythical-religious traditions, it is highly significant that the places where the heroes lived and performed their deeds are so specifically placed in the region, a fact that clearly attests to a profound and well-developed geographical orientation. The plots of the Xinguanos' great mythical history, in which are to be found the basis and the ritual form of their religious beliefs, according to legend center around the junction of the headwaters of the Xingu—the Morená, in the language of the Indians. It is their mythical land, enveloped in an aura of mystery and the supernatural. There lived Mavutsinim (a Kamaiurá name), the personage who created the mother of the twin heroes Sun and Moon and along one of the beaches scattered the various kinds of weapons used today, which distinguish one tribe from another.

The great lagoons of the region also appear in their stories and traditions. Some are said to be the former domains of legendary nations; others the dwelling places of monstrous animals who inspire real terror in the Indians. Their origin and subsequent histories are all connected with the prowess of one or another mythical figure.

The nebulous past of the Xinguanos generally begins, according to them, with a series of strange nations known to their ancestors: some had been encountered during the great expeditions they habitually made to the east; others in their own territory. Given the fantasy and obscurity that dominate the narratives presented in the pages to follow, we have decided to call them myths, without, at the same time, denying the possibility of their being true stories greatly altered by time and by the human mind's natural penchant for the marvelous.

The "Oí"

"Oí" is the name given by the Trumái to a very strange people, who, according to them, from time to time used to prowl around their former villages at Kranhãnhã on the Kuluene's right bank. The Oí were, according to the legend, very tall, and they had a curious habit of singing in chorus on their rounds and on the way home. They persistently spied on the Trumái, armed with large clubs which they carried over their right shoulders, but the Oí never assaulted the Trumái. The Trumái heard their chant so often that they learned it by heart, and it is intoned still at the great Javarí ceremony.

The Minatá-Karaiá

This story is more frequently told by the Kamaiurá.

They narrate that on one occasion the early explorers departed on a long trip. They went up a river for many days, until they reached an inhabited region. First they found many paths crossing and extensive fields of manioc, corn, and other crops. Suddenly they began to hear a high, loud whistle. Curious to know what it was, they walked in the direction the sound was coming from. After a while, they reached the village, which belonged to the Minatá-Karaiá. The village was full of people, and the men had a hole in the top of their heads that produced the whistle the Kamaiurá had heard from far away. The Minatá-Karaiá had another peculiarity: from underneath their armpits bunches of *minatás* [coconuts] grew, and they were constantly snatching the fruits off, breaking them against their heads, and eating them.

One day the Minatá sensed the presence of the Kamaiurá spying on them and gave chase. The Kamaiurá took to their heels and ran night and day without stopping, but the ferocious Minatá would not give up. They set fire to the underbrush, intending to create billows of smoke to chase the invaders out of their land. After crossing several fields, woods, and valleys, the Kamaiurá believed themselves saved and decided to set up camp and rest. Instead they glanced back and were surprised to see that they were being followed at close range by new clouds of smoke created by the Minatá-Karaiá, who had still not given up the pursuit. The invaders took flight again, finally ridding themselves of the Minatá-Karaiá when they reached the Paranajuva River, by which they returned to their villages.

The Tatu-Karaiá

This brief story is in some ways similar to the last one. The Tatu-Karaiá were also discovered by the early Indian explorers. One day, as these Indians were wandering across a vast open space that had traces of habitation, from a hilltop they spotted billows of smoke rising from the ground. On closer inspection they discovered that the columns of smoke originated from a number of holes in the ground. These holes were the dwellings of the Tatu-Karaiá, who, as they attempted to escape, were all killed at arrow point or by clubbings.

Tamacaví

Tamacaví was a great Kuikúru chief, who, according to the legend, was endowed with a colossal body. His arms were as thick as the thighs of a strongman, and his legs as big as the chest. Tamacaví's villages, on the banks of the Itavununo lagoon, were frequently attacked by hostile neighboring tribes. Tamacaví used to chase them away single-handed, not only by using his great physical strength but also by his deft archery. On one occasion, all his enemies joined forces against him and attacked him en masse. Tamacaví's people were totally massacred. He stood alone, continuing to resist his attackers. The latter, in large numbers, were running out of arrows and tried to subdue the great chief bodily, but he crushed them one by one. For an entire day Tamacaví fought the constantly renewed enemy, but finally he began to lose strength and sink into the marsh; soon they overpowered him, and after killing him, they devoured his flesh. But it was bitter and poisonous and killed everyone who ate it.

Coeviacá

The Indians narrate that Coeviacá was only one person, a very tall man with long hair who in the early days used to wander through the woods and fields. His job was to set fire wherever he went. Even today when the Xinguanos see smoke where they believe no one lives, they blame the fire on Coeviacá, the wandering incendiary of the woods.

The stories that follow, with the exception of the five-part myth of Sinaá, which comes from the Juruna Indians, are common to all groups in the area, with minor variations that are not significant enough to modify the meaning and development of the story. These rare and minor variations might provide material for a study on intertribal acculturation, but that is not the purpose of this work and we have set aside these details. What we intend to do is to acquaint the reader with general aspects of the spiritual life of these Indians, as revealed by their mythology.

The majority of the stories recorded contain no exceptions to the general rule about myths; that is, they encompass an interpretation of the world, a peculiar way of explaining nature and the origin of things, such as: the conquest of day; the procurement of fire; the formation of the rivers; the remarkable characteristics of specific animals; and also, magical practices and religious ceremonies.

Thus, the stories in general, through the feats, examples, and statements of their heroes, not only reveal a specific conception of the world but also explain and lay the foundations for the main spiritual, moral, and material traits of the culture in question—that is, of the community of tribes that has for centuries lived at the source of the Xingu.

We want to emphasize that the same story was heard more than once, always from different narrators. There were no pressures of time; instead, our interest was to transmit with the greatest possible accuracy everything heard and understood over a long period of time, twenty-five years of daily, hourly, and minute-by-minute communal living with the Indians.

We have attempted to transcribe the thought of the Indians as clearly as possible, adding nothing, neither inference nor conclusion, to their ideas. The occasionally incomprehensible or ambiguous points are part of the stories themselves that develop in that territory between the real and the unreal.

And last, we would like to point out that one of the most difficult things in obtaining this kind of data is to find the best informant. An Indian who speaks our language well and who readily offers to tell us stories or reveal information is precisely the least trustworthy for this purpose. True informants never come forward on their own, they speak only their own language, and when they are questioned, they even draw back. Furthermore, there are never more than one or two true trustees of the spiritual culture in each village. In gathering the data and stories collected in the present book, we were aided by the best informants in the area.

Part Two
THE MYTHS

MAVUTSINIM:
The First Man

(*Kamaiurá*)

In the beginning there was only Mavutsinim. No one lived with him. He had no wife. He had no son, nor did he have any relatives. He was all alone.

One day he turned a shell into a woman, and he married her. When his son was born, he asked his wife, "Is it a man or a woman?"

"It is a man."

"I'll take him with me."

Then he left. The boy's mother cried and went back to her village, the lagoon, where she turned into a shell again.

"We are the grandchildren of Mavutsinim's son," say the Indians.

[handwritten annotation:] constitutive Symbol : manner in which society denies its mortality ult reality • Death
Life : human mastery of ecology.

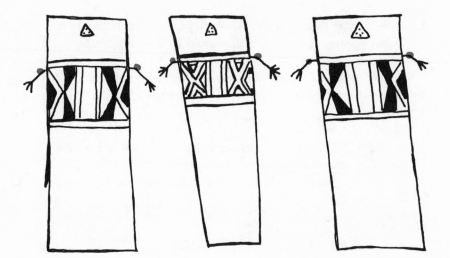

Kuarup logs

Life → Dead →Life   wood
2-marine toads 2

Disobedience = death

MAVUTSINIM:
The First Kuarup,
the Feast of the Dead

(Kamaiurá)

Mavutsinim wanted his dead people to come back to life. He went into the forest, cut three logs of *kuarup* wood, carried them back to the village, and painted them. After painting them, he adorned the logs with feathers, necklaces, cotton threads, and armlets of macaw feathers. Then Mavutsinim ordered poles to be fixed in the ground at the center of the village. He called for *cururu* toads and agoutis (two of each) to sing near the kuarups. On the same occasion, he brought fish and *beijus* [flat roasted bread] to the center of the village to be given out to his people. The *maracá-êps* [singers], shaking gourd rattles in their right hands, began to sing without pause to the kuarups, pleading with them to come to life. The village men kept asking Mavutsinim if the logs were actually going to turn into people or whether they would always be wood as they were. Mavutsinim answered that no, the kuarup logs were going to transform themselves into people, walk like people, and live as people do. After eating the fish, the people began to paint themselves and to shout as they did so. Everybody was shouting. The only people singing were the maracá-êps. Around midday the singing ended. The people wanted to weep for the kuarups, who represented their dead, but Mavutsinim would not let them, saying that the kuarups were going to turn into people and for that reason there was nothing to weep about.

On the morning of the second day, Mavutsinim would not let his people look at the kuarups. "No one can look," he said. Mavutsinim had to keep repeating it from moment to moment. His people must wait. In the middle of the night on the second day, the logs began to move a little. The cotton thread belts and the feather armlets were trembling, the feathers moving as if shaken by the wind. The logs wanted to turn themselves into people. Mavutsinim kept telling his

2 - Marine toads

2 - furred animals

Revulsion

| 55

people not to look. They had to wait. As soon as the kuarups began to
show signs of life, the singers—the cururu toads, and the agoutis—
sang to make them go and wash themselves as soon as they came to
life. The posts moved, trying to get out of the holes where they had
been planted. At daybreak, from the waist up, the kuarups were already taking human form, with arms, breasts, and heads. The lower
half was still wood. Mavutsinim kept telling his people to wait, to keep
themselves from looking. "Wait . . . wait . . . wait," he said over and
over. The sun began to rise. The singers never stopped singing. The
kuarups' arms kept growing. One leg was already covered with flesh.
But the other was still wood. Around midday, the logs were nearly real
people. They were all moving around in their holes, more human than
wood. Mavutsinim ordered all house entrances to be covered. Only he
stayed out at the side of the kuarups. Only he could look at them, no
one else. When the transformation from wood into people was nearly
finished, Mavutsinim ordered the villagers to come outside and shout,
make a commotion, spread joy, and laugh out loud near the kuarups.
Then the people came out of their houses. Mavutsinim suggested that
those who had had sexual relations with their women during the night
ought to stay inside. Only one of them had had relations, and he stayed
inside. But he was unable to contain his curiosity, and after a while he
came out too. In that very instant, the kuarups stopped moving and
turned back into wood.

Mavutsinim was furious at the young man who had failed to follow
his orders. He ranted and raved, saying, "What I wanted to do was
to make the dead live again. If the man who lay with his wife had not
come out, the kuarups would have turned into people, the dead would
have come back to life every time a kuarup was made."

After his tirade, Mavutsinim passed sentence: "All right. From now
on, it will always be this way. The dead will never come back to life
again when kuarups are made. From now on, it will only be a festival."

Mavutsinim then ordered that the kuarup logs be taken out of their
holes. The people wanted to take off their ornaments, but Mavutsinim
would not let them. "They should remain this way," he said. And right
afterward, he ordered them to be thrown into the water or into the
forest. No one knows where they were thrown, but they are at the
Morená today.

MAVUTSINIM:
The Origin of the Twins
Sun and Moon

(Kamaiurá)

M avutsinim told his daughters that he was going to the jaguar's village to look for *embira* fiber to make a bowstring. The women warned their father not to go, saying that the people over there were very dangerous. The next day Mavutsinim left on his trip. Near the jaguar's village, he found the embira trees and started to pull at the bark. As he pulled the bark off the second log, the jaguars heard the racket, came running out, and surrounded Mavutsinim.

Seeing himself surrounded, he went up to the jaguar chief and said, "What a surprise to see you here, Uncle. Don't let your people kill me, because I'm sending my daughters to marry you."

Hearing this, the jaguar sent Mavutsinim away. "Go fast or my people will kill you."

Mavutsinim left on the run. The other jaguars, who had seen their *morerequát* [chief] talking to Mavutsinim, asked where he was off to. The jaguar chief said, "He's gone now, and you'll never catch up with him."

Mavutsinim moved right along. At midday, he got to his village in the Morená. There he told his daughters what had happened to him, saying that he had almost been eaten by the jaguars.

"We knew it. That's why we asked you not to go," they said.

After explaining how he had saved himself, Mavutsinim asked his daughters which ones of them wanted to marry the jaguar. None of them did, because they were afraid of the jaguar's mother.

"If we marry him, she'll eat us."

"Very well. You're quite right."

The next day Mavutsinim went into the forest, telling his daughters he was going out to chop wood and do a number of things. In the forest

| 57

he cut hardwoods: two logs of kuarup, two of *camioá,* two of *mavu,* and two of *uaiacaêp.* He carried the logs back to the village and put them inside a tightly closed hut. Inside, he covered the logs with fragrant *enemeóp* leaves and began the incantation to turn the logs into people. He began by saying this: "I want you to turn into people." And the logs actually turned into people. But when Mavutsinim examined them, he saw that they had no hair or teeth. So he went into the forest and gathered some *buriti* [wine-palm] fiber to make hair with. After putting it on the girls' heads, he looked over his handiwork and did not like what he saw: the hair was too light. So he went out to search for the *tsitsicá* [black bird] and asked him for his hair. The tsitsicá gave it to him. Mavutsinim put this on the girls' heads and thought it looked fine, because it was really black. The teeth he made out of shells at first. After putting them in, he told the girls to laugh. They laughed, and he realized their teeth were too dark and looked very ugly. So he tried *mangaba* fruit seed. Again he told them to laugh. They laughed, and Mavutsinim thought they looked beautiful. Their teeth were now very light. Mavutsinim then observed, "They look all right, but those teeth aren't going to last very long. They'll begin to rot after a while, and they'll hurt too." After finishing the teeth, Mavutsinim made some buriti belts and went into the forest to look for embira to make a protective shield for their sexual organs. First he tried *pindaíba* embira, but he did not like it because it was too coarse. Then he tried *tameóp* [another inner bark] and was satisfied. That was soft and whitish. Finally, Mavutsinim went into the forest to cut *taquara* [bamboo] shafts to fashion the women's sexual organs. After that he went into the forest and brought back *jiquiá* [liana] to have it copulate with them. The jiquiá had relations with the eight girls. Mavutsinim was content and said, "Now they are really women."

And then he asked them, "Do you want to marry the jaguar?"

Five of the eight said yes. The next day they made ready to leave. Mavutsinim pointed them in the right direction, and before they set off he gave them this advice: "Wait for the jaguar on the shore. Better not go to his house. He comes to swim in the lagoon."

After hearing this warning, the five girls left. They had gone a fair distance when one of them realized she had forgotten her comb and went back to get it. She took such a long time catching up with them

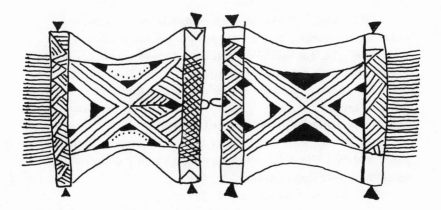

Comb

that the others went on, saying, "Let's leave her here. Who knows what
she'll turn into." *vanity*

And that one never did come back. She got lost and turned into the
iavurê-cunhã [elf of the woods]. Traveling on, the others came face to
face with the jabiru stork.

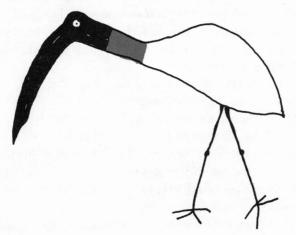

Jabiru stork

"What are you doing here? Would you point the way to the jaguar's village?"

"I'll show you, but first you must have relations with me."

During the contact the girls painted the jabiru's neck with urucu to make him ugly. The jabiru showed them the way, and they went on. Farther ahead they found a buriti palm. One of them climbed up to break off a new shoot to make a belt. The shoot, thrown from above, fell stem first and stuck in the ground. The girls on the ground sent a motuca fly to attack the one who had climbed up. As she tried to shoo the motuca away, she toppled out of the tree, fell sitting on the shoot's spike, and died. The three survivors took up their journey, and farther along they came upon the tapir.

"Where are you headed?" asked the tapir.

"We're going to the jaguar's village, and we want to know the way."

"I'll show you, but first I want to have relations with you."

The girls agreed, but the one who coupled with the tapir died. She died because the tapir's member was very big. So only two girls were left to continue the journey to the beach at the jaguar's village. There they climbed a tree to wait, sitting on a branch. A lot of people came out to swim. The two watched from the tree. Last came the *anum* [a black bird]. He left the lagoon with a *cabaça* [gourd] full of water on top of his head. As he was going back to the village, the girls sent a motuca fly to attack him. At the motuca fly's touch, the anum let the cabaça fall. The two girls thought it was funny and laughed.

The anum heard them and, turning around, saw the two young women perched up in the tree. He said, "Why are you hiding up there? Why don't you come down?"

Back in the village, the anum told the jaguar that there were two girls at the dock looking for someone.

"I think I'm the one they're looking for," said the jaguar.

Having said that, he went to the dock throwing whistling arrows, but the girls did not catch a single one. The jaguar went home, saying, "Maybe I'm not the one they're looking for."

Then the *auaratsim* [wolf] went to the dock to throw arrows too.

"Here comes another jaguar," the girls said.

When they caught the arrows, the auaratsim spoke, "I'm the one you're looking for."

And the girls went home with him. Halfway there they caused a wind to raise the auaratsim's hair and, seeing that his buttocks were red, one said to the other, "Did you see that? This is no jaguar, it's a wolf." At home, the auaratsim gave the girls fruit to eat. The wolf's mother explained that her son ate only fruit. He ate nothing else. The girls would not accept the offered fruit.

But later they decided to eat, remarking, "We'll have to eat this today. Tomorrow we'll ask for manioc flour at the house of our aunt, the real jaguar."

Next day, the auaratsim's mother, seeing that the young women did not want to eat fruit, told them to go to the jaguar's and ask for manioc flour. "They have that over there," said the old wolf. Bright and early the girls set off and stayed there to make beiju. The jaguar's mother told them that the auaratsim had no planting grounds and ate only fruit. At the jaguar's, everyone was getting ready for a hunt. The old jaguar, the lady of the house, asked the girls to come back the next day and help make beiju for the hunters. The girls set out on the day of the hunt. The jaguar went out too, but along the way he said he could not go on because his eyes hurt. His companions told him to go home. "Since you're ill there's no point in your coming along." But the jaguar was not at all ill. He had lied so as to be alone in the village. On the way back, as he was nearing home, the jaguar started to throw arrows in its direction.

"Let's catch the arrows," said the girls.

They left the hut and caught the arrows. Then the jaguar came up and took the girls to his house. There he put them to work, telling them to make beiju and manioc drink. In the afternoon the hunters came home. They had killed a lot of game: paca, deer, boars, and other animals. The auaratsim soon missed the girls and asked his mother where they were. On learning that they had gone to the jaguar's house, he told the old lady to go get them. She went, but the girls did not want to come back. They invited her to stay so that she could have some manioc drink. They mixed *pequi* thorns with the liquid they were preparing. As soon as the old wolf took a sip, she wound up with a mouth full of thorns.

"Go. On the way home you can pick them all out," said the girls.

When the auaratsim's mother left howling, the girls said to her, "You ought to turn into an animal so that you can keep that up."

That very hour, the old lady and the auaratsim both turned into animals.

The jaguar, in turn, said to the auaratsim, "It wasn't you who sent Mavutsinim away so he wouldn't be eaten. I was the one who saved these girls' father."

The girls stayed in the jaguar's house and married him. One of them, the younger, got pregnant and had a child inside her belly. One day, when the child was just about to be born, the husband went to the planting grounds to dig manioc with his other wife. The younger one, with the child in her belly, stayed home making beijus.

Her mother-in-law sat up in her hammock scratching her head and said, "Who wants to pick off my lice?"

"I can't right now, because I am making beijus," answered the daughter-in-law.

The old jaguar sat in the doorway and waited. When the young woman finished making beijus, she went over to pick the lice off her mother-in-law's head. She began to pick and eat the lice. At one point, she pulled a hair out along with a louse, and raising it to her mouth to eat, she tried to spit out the hair. The old woman turned around and told her daughter-in-law that she had spit because she felt disgust. It was no use for the daughter-in-law to explain that she was only spitting out the hair. The old lady, enraged, bit her daughter-in-law in the neck and killed her. Afraid for what she had done, she put the body on the ridgepole and ran to hide in the forest.

At the planting grounds, the other woman had a feeling that her sister had been killed and said to her husband, "How do you like that! Your mother killed my sister."

The jaguar was very angry when he arrived back home. He looked for his mother but could not find her. The old jaguar was well hidden. The jaguar took the body down from the ridgepole and asked the ants to pull the child out of her womb. There were two babies, still very tiny. The father made a large basket, and in it he put a gourd with the babies inside. The basket was hung high up, away from the floor. Then they buried the woman.

When the jaguar and his wife left for the planting grounds, the babies would climb down to eat fish and beiju. They were already getting bigger. The jaguar then made cloths to carry gourds with and left them near the basket where the babies were, to see if they would take them. But they did not. Then the jaguar made two little bows and arrows and put them with the cloth beside the basket. In his absence, the babies climbed down and picked the things up. In this way, the jaguar discovered that his children were male. Now he wanted to see the boys. So he and his wife pretended to leave. They went a little way from the house, then came back. Hiding, they began to spy. After a while the boys climbed down to the floor. The father wanted to grab them, but they hid behind one of the poles holding up the roof.

The jaguar, seeing this, said, "No, boys, you don't have to hide. You stay here on the ground."

They obeyed and stayed on the ground. From then on they took to walking from place to place killing *calangos* [lizards] and birds. The first time they killed a calango, they cut off its foot and thought it looked like a human hand, which seemed very interesting.

One day they killed a paca and roasted it. The smell of the roast reached their father's nose. He said, "It smells very good, I want to eat."

"It's for you to eat; that's why we killed it."

Another day the two brothers came across an armadillo, who asked what their names were. They answered that they had no names.

"Take mine then," said the armadillo.

The older brother became Tapeacanã and the younger Tapéiaú, which were the armadillo's names. On the way home they started calling each other by those names. Hearing that, their father asked, "Who gave you these names?"

"It was the armadillo."

The boys always went to the planting grounds of the *cuiatetê* [partridge] to pick peanuts. One day, when they were there, the cuiatetê appeared. Seeing him coming, one said to the other, "Here comes the owner of the peanut patch." Saying this, they ran and hid in a thicket.

The cuiatetê began to speak, "What silly boys these are, eating my peanuts. They have no mother, only an aunt."

When the boys heard this, they came out of their hiding place and asked the cuiatetê to tell them the story. "We want to know."

Then the cuiatetê told them everything. He told them that their mother was buried in the middle of the village; she had been killed by their grandmother, who now was hiding behind the hut where they lived. Hearing this, the boys said, "Now we know everything." And they went back home but did not go in. They sat down outside and started to cry. Their aunt asked them why they were crying and told them to come inside. The boys refused and went on crying.

At last the aunt said, "Who told you that your mother is dead?"

"We know that you are not our mother. Our real mother died."

They said that and went on crying. Then their father and their aunt came out to cry with the boys. Consoled a little by this, the boys went inside. There the aunt confirmed what the cuiatetê had said: their grandmother had actually killed their mother. The boys asked where their mother was buried. Their father showed them the spot. One of the boys asked, "What shall we do with our mother?"

"Let's see first, then we'll decide what we'll do," answered the other.

They went to the grave and stood there weeping, and then they began to call to their mother: "*Amá, amá, amá . . .*" From the depths of her grave their mother answered with a wail. Each time the boys called, they heard her answer. Then they began to remove the earth from the grave. They wanted to exhume their mother's body. Each time she answered, they dug more, until they discovered the body.

"What shall we do now?" one of them asked.

"Let us take everything out and see how it is," answered the other.

They lifted their mother out of the hole and saw that her neck was completely rotten. Seeing this, the older boy said, "There's nothing we can do for our mother. She is badly battered. If our father had told us this before, we could have cured her and she could have lived again."

Lowering the body into the grave, they said, "Now it will always be this way; people die and never come back. They will die only once."

After this second burial, they sent their father off fishing. The jaguar went out and came back in the afternoon with a lot of fish, and the next day he distributed it among the people. At that time there were chants to send the dead woman's spirit away. The next day the brothers again sent their father fishing, to end the mourning. The jaguar went out, and when he got back to the village, he broiled all the fish he had caught, to hand it all out again. After the distribution, the two boys were bathed with their father and their aunt, to end the mourning. The boy who had opened the grave to bury the dead woman asked the jaguar to tell everyone to paint themselves to pay homage to their mother.

When the ceremony was over, the two brothers dressed as calango lizards and went after their grandmother. They searched until they found her. The old jaguar, seeing her grandchildren, called them to play in her lap. She played with one first, raising and lowering him against her chest. The other, the elder brother, had tied a stone to the sole of his foot. When the grandmother lowered him to her chest, he gave her a good kick with his foot and killed her. Back home, they told their aunt what they had done. The grandmother was not buried. They left her right where they had killed her.

Then the boys told their aunt, "We made our grandmother pay for our mother. She had to die."

Then they went out to hunt deer. They killed one, counted its toes, and, seeing that it was not one of their relatives, they roasted and ate it, saying that it was an animal and therefore it could be eaten. On another walk they took, they found the *kuaráiuminhã* [little cricket], who asked their names.

"Tapeacanã is my name," said the older. "My brother's is Tapéiaú."

"Those are ugly names," said the kuaráiuminhã. "You ought to name yourselves after me."

"What's your name?"

"It's Kuát and Iaẽ. The older of you will be named Kuát [Sun] and the younger Iaẽ [Moon]."

The boys thought these were beautiful names and kept them. When they arrived home, they started to call each other Kuát and Iaẽ. Their aunt asked who had given them these names.

"It was our grandfather kuaráiuminhã," they answered.

The Sun and the Moon spent much of their time hunting. Every day they went out to hunt. Seeing this, their aunt advised them to stop bothering their father's people. "You're killing too much. You must stop doing this."

The jaguar, who also was annoyed at the boys, gave them a warning: "One of these days I'm going to transform you into people like us, to make you leave my people alone."

After this warning, the brothers considered what they were going to do. The Sun suggested to the Moon, "Let's gather taquari and turn it into a lot of wild men, so that they'll kill all the people around here."

They agreed and went out into the forest to cut taquari. They cut a lot and brought it back to the village. They cut the taquari into tiny pieces and scattered them around the huts. There was a lot of taquari. On a day chosen by the jaguar, the villagers grabbed the Sun and the Moon, and took them to the center of the village. When the jaguars began to squeeze the boys' hands to shape them into jaguar's paws, they screamed. At that moment, the taquari turned into people, invaded the village, and killed everybody there.

The Sun had shut his father inside the house. When everybody was dead, the Moon asked, "What will we do with our father?"

"We will send him away," answered the Sun.

They went to the house and said to him, "Now we are going to send you away."

"All right."

The Sun then gathered a pile of ashes and blew them over the hut. The jaguar was afraid and climbed up to the sky with his wife, the boys' aunt.

"And now, what are we going to do with all these people we made?" asked the Moon.

"We must send them away," answered the Sun.

To do that, the Sun and the Moon assembled everybody in the village clearing and told them to follow each other and go off, a few in each direction. When they left, they set fires, so that everything would burn in all directions. The Sun and the Moon stayed alone for a long time. When Mavutsinim, their grandfather, found this out, he sent for them. And they went to the Morená, where Mavutsinim lived.

There, their grandfather said to them, "When you go back, you must make your mother's kuarup [funeral ceremony]."

After a while, the brothers told their grandfather that they were going to have the kuarup. After giving his permission, Mavutsinim advised them, "You can go, but don't fight with the others. You must treat everybody well. You must be everybody's friends."

The Sun and the Moon, accompanied by their grandfather's people, then journeyed to the jaguar's old village, where their mother had died.

There they cut the logs for the festival. They made a great catch of fish, prepared beijus and manioc drink. When everything was ready, they sent the *pariáts* [messengers] to invite the fish and other people to the feast. Headed for the Morená, the *carícarí* and the gigantic *pirarrucú* fishes and the *pecaú* pigeons began their journeys. The guests asked what day they could leave. The pariáts said the next day. The next day, at dawn, the fish left in answer to the Sun's invitation. The other pariáts went to invite the village of the *caratú-aruiáp* [fish]. The chief of the caratú-aruiáp told the messengers that he could not go because he could not walk any more, but he would send two of his sons. These fish caught up with the others who were still in the Morená, and they all left together for the Sun's feast. They began their journey upstream. The first day they passed by Anariá. After that, by a place called Maracutaví. Here they had a scrape with the teeth of the *peixe-cachorro* [fiddlerfish]. This made them bleed. A little later, upriver, they passed by Iacaré and, soon after, by Iauapé and Kranhãnhã. There, they danced the *oát* [flute dance] during the night. The next day they reached the Marivarrét lagoon and slept there. Everybody was very happy that the two caratú-aruiáps were traveling with them, because they were great warriors. Some of the people stayed at the Marivarrét lagoon. Others went on by canoe or on foot. Farther along, they ran into the *catsinim* [a rodent], who was fishing. The fish began to swim past him. The catsinim eyed them. The spiny-finned *tucunaré* went by, then a little red fish called *ararapirá*.

Those in front said to those behind them, "Watch out for the catsinim fishing."

Hearing this, the catsinim was astonished. The ararapirá stuck his head out of the water and said to the catsinim, "We're on our way to the Sun's feast."

The catsinim was terrified of the water. The fish pulled him into the water, saying, "Don't be scared. You're not going to die."

The catsinim went along with the fish. Farther ahead, they stopped awhile to sleep. At that point, the *ariranhas* [otters] began to chase the fish. The fish hailed the catsinim, "Can you hear the singers?"

"Yes."

"Those singers have hands and feet like yours. Their legs and arms are just like yours. They are the same thing as you."

Cascudo

They said this and went on their way. Farther up, they found a waterfall. The *cascudo* [mailed catfish] wanted to jump but he got caught. Then the *acarí* fish tried, but he failed too. He jumped and got caught. Then came the *papa-terra,* who leaped over to the other side. The tucunaré also got over the obstacle. Then came the sons of the caratú-aruiáp. The fish who could not get by asked the caratú-aruiáp to lead the way. The way was opened and all of them got over the waterfall. Farther ahead, they found another waterfall and stood waiting for the caratú-aruiáps to catch up. These led the way, and the fish started to pass.

Once the waterfall had been negotiated again, they said to the catsinim, "Do you see, catsinim? The singers are just like you."

At this point they were approaching the Sun's village. They were almost there. They arrived in the afternoon and camped near the village. From the campsite, they asked for manioc drink. This was served to them and they ate it all. Then they asked the messengers who had come to invite them for fire. The pariáts took a long time, so five of the guests went to the village to get them. They leaned against the deer's house and kept calling for the head of the house. Two young women came out and said no one was there. They were the only people at home. The five went inside and asked if they could stay and have relations with them. The women agreed and they stayed. Meanwhile, the pariáts had brought fire for the guests, and told them that their companions were in the village with the women. The guests got angry and said that in that case their companions need not return. They took up their five hammocks and set them far away from the camp. The guests did not want their companions to come back.

Following the fish, the otters were beginning to arrive.

The next day, the guests began to paint themselves. The women too painted themselves. When the Sun appeared in full, the pariáts went to get the fish. They brought them all to the center of the village. The five who had gone courting the day before were not allowed to attend. When all were assembled in the middle of the village, the dance began. The Sun's folks were the first to dance. After that it was the fishes' turn. In the end, the catsinim joined the others in the dance. When the dance was over, the wrestling matches began. The Sun fought first with one of the caratú-aruiáps and lost. The other caratú-aruiáp defeated each of the best wrestlers in the Sun's village. After the first matches were over, the general competition began. The jaguar fought with the *poraquê* [electric eel] and snatched off all the ornaments on his arms. The Sun wrestled again with the great fighter and was thrown, falling head to the ground. At that moment the matches were over. When the Sun rose, he asked who had thrown him. They told him that the wrestler who had done it had already left. As soon as he had thrown the Sun, he ran and hid in a hole. After the fight, the people started to dance the *uruá* [flute dance]. The carícarí and the acarí fish danced, accompanied by women. The woman dancing with the acarí started tickling him to make him fall down. The acarí caught her arm and dragged her into the water. After the dance, manioc drink was served. At this point, the otters started to show up. The fish ran to hide. Only the catsinim was left in the middle of the village. Then the otters asked him where everybody was, saying that they could see a lot of tracks but no people. The catsinim said he did not know, and coming closer to the otters, he farted loudly.

The otters asked, "Where did that come out of?"

"My asshole," answered the catsinim.

The otters stayed at his side. Minutes later, the catsinim farted again.

The otters smelled the odor of feces and became curious, asking once more, "Where did you let this out?"

"Through my asshole," he said again.

Afterward, the catsinim drank some manioc drink and felt a bowel movement coming on. When he walked off to relieve himself, the otters followed to see where it would come out. They crept up on him and watched. Then they asked the catsinim if he could make a similar opening in them. They complained that they did not have one, and whenever they needed to relieve themselves, they had to vomit. So they said, "We want to be able to shit like you, not through the mouth the way we do now."

"All right," said the catsinim. "I shall make you just like me."

Speaking thus, he removed the string from his bow and sharpened one end. Turning to the otters, he said, "Now turn your ass upward and cover your face with your hands."

When the otters were in this position, he made a hole. One of them asked, "Will we die completely?"

"No," said the catsinim, "you'll die a little, but you'll come back to life again."

And the catsinim went on making holes. All the fish were hiding in the *tapãim* [men's house]. When the catsinim got ready to make a hole in the last otter, a fish spoke from the hiding place, "Catsinim, you will kill them all."

Hearing this, the last otter leaped into the water, and the catsinim was hardly able to reach her tail with the tip of his bow. The one who escaped gave birth to others, all with a little anus like the one that had been made in her. If the fish had not said anything, all the otters would have been killed.

The catsinim was furious with the fish when they came out of the tapãim and said, "If you hadn't said anything, I would have taken care of all of them."

The fish who went to the Sun's feast never came back. It was too far for them. Only the Sun and the Moon returned to the Morená, where Mavutsinim's village was.

Ariranha

KUATUNGUE:
The Origin of the Twins
Sun and Moon

(*Kuikúru*)

K uatungue went out to hunt and to gather embira to make a fish net. He was pulling embira off a tree when the jaguar arrived with his tribe. The jaguar was in the lead, his people behind. As soon as the jaguar's people spotted Kuatungue, they began to encircle him. Kuatungue, afraid of being eaten, wanted to escape before the circle closed around him. The jaguar's people were moving closer and closer around Kuatungue, when he saw the jaguar and went over to talk to him.

"What are you going to do with me? Do you want to eat me? Don't do that. I have beautiful daughters and I'll give them to you."

"Get out of here fast," answered the jaguar before the others arrived. He said that while the others were getting closer and closer. Kuatungue ran off. The jaguar's people closed in and asked, "Where is he?"

"He ran off."

"Why didn't you grab him?"

"I didn't see a thing."

Kuatungue was running fast and soon began to get tired. Everything was dark. The sun did not exist at that time. Kuatungue got home very late and very tired. He had two daughters, beautiful girls. Kuatungue was beginning to fret about his promise to the jaguar; how could he bear to give him one of his daughters?

"What am I going to do?" Stretched out, he thought of nothing but his promise. The next day he got up early and went to the forest looking for *uégovi* [tree], the chief of the trees. Walking quite a distance, he found a *pau-amarelo* [yellowwood] or *vatá*, from which he cut two logs. Farther on, he found a *pau-de-leite* [milkwood] or *icú*, from which he also cut two logs. And last, he cut two logs of uégovi, the wood he had been looking for in the first place. Having done this, he started to carve, in the logs he had cut, images of people with legs, arms, and heads. After he had finished his work, Kuatungue brought the logs home and hid them well behind the bushes. Then Kuatungue made a stool, which he put near the effigies in the bushes. He also left hammocks ready to be used there. When it got darker, Kuatungue went to sleep. In the middle of the night the logs began to turn into people. When he woke up, Kuatungue could hear the sound of talking coming from the bushes. Stealthily, he crept over to see if the logs had actually turned into people as he had wanted them to.

Seeing that everything had turned out as he had hoped, he said, "Aha! My daughters, I am your father. I was the one who made you. How are you? Are you healthy or feeble?"

"We are very well. We are strong."

Kuatungue examined them closely and saw that they had no hair. "Oh! What am I going to do?" he worried. He took off in search of something to make into hair. First he brought fibers of palm shoots and hung them on the girls' heads. After inspecting them, he decided that it wasn't quite right. He thought the fiber looked too white. He went out after something else, finding a kind of grass in the water that seemed better. He brought the grass and also dry corn silk. He hung it all on the girls' heads and decided this time it would do.

The girls laughed, and he saw then that they had no teeth. Kuatungue went out to get some and came back with piranha teeth. He put them in the girls' mouths, and brought food to see if they were properly set in and how they ate. He noticed that they gobbled very fast, like otters or even piranhas. This displeased Kuatungue. He took their teeth out and went to look for something better. Then he found mangaba seeds. Back home, he put the mangaba seeds one by one into his daughters' mouths. But before installing the teeth, Kuatungue put a little insect in the seeds. And that is why teeth rot and don't stay healthy for a lifetime. Then Kuatungue told them to laugh. They laughed, and he thought the teeth looked fine.

Kuatungue left again, this time in search of embira to make a vaginal shield for the women. He walked a long way, until he reached the pindaíba village. When he got there, everybody was wrestling. He waited for the wrestling to end. They all recognized Kuatungue and asked, "What do you want?"

Kuatungue went to the center of the village, and when everybody was standing around, he spoke. "I have six daughters. I need embira to make shields for them. Whoever wants to come along, let's go."

Kuatungue went home crestfallen because no one wanted to go with him. But he wasn't angry. At his house, he described what had happened to him. Next day he left on a new search. He walked and walked until he came to the village of the white embira [*túim*]. There, too, everyone was wrestling. He waited for the matches to be over, and standing in the center of the village, he said, "I have six daughters and I need embira to make shields for them. Whoever wants to come along, let's go."

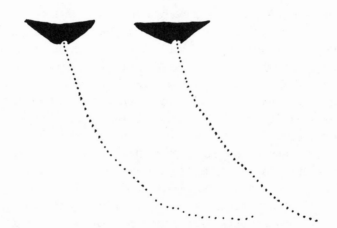

Vaginal shields

Everyone accepted Kuatungue's invitation, but only six people went with him to the village. There Kuatungue peeled the bark off the logs, stood them up, and put them to dry near the fire. When the embira was quite dry and white, Kuatungue made vaginal shields. Then he explained to his daughters how to use the shield [*túim*], recommending that they take it off to urinate, so that the fiber would not rot. Then Kuatungue told them all to go to sleep, so that they could rise early and go bathe. He also taught them how to sit up. At dawn the girls rose, went to bathe, and talked a lot.

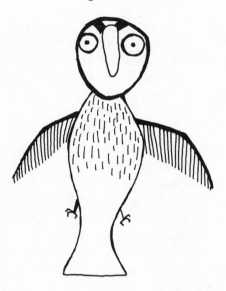

Owl

They had an owl. When the owl hooted, they started to laugh. One of them asked, "Oh! My father, can't you hear the bird hooting? What is he hooting about?"

"Oh! My daughter, when I went to collect fiber to make a fish net, I came across a jaguar and he almost ate me. So I said to him, 'Don't eat me and I'll let you marry my daughters.' How do you feel about it? Do you want to go?"

They were sad and told him they did not want to, they would rather stay. When Kuatungue spoke again, he was very stern. In the end, the young women consented. When everything was ready, they said goodbye to Kuatungue. They traveled till noon. Until that time, they could not find any water. Each one of them was carrying a small mat made of the thickest part of the buriti's stalk. In the afternoon they found water, but it was foul. It was dirty and poisoned. One of them, being very thirsty, drank it and died. The others had no intention of trying that water; they preferred to stay thirsty. At night they were so tired that they went to sleep right away. But before they did, they buried their sister who had died. They cried a lot. In the morning they continued their journey.

After walking quite a distance, they met the kingfisher, who said, "Where are you going?"

"We are going to the jaguar's place. Is it very far?"

"Yes, it's quite a way. It will take you five more days to get there."

They said goodbye, but just as they were about to leave, the king-fisher grabbed one of the girls as payment for his information. The other four left. The fifth had relations with the kingfisher and then ran off to catch up with her sisters. Traveling some distance, the five sisters came across an *irara* [weasel-like animal] collecting honey.

"Where are you headed?" he asked.

"We're going to the jaguar's place. Is it very far?"

"It will take you four days to get there."

The irara offered them honey and the girls accepted. One of them choked on it and fell to the ground in a fit. The irara took advantage of the occasion and had sexual relations with her. It had been he who blew on her and caused her to choke. As soon as he had finished with her, the woman recovered and proceeded on her trip with the others. They walked a little farther and then stopped to rest for the night. Next day, after traveling some distance, they came across a tapir.

"Where are you headed, girls?" asked the tapir.

"We are going to the jaguar's place."

"Who sent you?"

"Our father did. Is it still very far?"

The tapir pointed out the way, but he wanted to have relations with them as a reward for the information. The women did not want to, but the tapir grabbed one of them. She died because the tapir's penis was huge. The others began to weep and went to have a look at their dead sister. Since she had split right up the middle, the women could see that they were all made of wood.

"Aha! So that's why our father sent us. We aren't people. He doesn't like us. That's why he sent us to the jaguar."

After their sister's death, only four of them were left. They went on till they came across the *tatupeba* armadillo. He gave them directions to the jaguar's place and said that it would take them two days to get there. Just as they were about to leave, the armadillo grabbed one of them because he wanted to have relations with her. Discovering that his penis would not harden, the armadillo told them to wait while he went home to fetch something that would enable him to have relations. As soon as he left, the women fled.

"Let's leave right now," they said.

After a little while, the armadillo came back and called, "Hey you! Where are you? I'm back." Tired of shouting, the armadillo got mad and yelled, "Run off, will you? You'll die on the way."

Then, his penis hard and dangling, the armadillo went home in anger.

Everything was dark and cold, since there was still no sun. The sun had not yet been born. The four women continued their journey. They walked until they found a shallow stream with a slippery bottom. This slowed down their progress; in the stream, the young women bathed and drank a lot of water. However, one of them slipped, hit her head against the bottom, and died instantly. The others wept copiously, buried their sister, and went on their way. Now there were only three of them.

Farther ahead, they found a deer standing in their path. He was fully adorned and beautiful. The girls stopped to look at him. They liked him. He was very handsome. They had some salt with them and wanted to give it to the deer. "Oh! Young man, here's some salt, do you want to eat it?" •

The girls wanted to put the salt in his hand, but he would not open his fingers. He told them to put the salt on the back of his hand, because if they placed it on his palm, the cold salt would make him weak. Then he asked, "Where are you headed?"

"We're going to see the jaguar and marry him. Our father told us to."

"Do you know where the jaguar lives?"

"No, we don't."

"You're getting closer. In one night you'll be there. When you reach the water, you will see two paths, one to the jaguar's house, that's the straight path; the other goes to the wolf's, and it turns off in the other direction."

The girls went on their way. Farther on, they found a buriti palm. One of the girls told another to climb up and strip off the shoot's fiber to make a vaginal shield. One of them climbed it and from above threw the shoot down. It stuck in the ground, point upward. As the girl descended, the others started to throw bits of their fingernails at her. The fingernails turned into motuca flies and stung the woman in the tree. To shoo the flies away, she swatted at them with one hand, but she couldn't hold on with the other alone, so she fell on the palm shoot, which had stuck in the ground, point upward. This killed her. The other girls buried their dead sister and went on their way. There were only two of them left.

After some distance, they came to a stream near the jaguar's beach, which was his bathing place. The two paths started there. The young women climbed into the trees and waited to see who would come to bathe. After a while, a *seriema* [a crested, crane-like bird] with a gourd came to fetch water. The seriema was the wolf's wife. She set about bathing, and the two women watched from the tree. After bathing thoroughly, the seriema came out of the water and started talking to herself. "My body is lovely. My hair is long. I'm strong. My legs are nice and sturdy. Everybody says I have no hair and my legs are thin."

The two girls heard this and laughed. As the seriema was leaving, the girls peeled off bits of fingernail and threw them at her. The nails turned into motuca flies and stung the seriema. She tried to shoo them away, and in the process let the gourd fall and break. The seriema went to get another gourd and filled it with water again. As she was about to leave, the girls threw more bits of fingernail at her. When they turned into motuca flies, they stung her again, and she dropped the gourd, and again it broke. This time the seriema heard the two girls laughing and got angry. The girls saw that the seriema suspected something. When she got home, the seriema told her husband what had happened.

"There are strangers nearby. They threw something at me and made my gourds break. I think these people came to marry you."

The women climbed down from the tree and decided to leave. They agreed to take different paths. One would take the jaguar's path, the other the wolf's path. The older, because she had been made out of the lower half of the trunk, took the first trail, her sister the second. This was their plan: whichever of them took the wrong path and failed to find the jaguar would look for the other, who would have taken the right path. The older sister found the wolf's house and was captured by him. The wolf liked her. The younger sister reached the jaguar's house and introduced herself. "My father sent me."

"Ah! Yes, I know. I met your father. Where is your sister? Why didn't you come together?"

"We didn't know the way to your house. My sister took the other trail and must have found the wolf's house."

The jaguar then spoke to his tribesmen. "In a while we shall go out to hunt."

They nodded. As they were about to leave, the jaguar took a few steps and said he could go no farther because he was injured. "My people, I can't come because I'm hurt. You'll do all right without me. Don't fight with anyone."

He had injured himself deliberately so he could stay behind. He wanted to find the girl who was at the wolf's house. Coming back from the forest, the jaguar shot whistling arrows toward the girl, who was sitting in the wolf's doorway. He kept shooting the same arrow and picking it up as he walked along. Close by the house, the jaguar threw his arrow, and it fell right in front of the girl. She picked it up. When he came to fetch it, the jaguar grabbed the girl by the wrist. "Hey, girl, what are you doing here? Why didn't you stay with your sister? Your father sent you to me."

The wolf's mother, who was an old woman, followed after the jaguar as he made off with the girl. The old wolf said, "Why are you taking my son's wife? That's my son's wife you're taking."

The jaguar said, "She belongs to me. Her father sent her to me."

And turning to the girl, he said, "Don't look at the old woman or her head will fall off."

Just as they came to the jaguar's house, the girl looked back at the old woman. The old woman's head fell off.

"That girl doesn't have long to live. She'll die soon," said the old wolf.

The people began to return from the hunt. The jaguar brought manioc drink to the hunters. The wolf found out that the jaguar had taken his wife away, which made him sad. But the old wolf, his mother, was angry.

The jaguar asked the girl, "Listen, woman, did the wolf meddle with you?"

"No, he didn't."

"Did he lie with you?"

"Yes."

"In that case he did meddle with you. You will have to drink some bark and root medicine to make you vomit."

The jaguar went into the forest, brought back the medicine. And the girl drank it and vomited. The girl was already carrying the wolf's child. The jaguar gave her the medicine to make her vomit, so that his own son wouldn't come out a halfbreed. Later the same girl became pregnant by the jaguar. Her sister would not get pregnant.

One day, when her time had almost come, the pregnant woman was sitting in the entrance to her house, spinning cotton. Her mother-in-law, the jaguar's mother, was sweeping the house. She passed wind and barked angrily at her daughter-in-law, "Why didn't *you* sweep first? This is your husband's house. Why don't you sweep?"

The daughter-in-law spat out the cotton threads that were in her mouth, but the old jaguar thought she was spitting because of her farting and snarled, "Did you spit because of me?"

The old jaguar, very angry, peeled a piece off her fingernail and threw it at her daughter-in-law, cutting her head off. Her daughter-in-law thrashed about on the floor next to her head. At that moment her sister came in. She began to weep and said to the old jaguar, "Why did you do this? Why did you do this?"

Then she picked up her dead sister, placed her in the hammock, and put her head back where it belonged. The jaguar was away at his planting grounds. When he came home and saw what had happened, he asked, "What happened?"

"It was your mother who did this."

When the woman ran to help her pregnant sister, who was dying, she saw that two children were coming out. The two boys who were born were: Rit [Sun] and Une [Moon]. Until then everything was dark. The sun did not exist at that time. Since Rit was the sun himself being born, it got lighter as he grew. Thus, only when Rit reached adulthood would light be its brightest.

The jaguar, seeing all that, was very sad and said, "Why did you do this, my mother?"

He took his mother to a place near the stream. There he made a little hut, left some food, and gave the place to his mother. So people would leave her alone, he surrounded the hut with snakes, wasps, and pineapple thorns. Back home the jaguar had no idea where to put the dead woman's body. The two children were already being taken care of by their aunt. At length the jaguar decided to put the dead woman on top of the house.

It did not take the two boys very long to grow up. They grew rapidly. Two moons went by and they grew; three moons and they still grew. After three moons, they were already standing up. After ten moons, they were walking and crying. Their aunt was getting annoyed and said over and over, "Don't cry. Here's some food: beiju and manioc drink. Keep quiet. Go and fetch peanuts from the partridge."

The two boys headed toward the field. They found the peanuts and ate a lot of them. Meanwhile, the partridge arrived and flew into a fury. "Who is messing up my peanut garden? Who is picking my peanuts? Where have these children come from? Oh! I understand . . . You don't know anything. Your mother is dead. It was your grandmother who killed her. The woman there isn't your mother; she is your aunt."

The boys listened in silence to everything the partridge told them. The partridge went on: "Do you think she is your mother? No, she is not. She is your aunt. You don't know anything. It was your grandmother who killed your mother. She is on the roof of your house. Your father was the one who put her there. She is dead. Your father hid your grandmother near the stream. He is very ashamed."

In this way the boys learned that that woman was not their mother but their aunt. They rushed from their hiding places and grabbed the partridge. "What did you say?"

The partridge was afraid of them and said, "I didn't say a thing. I only told you to stop picking my peanuts."

"No, that wasn't what you said. You said something else."

"No, I didn't say a thing."

The boys clung to the partridge firmly. When they loosened their grip a little, he told them, "It was your father who put your mother on your roof. Your grandmother is hidden in a hut by the river. If you go there, watch out for the snakes."

This made the boys angry, and they said, "We shall no longer call him father. Now we will only call him chief."

The boys grabbed the partridge by the neck and hurled him into the field. He plunged to the ground with his neck stretched out and at once started to whistle, just as the partridge does today. The boys went off. They conferred as they walked. "Shall we visit our grandmother? Shall we kill her?"

When they reached their own house, they did not go in. They stayed outside. The aunt appeared and said, "Come in, my sons. Did you gather a lot of peanuts? Did you eat well? Why are you crying? Don't stay outside."

"No. You are not our mother. You are our aunt. Our mother died. Our grandmother killed her. Our father was the one who put her on the roof. The partridge set us straight."

When their aunt went inside the house, the jaguar asked what the children had said. The woman answered, "They said I was not their mother, and they said their mother was dead and their grandmother killed her. They know everything."

"Who told the boys all these things?"

"The partridge."

The two boys went off to search for their grandmother. They looked and looked, until finally they found the hut. The partridge had given them every warning. He told the boys to watch out for the snakes, the wasps, and the pineapple thorns around the hut.

"Let's summon the eagle. He likes to catch snakes," one of the boys recalled.

The eagle came and swept down on the snakes. Now they had to deal with the wasps. The boys remembered a little bird that ate wasps and called upon him. That left only the pineapple thorns. For these, they called upon the tapir, who liked to trample everything underfoot. The tapir came and trampled all over the thorns until the path was cleared. Then the boys went up and uncovered the door to the hut.

The old jaguar said, "Oh! My grandchildren, come and lie here with me."

The boys went inside. The old jaguar embraced both of them and began to play with them. The boys had tied stones to their feet. At first, when their feet touched their grandmother's chest, the boys pretended to be playing. The old jaguar played with them one at a time.

"Oh! My grandmother, we were looking for you."

The grandmother said, "It was I who killed your mother. I killed your mother. I didn't like her."

Meanwhile, the boys started to hurt their grandmother. They kicked her chest harder and harder. Finally they kicked her so hard that she died. Then they said, "What are we going to do? Shall we set fire to the whole thing? How will we manage? Shall we set the whole thing on fire and say we did it to kill the wasps?"

The boys went home and said, "Chief, give us some fire."

"What for?" he asked.

"To kill wasps."

"Where have you been?"

"In the forest."

"Be careful, my sons, it's dangerous. The animals can eat you."

The boys took the fire and left on the run. At the water's edge they set their grandmother's hut on fire. The fire burned everything. The two boys hid, fearful that something would explode out of their grandmother's body and hit them. Rit told his brother Une to keep himself well hidden and not to watch. "Be careful. A piece of our grandmother might hit you."

Une stayed hidden behind a tree for a while, but a foul piece of the old woman popped out of the fire and hit him on the nose. When the fire was spent, they came out of hiding. Rit said, "Why did you watch? I told you not to, but you wouldn't believe me."

Rit covered his brother's nose with his hand, which healed the wound quickly. Now Une's nose was flat and closed up. Once it had been like Rit's, large and straight. The two boys went home. Their aunt asked, "How did it go? Did you burn the wasps?"

"Yes. We finished them off."

Their father, the jaguar, was suspicious that they had found their grandmother. He decided to go and have a look. When he got there, the hut was nowhere to be found. Everything had been burned to the ground. "That's what I thought," the jaguar said to himself.

"Did you set fire to your grandmother, boys? What did you do to your grandmother? That was not kind of you."

The jaguar did not make an issue of it because he feared his sons, who by now were nearly full grown and very clever. They already knew more than their father.

The jaguar said to his wife, "The children burned their grandmother. I went to see, and there was nothing left. Everything was burned to the ground. That's what they wanted fire for."

Rit and Une were very angry. Rit said to his father, "Chief, tell your people to gather taquari to make arrows for us."

From the time the partridge had told them the truth, Rit and Une had not addressed the jaguar as father, only as chief.

The jaguar consented and went out calling to his people. "My tribesmen, go and gather taquari to make arrows."

His people heard him, consented, and that very hour went out to gather taquari. When they returned, the jaguar's wife, the boys' aunt, provided everyone manioc drink. She brought the manioc drink pot by pot to the center of the village. As they sipped, the jaguar questioned his sons, "All right, my sons. What do you want?"

"You must tell your people to begin making arrows at once," Rit answered.

Everybody began making arrows at once. Meanwhile, the jaguar's wife went on distributing manioc drink. Rit and Une sat at the doorway. As the capybara passed, carrying a gourd for the jaguar, Rit shot him in the leg with an arrow. The capybara died immediately. Rit then gave his aunt the animal to roast. When it was cooked, Rit carried it to the jaguar to eat, and said, "Chief, you must eat this. If you eat any more people, there won't be anyone left. You have to change your diet. From now on you have to eat deer, capybara, fish, and other things."

The jaguar ate it up, and Rit asked, "Chief, did you like it?"

"Yes, I did."

When they had run out of arrows, Rit said to his father, "Chief, tell your people to start making cudgels."

Rit burned the taquari left over from the arrows, purified the ashes into salt, and gave it to his aunt to put on food. The aunt, the jaguar's wife, ate it and got pregnant.

Later the cudgels were finished. The jaguar handed all the cudgels and arrows over to his son. Then he asked, "Well, my son, are you pleased?"

Rit said yes and ordered that everything be taken into the forest. Then he had a talk with his brother Une. "How will we do it? Shall we take her down from the roof?"

Rit sent for his friends, Kuatungue, Caiãnamá, and Caiãnamá's sister, Babanhiço. When they came, Rit arranged to get his mother down from the roof. With great care, they lifted her down. She was almost dead. She was terribly weak and thin. Gently, and very slowly, they took her inside and put her in a hammock. Cautiously they gave her some manioc drink and beiju. Rit asked, "My mother, how are you? Are you going to die? Have some more manioc drink. Can I lie here beside you, Mother?"

Rit lay beside his mother. "My mother, if you are going to die, will you tell me? Will you tell me? Will you tell me if you're going to die?"

As he lay beside his mother in the hammock, Rit's weight squeezed her so tightly that she died. Everyone wept at her death. Rit sent for the *tatu-pequeno* and *canastra* armadillos, and the beetle and the *mamangaba* bumblebee, and told them to dig a hole to put his mother in. The burrowers wanted to bury Rit's mother in the center of the village, but Rit was against it. They insisted, and still Rit refused. So they suggested making two graves connected by a tunnel underground. Finally Rit agreed to this, and got ready to paint and adorn his mother for burial. The two armadillos, the beetle, and the bumblebee told Rit that he could bury his mother just as she was. Rit said he would, but suggested that they wrap her up in the hammock and carry her slowly, singing chants along the way. Rit checked the lengths of the hammock and of the tunnel between the two graves to make sure they were the same. Then they slowly bore the dead woman's body to her grave. Everyone keeping her company was weeping. At the graveside, they lowered the body to the ground. Then the bearers gently let the body down into the hole, and there at the bottom, they spread out the hammock in the tunnel between the two holes. Then they covered the body with a mat and filled the grave with earth. Everyone was still weeping, including Kuatungue, who had come at Rit's request, which had been conveyed to him by the *graxaim* [wild dog]. The armadillos, the beetle, and the bumblebee also wept. The tatu-pequeno armadillo had a fit, fell over, and started having convulsions. Those who were weeping began to laugh. Rit laughed too. Then he said, "Everybody is laughing. That's better, otherwise the sadness is too much. It's enough to be sad for five days."

After burying Rit's mother, they all went back home. Rit's aunt was

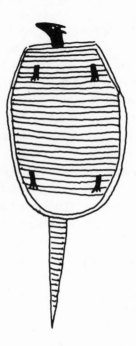

Armadillo

about to give birth. Rit said to her, "Oh! My mother, are you giving birth here? Better go into the forest where the arrows and cudgels are being kept."

Rit led his aunt out there. The aunt began to give birth, but she was giving birth to fully grown people. As soon as they were born, Rit handed them bow and arrow, and they came out ready to fight, stamping their feet and crying Oooooooooooo . . . Rit handed out arrows until he had none left. He gave away many bows. When there were no more, he started giving out cudgels, till he ran out of those too. Each of them had one. There were plenty of them. Suddenly, they decided to kill Rit. But he said, "All of you are my sons. You can't do that."

The jaguar had no idea what was going on. Rit didn't tell him. Instead Rit ordered everyone to stay in the forest and keep quiet. At this time there was already something like day; there was light. The great sun was being created.

On her way home, Rit's aunt captured a baby opossum and brought it with her. The jaguar asked, "Was the child born?"

The jaguar's wife held out the baby opossum and said, "Everything is fine. Look, doesn't he look like you?"

"Yes, he's just like me."

The woman gave her breast to the baby opossum. Meanwhile, the mother opossum was frantically searching for her child. "Who stole my baby? Who could it be?"

The mother opossum looked and looked until finally she came to the jaguar's house. There she found her baby in the lap of the jaguar's wife. The opossum grabbed her baby and ran off. The jaguar said to his wife, "You lied to me. That baby wasn't mine. You stole somebody else's baby. That was not my son."

The jaguar's wife was ashamed that she had lied to her husband. The jaguar was sad. "Where did you put my son? Where did you leave him? Did he die? Where did you bury him?"

The jaguar's wife did not answer. Rit had told her not to say anything, not even if the jaguar asked. Everybody went to sleep: the jaguar, his wife, Rit, Une, all of them. Rit told the people who had been born to keep quiet and at nightfall to surround the jaguar's village. At daybreak, Rit instructed, they were to attack the village. As soon as it began to get light and the villagers were leaving to bathe, the attack began. Everybody was shooting arrows, running, and screaming. The jaguar's tribesmen all died, except for the agouti, who was very clever and took flight. During the fight, Rit summoned his father and his aunt, and said, "Sit here on this bow. I'm going to send you to the heavens. That is our place. Go there. The fight has begun, and your people will all die."

When the fighting was over and the jaguar's people were all dead, the warriors gathered in the center of the village. There they decided to kill Rit and his brother Une. Rit spoke, "How can you do that, my sons? I made you. How can you kill your father? If it were not for me, you would never have been born."

They all nodded and said, "That is very true. He is our father. We may not kill him."

Rit divided the people and to each group of three, he gave a name: these he called the Suiá; those the Aviotó; these the Juruna; and thus the rest of them were named: Turrivissurrú, Iarumá, Pitado, Atuvúoto, Tavugli, Kamaiurá, Waurá, Naruvoto, Trumái, Caiabí, Meináco,

Auetí, Kalapalo, Kuikúru, Aipatse, Iaualapití, Tsúva, Auaicü, and others.

After dividing them, Rit added, "Not all of you will stay here. You will go far away, each in a different direction. Whenever you find other villages, fight with them."

After this, Rit and Une went to the Morená.

KUÁT AND IAÊ:
The Conquest of Day

(*Kamaiurá*)

In the beginning it was all dark. It was always night. There was no day. People lived around the termite hills. Everything was very confused. Nobody could see a thing. The birds defecated on top of people. There was no fire, there were no clearings, there was nothing. Only those fireflies around the termite hill existed. The brothers Kuát and Iaê, the Sun and the Moon, did not know what to do with their people: they were all dying of hunger because they could not work to get food. The brothers were hungry too and always thinking about how to make light. They wanted to create the day, but they could not think how. After much thought, they made an image of the tapir and filled it with manioc and other things that would rot and stink. After a few days, the effigy began to reek. Everything inside had spoiled and maggots were crawling all over it. The Sun wrapped the maggots up and gave the parcel to the flies, telling them to take it to the birds' village. The flies flew off and landed in the birds' village with the package of maggots. The birds surrounded the flies to find out what they had brought. The *urubutsin* [king vulture], the birds' chief, told them that the Sun intended to trick them so that he could steal the day. The urubutsin's village already had the day; they had light. The urubutsin ordered stools to be brought for the flies to sit on. Once they were seated, the chief asked, "What did you come here for?"

The flies answered him, but the urubutsin could not make out what they were saying. Nobody could understand the flies, as no one knew their language. One by one the birds questioned the flies, but none of them could understand what they said. The answer was always hum, hum, hum. They called the *xexéu* [oriole] bird to see if he could do any better.

"I doubt that I'll understand them," he said.

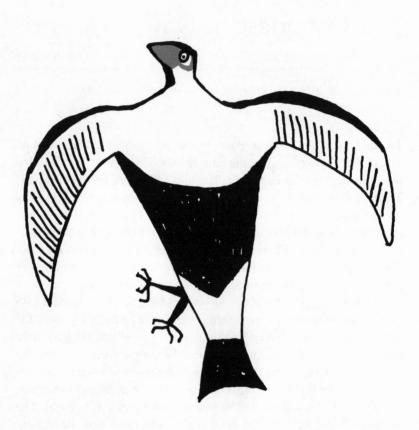

Urubutsin

In fact, he too failed to understand them. So they called a relative of the xexéu, the *diarrú* [congo kingbird]. The flies said something three times and he understood none of it. He told the others that he hadn't understood a thing. The other birds, his friends, had thought that he might understand the language of the flies because the xexéu speak many tongues. Then they called the *jacubim* to perform magic, but he too was unable to make anything out of the hum, hum, hum of the flies. Many other birds questioned the flies, but nothing came of it. Finally they called upon another relative of the xexéu, the *iapí-aruiáp* [a lesser variety of congo kingbird]. He was able to understand them. The flies then showed the package they had brought, saying that down below, where they came from, there were lots of rotten things that were good to eat. In fact, so many things that nobody could possibly eat it all. Then they handed over the package of maggots to the birds, who consumed it all and immediately asked the flies when they could go and eat what was down there.

"You can come this very day," they answered.

The urubutsin was always carrying on about how dangerous it was down there, and before they went, they must all cut their hair. The birds shaved themselves bald and started the trip down. The urubutsin was the last to leave. The Sun and the Moon had hidden themselves inside the tapir effigy. The urubutsin went to sit at the place the Sun had prepared for him. The birds arrived and began to eat the insects. One hawk did not rush to the carcass. He perched at a distance, watching. The Sun, who was spying through holes in the effigy's head, met the hawk's glance. The hawk saw the movement from his perch and warned the birds that the tapir's eyes had moved. The birds instantly took flight, abandoning the effigy, but after a while they came back and went on eating the grubs.

Then the Moon said to the Sun, "Get ready, here he comes."

As soon as the urubutsin landed on the carcass, the Sun grabbed one of his feet and held it fast. Seeing that their chief had been captured, all the birds took off together, abandoning the tapir's carcass.

The hawk, who had been watching from a distance, said, "Didn't I tell you I saw the tapir open his eyes?"

Then the Sun told the urubutsin, "We're not going to kill you. We only want the day. That was the reason we called you."

The birds flew back to their village. Only the jacubim and the guan stayed behind. The urubutsin ordered the jacubim to go and bring back the day. The jacubim flew off and after a while came back wearing an *aravirí* [armband] made of blue macaw feathers. The day began to dawn a little, and the Sun asked, "Is this the day?" The Moon told him it wasn't, it was only a blue macaw feather. As soon as the jacubim alighted, everything got dark again. Back in their village, the birds were very sad, thinking that the Sun had killed their chief. The urubutsin, trapped by the Sun, told the jacubim to go home again and this time bring back the real day. The jacubim left and returned with the crest of the *canindé* macaw, the yellow one.

As he flew back, it cleared up a little, and the Sun asked, "Is this really the day?"

"No, this is not the day. It will get dark again as soon as he touches the ground," said the Moon.

And in fact as soon as the jacubim touched the ground, it got dark again.

"What did I tell you?" the Moon said. "It still is not the real day."

The jacubim, sent away again by his captive chief, left and returned with a headdress of parrot feathers. Again it began to get light. This time, the Sun thought, it really must be the day. But the Moon said no, it would get dark again, and sure enough, as soon as the messenger landed, it got dark again.

So the Sun said to the urubutsin, "If you do not send for the real day, your people will think we have killed you here."

Hearing that, the urubutsin told the jacubim to bring the real day. The jacubim left and flew back covered with parrot feathers.

"Is this it?" asked the Sun.

"No," said the Moon, "it's the same thing as before."

The Sun said to the urubutsin in an ingratiating tone, "*Tamãi* [grandfather], send for the real day so that you can leave."

The jacubim went off again. This time he flew back decked out in a headdress and armbands of red macaw feathers.

The Sun asked, "Is it right this time? Is this really it?"

"No," repeated the Moon, "it's a red macaw's feather, and this is still not the day."

At this point the urubutsin spoke in a different tone to the guan, "Now go get the real day, because I'm tired of staying here."

The guan left and came back all decked out with a headdress, earrings, armbands and leg ornaments. He glided down.

The Moon said, "This is the day. That is the true red macaw. The other one wasn't pure."

When the guan landed, everything became bright. Pleased at last, the Sun said to the urubutsin, "I did not call you, Grandfather, to kill you. It was so you could give us the day. All my people were dying of hunger in the darkness. I needed the day for planting, for hunting, and for fishing."

Then the urubutsin began to instruct the Sun and the Moon, saying, "In the morning the day is born, in the afternoon it starts to fade, and then it disappears all at once. When this happens, don't think we took it back. Don't think that. The day appears, and afterward comes the night. It will always be this way. When the night comes, don't think that it will stay dark and that we stole the day from you. Don't be afraid. It will always come back."

Then he went on, "The night is for sleeping. The day is for working: to make gardens, hunt, fish, and do all kinds of things. Sleep at night and work during the day. Always."

When the urubutsin finished speaking, the Sun began to adorn him. He shaved the top of his head with a stone, painted it with urucu, and bound a white cotton string around it. Before leaving, the urubutsin said to the Sun and the Moon, "When you kill a big animal, put it where I can see it, so that I can come and feed."

After he spoke, the urubutsin opened his wings and flew away.

KUADÊ:
Juruna Kills the Sun

(*Juruna*)

Kuadê, the Sun, was also a person. He lived far away and spoke another language. The Juruna often traveled near his house. Where the Sun lived, there was a hole in the stone that was always full of water. It was a trap for catching animals. Any animal that put its head in the hole to drink got stuck. Every day the Sun went to see if he had caught anything. When he found something, he killed it and took it home to eat. Fishing he did at night only, shining a light from his rump into the water. He would get furious and kill anybody who claimed to have seen his light. There once was a young Juruna who did not know about the Sun's trap, the hole in the stone. Passing by one day, and being thirsty, he went to get a drink, and his hand got caught.

The next day, when he saw the Sun making his daily rounds, the youth pretended to be dead. He lay there stretched out, not moving a muscle. Even his heart stopped beating, out of fear. The Sun came up and inspected him. He opened his mouth and eyes, felt his chest, and saw that everything had stopped as in dead people. So the Sun freed the young Juruna's arm from the hole and put him inside a basket for carrying. But before raising the basket to his shoulders, to see if the youth was truly dead, he scattered ants all over him. The Juruna put up with the ants without moving until they began to bite his eyes, and then he stirred a little. The Sun's cudgel, which was standing nearby, saw him move and was going to smash him, but its master would not let it; he insisted that the Juruna was really dead. Then the Sun carried the basket with the body to a spot near his house and hung it from the branch of a tree. The next day he told his son to bring the basket into the house. The Sun's boy went out, but the Juruna was nowhere to be found. He had escaped during the night. On learning this, the

Sun hurled his cudgel after him. The cudgel left flying and at length struck a deer. The Sun said that was not what he wanted and went after the fugitive himself. Finally he found him hidden in the hollow root of a tree. The cudgel went up to the tree and proceeded to pound its trunk. Realizing that he wasn't getting anywhere with this, the Sun cut a stick and started poking around inside the hollow. He wounded the Juruna from head to foot, but still he would not come out of his lair. It was getting late, so the Sun covered up the hole with a stone and said to the cudgel, "Tomorrow we'll come back and finish him off."

At night, with the Sun far away, all kinds of animals—tapirs, wild pigs, deer, monkeys, pacas, agoutis—came to help the young Juruna out of the hole where he had hidden. From inside, he begged them, "Uncover this trunk so I can leave."

The animals started to burrow. Whenever their teeth were ready to break, they would bring other animals to keep on digging. Finally the tapir succeeded in making a little hole. The Juruna put his head out and asked them to dig a little more. The agouti and the tapir made the hole wide enough for him to get out. When the Sun arrived, the Juruna was nowhere to be found. By that time, he was practically in his own house. At home, he told his relatives about his adventure, saying that he had come very close to being killed by the Sun. After three days, he told his mother he was going out to gather coconuts. In tears, his mother begged him to stay. "Don't go, my son, because the Sun will kill you."

The young man cut off all his hair and painted his body with genipap. He went to tell his mother that the Sun would never recognize him as he was now. "Don't worry, the Sun will not recognize me. I'm different now."

He said this and marched off into the forest. He climbed the first inajá palm he could find and stayed up there gathering coconuts. The Sun happened to be passing through the neighborhood and thought he saw a monkey up in the palm tree. But when he realized that it was a person and that, in fact, it was the young Juruna, he said, "I almost killed you the other day, and now you really are going to die."

"I am not the person you think I am. I'm somebody else," said the young man from above.

But the Sun knew and replied, "It's you, all right. Come on down, you're going to die right now."

Then the Juruna, from the top of the palm tree, asked the Sun first to catch the coconut bunch he was about to throw. "First catch this bunch I'm throwing down."

"Throw it," said the Sun.

The youth threw the bunch and the Sun caught it. It was a small bunch, that first one. Up in the palm tree, the Juruna called again, "Catch this one too."

And from up there he threw a huge, heavy bunch. The Sun was waiting with his arms stretched out. The coconuts struck him right in the chest and killed him on the spot. At the Sun's death, everything got dark. The cudgel, at the death of its master, ran away and transformed itself into a snake, the *salamanta* [ringed boa], or *uandáre*

Snakes

[Sun's cudgel]. The blood pouring out of the Sun turned into spiders, ants, snakes, centipedes, and other creatures. The snakes and spiders that covered the ground would not allow the Juruna to climb out of the palm tree. So he began to swing from tree to tree, like a monkey, and would not come down until he saw that the ground was clear. Once on solid ground, the youth looked for his trail and went home to his village. When he got there, he said to his mother, "I killed the Sun."

"Why did you do that? I was right to tell you to stay home. Now everything is dark," the frightened mother complained.

The children were all dying in the darkness, since no one could fish or hunt or work. In the Sun's village, his wife realized that he had died. She said to her three sons, who were starving, "Your father died because he liked to kill people. Which of you wants to replace him?"

First she tested the oldest of the three. As soon as this one put on his father's feather headdress, he thought it was awfully hot. He went up and up, and when it was almost dawn, he couldn't stand the heat any longer and came back down. Then it was the second son's turn. He put the feathers on his head and started to ascend. He went a little past where his brother had given up, but in the end he couldn't stand it either and came down complaining of the heat. Now it was the youngest one's turn. His mother asked him if he wanted to replace his father. He said he did. He adorned himself with the feathers and rose up, but since the heat was frightful, he walked very fast and immediately hid himself on the opposite side.

When he came home, his mother said to him, "You stood it pretty well, but next time you'll have to walk slower, to give people a chance to fish and hunt and work. You mustn't run."

The Sun's youngest boy made the walk once again, and this time he went slower. His mother suggested that he rest awhile when he reached the summit in the middle of the route, and that he come down slowly, resting awhile there too, before going in on the opposite side. When the mother saw her son making the entire journey exactly as it should be done, she wept and said, "Now you've taken over your father's place and you'll never come back to me."

The son, in his turn, answered from above, "Now I can no longer return home to live with you. I must always remain up here."

Upon hearing this, his mother wept again.

KUAMUCACÁ:
The Sun and the Moon
Help to Kill the Jaguars

(Kamaiurá)

Kuamucacá's village was having a festival. It was the festival of the *namim* [ear]. The chanting and dancing began in the afternoon and lasted all night long, till the morning of the following day. The last night of chanting and dancing, Kuamucacá told his people that the next day a hole would be made in the boys' ears. At daybreak, the boys were brought to the center of the village, where their ears were to be pierced. The Sun and the Moon, who in their own village had been listening to the festive songs from the start, turned up that morning in Kuamucacá's village. When the two of them appeared on the path and were coming closer, Kuamucacá quickly told his people to take care not to pass remarks, because their guests could cause them harm.

Upon arrival the Sun said, "We have come to visit you."

In the village everything was ready to begin the ear-piercing ceremony. The boys were seated on the men's laps, the people were all ornamented, and the bone needles had been sharpened. Kuamucacá, wanting to please his guests, asked them to pierce the boys' ears. The Sun and Moon accepted the offer and, taking up miniature bows and arrows, got set to shoot the ears of the children, who were all sitting in a row in front of them. When he saw this, Kuamucacá ran over to stop them, saying, "This way you won't pierce ears, you'll kill all the boys instead."

He said that and went over to show them how to do the job. After showing them how the needle made of jaguar bone was used, he repeated that it could not be done with an arrow and handed the needle over to his guests, saying, "Now you can help us."

From then on, everything went well. The ears of all the boys were pierced. Once the piercing was done, the boys were taken into the houses. There were many of them. The chief's house was crowded. The boys climbed into the hammocks and began to fast. For three days they drank only small portions of *cauim* [fermented manioc drink]. When the fast was over, the older boys drank a liquid to make them vomit, so that they could go back to eating fish and other foods again.

The Sun and the Moon stayed on in Kuamucacá's village. During the period of confinement, the boys, to amuse themselves, began to make small arrows and asked the guests, the Sun and Moon, to help, giving them some bamboo arrow shafts to work on. When he found out about it, Kuamucacá got furious. The Sun and Moon made off with the shafts, following the path some distance from the village. There they hid and made the shafts into five *guariba* monkeys, sending them to attack the village. By afternoon the guariba warriors were closing

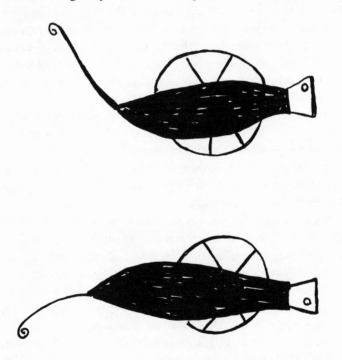

Monkey spirits

in on the houses. Kuamucacá went out to meet the animals, cajoling them and asking them not to attack. With fruits in his hand, the chief lured the monkeys into his house. And he shut them inside, after persuading the monkeys to eat the fruit.

The boys in confinement, still playing, began to throw wax balls back and forth, and also at the Sun, who happened to be nearby. Before throwing the ball back, the Sun stole a piece of it, joining the Moon back on the trail. Out of the wax he made a wild macaw and sent him to attack the village. Kuamucacá met him with a coconut in his hand, asking him to calm down. The macaw came closer and closer, till he ate the coconut offered to him. Kuamucacá, as he had done with the monkeys, trapped the macaw inside his house. The boys, who were still playing with wax, threw another piece at the visitor. Kuamucacá got furious with the boys. He said, "I told you not to do this and you did it."

The Sun and the Moon went back to the trail with the wax they had caught, and there they made a flock of birds called *tapemucarép* [parakeet]. That afternoon, the birds descended on Kuamucacá's house. Kuamucacá cautiously approached them, showing corn in his hand. They came close and were also trapped inside the house with the other animals.

Kuamucacá had a young sister who was in confinement. Every day he told his sister not to leave the house. "Don't go outside to bathe because the Sun and Moon are here," he repeated to her incessantly. But one day, in spite of his warnings, the girl went off to the lagoon to bathe and forgot one of the string ornaments she wore on her legs. The Sun, finding the string, brought it to the trail.

Kuamucacá gave his sister a stern scolding, saying, "Why did you do this? I told you over and over not to go outside."

After stealing the girl's string, the Sun and the Moon told Kuamucacá that they were going fishing. From a distance, they caused Kuamucacá's house to be enveloped in a layer of stone so that no one could get out. Then they transformed the string into a gigantic snake. The snake was meant to devour all of Kuamucacá's people. As soon as the snake was created, it slithered up to the stone house and said from outside, "Kuamucacá, hand over your people, so I can eat them."

Kuamucacá grabbed five boys and gave them to the creature. The snake gobbled up all five of them. In a short time, the snake came back and asked for more people. Kuamucacá gave him three more, and the snake ate them too. Minutes later, the reptile was back, asking for more. This time, Kuamucacá cut a number of logs and gave them to the giant snake. He ate them and slithered off, and it was a long time before he came back.

Meanwhile, Kuamucacá told his people that they had to escape immediately. "If we stay here another day, we will all die," he said. So they all cut their hair and began to paint their bodies with urucu and genipap, and adorned themselves with feathers to be able to leave right away. Kuamucacá asked the blue macaw to make a hole in the roof so they could leave. The macaw started to cut through the straw, but as soon as he reached the stone, it broke his tooth. And that is why people's teeth break and are so painful. Seeing that the macaw could no longer cut, Kuamucacá asked the tapemucaréps to continue the job. The parakeets set to work. They pecked and pecked till they pierced through the stone. Everybody was delighted and went on painting their bodies. The tapemucaréps called Kuamucacá to check that the hole they were making would be big enough for everybody to get out. Seeing that it wouldn't be, they set to work again and widened the hole.

Two men left first and stayed on top of the hut. From there, they shot an arrow into the sky. The arrow buried itself up there. They shot another, which joined the first. They kept on shooting them, until a string of arrows reached from the sky down to where they were. Then all the people began to leave the house through the hole. The guaribas left first. Kuamucacá asked them to lead the way, singing. After them, others climbed up the string of arrows that linked them to the sky. They went higher and higher. The guaribas never stopped singing as they led the way, and Kuamucacá's people followed, shouting. The Sun and the Moon heard the monkeys' chants and were furious because they were meant to have devoured Kuamucacá and clearly they had not done so.

On the roof, there remained two brothers and a sister of Kuamucacá. When it was her turn to climb up, the girl got frightened and balked. The brothers wanted to carry their sister, but she could not overcome her fear. She tried several times, but her nerve failed her. The boys, seeing that their sister was never going to make it, left her behind and went up the rope shouting.

Hearing the shouts, the Sun said, "You may be climbing now, but you'll all die up there."

It took the giant snake some time to come back after he had eaten the logs, but at length he returned, asking for more people. He called and called, but as no one answered, he said, "I am coming up after you." And up he went. When he was almost on top of the house, the girl cut off the tip of his tail and the snake slithered back down. As he dropped back, the girl cut him to pieces. She kept on hacking at him till his head fell off.

At that moment the Sun and Moon arrived at Kuamucacá's house and saw the pile of snake pieces. Spotting the girl, they asked her, "Why didn't you leave too?"

"I was afraid of going up."

As she said that, she started to cry, because of her brothers. The Sun urged her to go up, but she had no courage. Then the Sun told her to go away. She ran off, and the Sun transformed her into a bird, the scaled dove. As she took flight, the Sun said, "Now you will always live as a bird."

Having done this, the Sun and Moon gathered up the pieces of snake and threw them into the water. As they fell in, they became all different kinds of snakes. Then the Sun and the Moon climbed up the string of arrows in pursuit of Kuamucacá. Up there, they found the people painting their bodies. Kuamucacá asked them to paint themselves as well. The Sun and the Moon painted themselves and said, "We came after you because we missed you very much."

Then they all headed for the jaguars' village. Kuamucacá wanted to fight them and take away their village. They came to the village shouting, but there was no answer. They went into the village and shouted again, but no one answered. The wife of the chief of the jaguars came out of her house and told Kuamucacá that there were no men there. They had all gone fishing. The village women talked among themselves and said, "We could easily marry these men since our husbands are away." Of the chief's two wives, one married the Sun and the other the Moon. The rest of them married Kuamucacá's companions. Almost all of them got married.

The jaguars raised pigeons. The village women had asked every-body to leave the pigeons alone, but one of Kuamucacá's companions grabbed one of them. A handful of feathers came loose, was caught by a gust of wind, and floated off to where the fishermen were. The jaguars immediately realized that there were strangers in their village. The jaguar chief sent a puma to see if it was true. The puma hid and saw that indeed it was. He returned as quickly as possible and warned the tribe that their village was full of strangers. The jaguars immediately quit fishing and turned to go home. The Sun and Moon hid in the tapãim. The rest of them hid inside the other houses. The jaguars be-

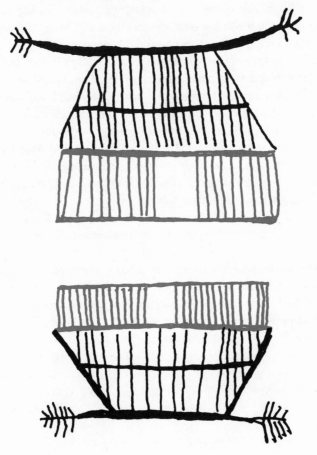

Houses

gan to appear. Five of Kuamucacá's companions, who were outside the houses because they had no wives, were killed right away. On killing them, the jaguars asked their women where the others had gone. They said that those five men were all there were. The jaguars did not believe this and went inside the tapãim to get them. As soon as they were inside, the Sun and Moon shot arrows into their eyes and killed them. The *jagua-tirica* [spotted leopard cat] had followed the other jaguars into the tapãim, but when the Sun shot his arrow, he jumped back and was not hit. Since the jaguars, because of this, were no longer coming into the tapãim, the Sun, Moon, and Kuamucacá's men left their hiding places and attacked the jaguars, killing them all. If it had not been for this massacre, there would be many more jaguars today. After killing them all, Kuamucacá's people gathered their carcasses in the center of the village and asked the Sun if they could pull out the jaguars' claws to make necklaces. The Sun and Moon said yes and even took some for themselves. Then Kuamucacá and his people asked if the jaguars could be eaten. The Sun refused to let them do this. And that is why jaguars are not eaten even today. Kuamucacá and his people stayed up in the heights. The Sun and Moon spent a long time with them. After their long visit, they spoke with Kuamucacá and told him that they wanted to go back to their own village, because they missed their wives very much.

"We must go back. It's been a long time since we left our village. You stay here, but don't fight with other people any more," the two of them said.

As they were leaving, Kuamucacá asked them to remove the arrow ladder by which they had gone up. The Sun and the Moon went down and then took away the ladder. When they saw Kuamucacá's house, they missed him. From there, they returned to the Morená.

KANASSA:
The Conquest of Fire

(*Kuikúru*)

The Indians did not have fire. Kanassa decided to search for it. He walked around a large lagoon. In his fist he was carrying a firefly. Tired of walking, he decided to go to sleep. He opened his fist, took out the firefly, and put him on the ground. As it was cold, he crouched down to warm himself in the firefly's light.

The next morning Kanassa came to the land of the curassow and found him making feather ornaments. The curassow was aware that someone was approaching. Recognizing Kanassa, he said, "Kanassa, some wild Indians are showing up around here."

"Nonsense. I just came from over there and didn't see a thing. That's only my people over there. There's nothing at all."

"I'm making this ornament so as to be ready when the wild Indian comes and I have to fight him."

"How are you going to wear this?"

"On top of my head."

"Then put it on so I can see."

The curassow put the ornament on top of his head and strutted around to show Kanassa. Kanassa stretched his arm out toward the curassow and said softly, "This ornament will never come off his head; it will always stay there." Then Kanassa left in a flash. The curassow started to take off the headdress but he could not. And from that moment all curassows wear headdresses. Kanassa kept moving till he came to the land of the *cuiará*, the small alligator of the scrublands.

The cuiará, seeing Kanassa, said, "Hey, Kanassa, are you taking a walk? Listen, there are wild Indians around here, so watch out."

"No, there is no such thing. There are only my people wandering around here."

The cuiará was making a manioc grater, and Kanassa said to him, "How are you going to carry this grater?"

"On my back."

"Then put it on so I can see. Put it on your tail. It won't work on your back."

The cuiará, as Kanassa suggested, put the grater on his tail and pranced around to show his guest. Kanassa stretched his arm out toward the cuiará and said softly, "This grater will never come off his tail. He'll be like this all his life." From that moment all cuiarás have had flat, rough tails, just like a grater. Having said this, Kanassa left in a flash, leaving the cuiará in a fury, trying to pull the grater off his tail.

Kanassa still had the firefly clutched in his hand. It was the only light he had. Kanassa kept moving till he came to a beach. There he met his relative, the *saracura*. Kanassa was glad to see her. Looking at the water, Kanassa said to the saracura, "How can I get across the lagoon? I think I will make a clay canoe."

And that's what he did. He made a big canoe and climbed aboard with the saracura. They made clay oars and pushed off. After a while they came across the duck, who was also crossing the lagoon, with his entire family, his wife and five children, in a small canoe made of *jatobá* [courbaril tree] bark. They met midway, in the center of the lagoon, just when the *banzeiro* [large wave] was about to start. Water was already coming into the duck's boat. Kanassa liked the duck's

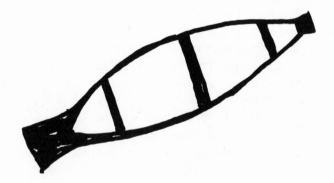

Canoe

canoe but didn't say a word, thinking, I'll figure out a way to get that canoe. And he said, "Where are you headed? I fear your canoe is going to sink, with so many people in it. If you want to trade, I wouldn't mind. My canoe is big and strong. Yours seems very dangerous."

"All right, that makes me happy. You are a good man, Kanassa," the duck answered.

The duck did not realize Kanassa's canoe was made of clay. Kanassa, aided by the saracura, grabbed the bark canoe and rowed away energetically. From afar, Kanassa stretched out his arm toward the duck's canoe, blew hard, and said, "Sink, canoe. Sink now. Banzeiro, be strong."

The duck's canoe could not stand up against the banzeiro and sank to the bottom. The duck was screaming with rage. "Kanassa, bring back my canoe. You lied to me. This one is no good, it's made of clay."

The duck and his family were terrified of the water. They did not know how to swim. When their canoe began to sink, they screamed and screamed, and kept struggling on the surface of the water. Suddenly it occurred to them that they weren't sinking, and they began to enjoy it. Today all ducks like being in the water. Kanassa and the saracura got to the other side of the lagoon.

Kanassa drew an *arraia* [ray or skate] in the mud at the water's

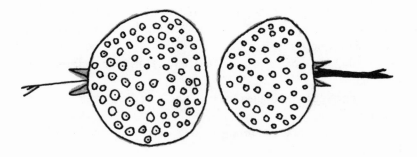

Arraias

edge, but as it was dark, he couldn't see and stepped on his own drawing and was wounded by it. As soon as she stung him, the arraia plunged into the water. Kanassa was mad at the arraia and complained, "I just made her, and already she's hurt me. It's all the firefly's fault, because he doesn't give any light."

Kanassa started to throw away the firefly, but then he remembered something and said to the saracura, "Blow on the fire."

"What fire? There's no fire here. The fire is over there with its master."

"Who is the master of the fire?"

"It is the *ugúvu-cuengo* [king vulture]."

"What is this ugúvu-cuengo like?"

"He's a kind of *uruágui* [ordinary vulture], but very large and hard to find. He has two heads. He will live only in high altitudes. And he will come down only to eat people."

"How would a person go about catching him?"

"The only way is to kill a large deer, a *cervo,* and hide under his hoof till he rots. When the ugúvu-cuengo comes, the thing to do is grab his foot and never let go till he gives you fire."

Kanassa decided to follow the saracura's advice, but he did not have to kill a deer. Instead he drew a picture of a big deer, hid under his hoof, and stayed there. For three days he hid inside the carcass, waiting for the master of the fire. After a while the ordinary vultures began to arrive. The ugúvu-cuengo was perched in a tall, dry tree. The vultures, making a terrible racket, shouted to him, "You can come. It's all right. We're waiting for you to come so we can start eating."

The ugúvu-cuengo, suspicious, was watching the carcass from above, stretching his neck to get a good view. Down below, the others went on shouting, "Come down. It's all right. Hurry up because we're starving."

The ugúvu-cuengo shouted back, "Drag the carcass over here to the tree trunk."

The vultures obeyed, but when they started to pull it, they saw Kanassa hiding.

Kanassa said softly, "Psst! Don't say a word. Get him to come over here."

The vultures went on shouting at the ugúvu-cuengo until he flew down from the big tree to the ground. With him came a great light. On the ground the ugúvu-cuengo examined the carcass well and, seeing nothing, started to eat. He told everybody to eat with him. The deer was very big, and they all began to eat it from back to front. When they got to the forepart, Kanassa, who was hidden in the dead deer's hoof, grabbed the ugúvu-cuengo's foot and said, "O Chief, I've captured you because my people need fire and only you know where it is. Don't be afraid. I'm not going to do anything with you. I only want you to show me where there is fire. You are the master of the fire."

The ugúvu-cuengo was not very angry. He called his son, a little black bird, and said, "My son, you must go find some fire up there in the sky. I'm caught here by Kanassa, who wants to know where there is fire. Go get it in the sky. Put fire in pindaíba fiber and take your time coming back. If you fly too fast, the fire will go out."

The bird went to get the fire in the sky and drifted down slowly to keep it from going out. But he brought only an ember. When he arrived, the ugúvu-cuengo told him to blow on the ember and light the fire. Afterward, the ugúvu-cuengo gave it to Kanassa, who immediately released him. When the fire was lit and burning bright, lots of frogs came out of the water and gathered around. "Where did this come from? Who brought it?" they asked.

The frogs had water in their mouths. As they were leaving, they squirted it on the fire and fled to the water. But this did not put the fire out completely. Kanassa revived it quickly. The frogs came out of the water again, but before they had a chance to reach the fire, Kanassa frightened them off.

The ugúvu-cuengo had already flown back to his dry tree nearby. From there, before flying off into the distance, he said, "Kanassa, when the fire goes out, break an arrow into pieces, crack them in half, tie one on top of another securely, and stick them fast in the ground. Afterward, find an urucu branch and stick one end into the pieces of arrow and spin it hard until you make the fire spring up."

From way up, the ugúvu-cuengo was still shouting to Kanassa. He was so far up that almost nobody could hear him. "Find a liana at the edge of the water, cut it open, and put it out to dry. It is very good to help you light fires with."

Now Kanassa had to carry the fire over to the opposite shore. For this he summoned the snakes, poisonous and non-poisonous, to carry the fire to the opposite shore of the lagoon. The snakes entered the water, carrying the fire, but in the middle of the crossing, one by one they got tired, and they lost the fire in the banzeiro. Only one, who was very speedy, was able to reach the other shore: the *itóto*. Kanassa crossed the water too, and on the other shore he gave manioc drink and beiju to the itóto, the snake who had borne the fire.

IANAMÁ:
The Conquest of the Jakuí

(*Kamaiurá*)

Ianamá lived a little above the Morená, the junction of the head-waters of the Xingu. Every day he went up the Kuluene to fish at the Kranhãnhã. He went and came back the same day. One of the times he went, while he was up in a tree waiting for fish, he heard the flutes of the *jakuí* [water spirits]. The jakuí were playing in the depths of the water, where they live. That is why Ianamá could only hear them and could see nothing. From that time on, whenever he went to the Kranhãnhã, Ianamá always came to listen to the jakuí playing in the depths of the water. Whenever he went fishing, he would always hear the sound of the flutes. And he said to himself, "Who could be playing here? I can't imagine who it might be. I wonder who?" To hear better, Ianamá would climb the tree where he had first heard the jakuí. Occasionally he would come down to shoot a fish, but then he would climb right back up to go on listening to the flutes.

One day he closed off the mouth of the lake, so as to catch fish with the *püa* [fish trap]. He caught a lot of fish that day. In the afternoon, at the time they always started playing, the jakuí first played on the surface, then in the depths, until they were very close to Ianamá's weir. At night, when Ianamá went back to Tacoatsiát, his village, he told his grandfather, Mavutsinim, what he had heard in his fishing weir there in the Kranhãnhã.

When Ianamá found out that the jakuí were the source of the music, he asked his grandfather what he could do to catch the jakuí, whom he heard playing every day as the sun was going down. Mavutsinim told him to make a big net. Ianamá worked on the net for three days, from morning to night. As soon as he finished it, he took it to his grandfather. The net was very big. After inspecting it carefully,

Jakuí

Mavutsinim said, "It's fine. Now make five cigars and a little pepper pot to take with you."

At dawn the following day, Ianamá set off for the Kranhãnhã carrying the three things his grandfather had advised him to take: the fish net, the cigars, and the pepper. When he got there, he fitted the net very tightly over the mouth of the lake and sat down to wait for the fish. When they swam up and tried to pass through the net blocking the mouth of the lake, they were pierced by Ianamá's arrows. He killed various kinds of fish: *corvina,* tucunaré, peixe-cachorro, *bicuda,* and various others. Ianamá spent the entire day fishing and grilling his catch. It was late at night when he began to hear the flutes of the jakuí, who were approaching and playing in the water's depths. Gradually they came closer and closer. At dawn, when the curassows were starting to snore, the jakuí were almost touching the net. From the sound of their flutes, Ianamá could tell that they were right under his nose. They came that far and then the jakuí began to turn around, playing their flutes all the time. Ianamá stayed there until he couldn't hear the flutes, which were getting fainter and fainter.

Because he had heard them so often, Ianamá knew all the jakuí songs by heart. He never missed a day at the Kranhãnhã, where he left his net stretched out to catch the jakuí. For their part, the jakuí always did the same thing: they came close to the net, and then they began to turn back. On one of his trips to the Kranhãnhã to fish and wait for the jakuí, he heard the flutes earlier than usual. When he first heard them, they were far off. Then they moved closer and closer. At dawn the jakuí were almost at the mouth of the lake, where Ianamá was standing. As it began to get light the jakuí fell into the net. Ianamá saw that they were thrashing around in it, and immediately he began to draw the net in, gathering it into the canoe. As he pulled the flutes in, he blew cigar smoke on them and said, "I'm going to take you with me. I won't kill you. I want you for myself."

Saying that, he scattered pepper over the flutes and headed back toward Tacoatsiát. There, when his grandfather Mavutsinim saw the flutes, he said, "This is the jakuí itself." Then he told Ianamá to make more wooden flutes exactly like the ones he had brought with him.

Mavutsinim said, "The ones you brought are the true jakuí. We must keep them safe."

Following his grandfather's advice, Ianamá went into the forest to cut taquara bamboo to make flutes. He made three flutes, but none of them would play. He then fashioned them out of wood, but those wouldn't make noise either. He tried the *ivurapaputã,* another type of wood, but like the others before, it was no use. He made flutes out of every kind of wood he knew, but none of them worked. They wouldn't make sound.

One day, when Ianamá went hunting, an agouti came up to him. Ianamá said, "If you were as smart as those wise people who know so many things, you wouldn't show yourself in front of me like this."

After making this observation, Ianamá aimed his bow at the agouti.

"Don't do that to me, so I can tell you what I know."

"Well then, tell me what you know," said Ianamá, inviting the agouti to have a seat.

When the agouti had made himself comfortable and had had a smoke, he said, "The wood for making the flute of the jakuí is the *irracuitáp,* and you can use *imurã* too."

After this revelation, Ianamá gave the agouti some pepper. He wanted him to befriend the jakuí with it. The agouti accepted the pepper and left. And Ianamá went off in search of irracuitáp. Once he had found it, he cut three pieces to make new flutes with. These were good ones. They made sound. The next day he made many more. He filled the tapãim with flutes. When everything was ready, he began to play the real flutes. The Sun and Moon heard him from their own village. Ianamá played every day, and the Sun and the Moon always heard him. After listening for a while, they appeared in Ianamá's village to get a good look at what he was playing. When Ianamá saw them coming, he told his people not to say anything. "Don't say a word or else they might do something mean to us."

When the Sun and the Moon came into his village, Ianamá asked them if they had come to visit.

"Yes, we came to see you and find out what you are playing. We keep hearing it."

Seeing the flutes in the tapãim, they asked Ianamá to give them a few. Ianamá considered their request and decided to make them a present of three of his flutes, the ones he had made himself. Accepting his gifts, the Sun and Moon left.

At night, Ianamá was playing the real jakuí, the ones he had gotten at the Kranhãnhã. These flutes he kept hidden. The Sun and Moon, hearing Ianamá's flutes, which were very different from the ones he had given them, went again to Tacoatsiát, Ianamá's village, saying that they wanted to see the flutes he had been playing. "Show us your flutes," they said.

"These are the ones I play," Ianamá answered.

Saying that, he showed them the flutes he had made himself. The real flutes, the ones he had caught in the net, were the ones everyone heard. But the ones he had given to the Sun were never heard. At the Morená, Mavutsinim, the Sun's grandfather, explained to him why Ianamá's flutes were heard and the Sun's were not. Old Mavutsinim said, "The ones Ianamá plays are not the ones he made. He caught them fishing at the Kranhãnhã. They are not made of wood. They used to live in the water. They are the real jakuí."

With that, the Sun and the Moon learned the truth and began to plan how to steal the flutes from Ianamá. After talking it over, they decided to stage a big festival and invite Ianamá, to poison him. They went to the forest and gathered lianas for killing fish and used it to make the poison. They filled two large gourds. After preparing themselves, the Sun sent the pariáts to invite Ianamá to the festival he was giving. The carí fish was chosen to be the head pariát. The carí arrived shouting at Ianamá's village. Ianamá heard the pariát's shouts from a way off and told his people that the Sun planned to poison them, and it would be dangerous to go to the festival they were about to be invited to. Ianamá asked the head pariát, the carí, to have a seat and went over to talk to him. Finally he said, "What day should we go to the feast?"

"This very day."

The messenger said this and went back to the Morená, the village of the Sun. Ianamá spent another day in his village. The next morning he got ready to travel with his people. He came to the village of the Sun at night and camped near it, at the site the pariáts had prepared for them. After a while the pariáts went to call their guests to dance. The guests went to the center of the village and danced. They were all decked out in feather headdress and necklaces. They danced the uruá in the *ocaríp* [center of the village], and the jakuí inside the tapãim.

The Sun asked Ianamá to dance by himself. After his dance, the Sun had fish and cauim served to everybody. The guests returned to their camp and danced the jakuí during the night.

The next day, they painted themselves and went back to the center of the village, led by the pariáts. Ianamá sat on a stool because he was the chief. His people, after a short dance, were challenged to a wrestling match, and all of them fought. The gourds with poison were there, ready for them. After the matches, they were served with manioc drink. Ianamá, sitting on his stool, was invited into the tapãim by the Sun. There the Sun asked him, "Are you inside?" Ianamá said he was. Seconds later, the Sun asked other questions: "Are you well?" "Are you still there?" "Are you still alive?"

Ianamá knew perfectly well why the Sun was asking these questions and kept on saying that he was fine. And he went on drinking the poisonous cauim that they were serving him. He could not stand it any more, but still he held on. Most of his people had fallen. Some of the stronger youths went out to have intercourse with the Sun's wives. They took off their ornaments, laying them on a stool, and went out dressed in the skins of the lizard and the mouse. They surrounded the

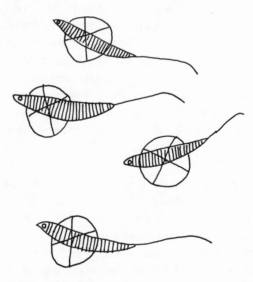

Spirits of lizards and mice

Sun's house and asked the women if they might come in. The women answered from within, "Come in, we're all alone here." Two of them went inside and lay with the women. This is why Ianamá brought the lizard and the mouse, who can get in anywhere. When they came back from the Sun's house, Ianamá asked them if they were all well. "We are well," his people answered.

Those who had survived the poison that the Sun had made were the bees and the acarí. Ianamá's people were mostly bees, while the Sun's people were fish. The Sun, after going to his house and beating his wives, went back to Ianamá. As he came up, Ianamá said teasingly, "Your poison is no good, it's too weak. Or maybe you were trying to fool us."

The Sun and Moon were extremely vexed, not only with their wives but also with the poison they had made that had not worked.

When Ianamá was ready to go back to his own village, he said to the Sun, "You will never succeed in killing us. Your poison can't hurt anybody. And you won't be able to hurt us in my village either."

Saying this, he left for Tacoatsiát. When he got home, his grandfather said, very pleased, "The Sun didn't have a thing to kill you with, did he?"

The day after his return, Ianamá began to make a poison for the Sun, to give him when he came to the festival that Ianamá was going to hold. When he had made the poison, he informed the Sun and Moon that the festival at Tacoatsiát would take place in five days' time. The *morenaiáts* [masters of the Morená], thus hearing of the approaching festival, waited to be invited. Ianamá sent for the carí fish to be head messenger. When he came to the Sun's village, the carí was taken to the center of the village, where he sat on a stool and waited for the chief. The Sun came out of his house and went to greet him. After a few pleasantries, he asked the carí what day he could leave with his people for the festival. The carí said the following day.

At daybreak, the Sun, the Moon, and their people left for Ianamá's village. When they arrived at Tacoatsiát and camped by the village, the pariát who had invited them brought them fish and beiju. They passed the night dancing. Early the next day they painted themselves for the festival. Mavutsinim, Ianamá's grandfather, went to the Sun's camp to ask him to make a nice festival without any quarrels. The Sun brought his people to the center of the village. Mavutsinim led the way. The Sun and Moon were wearing the garb of the piranha. They were very ugly and fierce. Their people were all wearing the skin of animals. Mavutsinim told Ianamá that he must not go out to take food to his guests. "Send your wife," the old man advised. Ianamá's people, hearing this, frowned on having women instead of men carry manioc drink to their guests. "Only men should carry manioc drink," they said. "We ourselves will bring manioc drink to the Sun," they added. If Ianamá went, he would never come back. The guests were all dressed as wild animals. The manioc drink was brought to them by one of Ianamá's men. At that moment Mavutsinim again begged them not to quarrel, but seeing that they were all enraged, he blew in their direction, forcing them to go back to the Morená, where they lived. When the wind hit them, they all spun around, breaking pots and spilling manioc drink.

When the Sun, driven by Mavutsinim's blowing, left with his people, Ianamá said, "How can the Sun kill me? He can't kill me. It should have been him who found the jakuí. He, who is greater than I am. I found it, and that is why he is angry."

The Sun wanted to kill Ianamá to steal the jakuí, but he never managed to do it.

THE IAMURICUMÁ WOMEN AND THE JAKUÍ: Women and Men Fight for Possession of the Jakuí

(Kamaiurá)

The Iamuricumá women played a flute called the jakuí. They played, danced, and sang every day. At night, the dance took place inside the tapãim [flute house], so that the men could not see. The flutes were forbidden to the men. When the ceremony was performed during the day, outside the tapãim, the men had to shut themselves indoors. Only the women were allowed outside, playing, singing, and dancing, decking themselves out with necklaces, feather headdresses, armbands, and other ornaments today worn only by the men. If a man by accident saw the jakuí, the women immediately grabbed him and raped him. The Sun and the Moon knew nothing of this, but in their village they were always hearing the chants and shouts of the Iamuricumá women.

One day the Moon said they had to go see what the Iamuricumá were up to. They decided to go, and they went. They came close to the village but stayed a way off, watching. The Moon did not like to watch the women's movements: the old ones playing the *curutá* and dancing, others playing the jakuí, still others shouting and laughing out loud. To get a better view, the Sun and Moon went into the village. The women were having a festival.

As the Sun and Moon came closer, the chief of the women said to her people, "Don't say anything, or they'll do something to us."

As soon as they got there, the Sun said to the Moon, "I can't stand to hear women playing the jakuí. This can't go on."

Then they discussed how to solve the problem, and the Sun said to the Moon, "Let's make a *horí-horí* [bull-roarer] to frighten the women away."

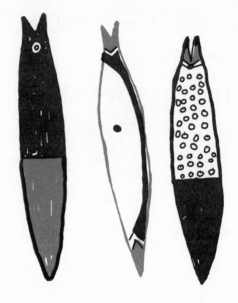

Horí-horí

"Let's do, and stop this thing. This is a dreadful state of affairs."

Having said that, they left to make the horí-horí. It took them an entire day. When the bull-roarer was ready, the Moon asked who would attack the women with it, to frighten them.

"Let me take it," said the Sun.

And he began to adorn himself with feather armbands, headdresses, and other things. After covering himself completely, he went off in the direction of the Iamuricumá women. The Moon waited in the village. As he got close, the Sun started to whirl his giant bull-roarer over his head. The women went on dancing, but they were starting to get frightened by the approaching roar. When they turned around and saw the Sun making his frightful horí-horí roar, they were terrified. The Moon shouted to the women to get inside their houses. They abandoned everything on the spot and ran inside. The men, in turn, came out of their houses shouting with joy and grabbed the jakuí. Seeing what was happening, the Moon said, "Now everything is all right. The men will play the jakuí, not the women."

At that very moment the men began to play and dance instead of the women. One of the women, who had left something in the middle of the village, asked them from inside her house to bring it to her. When the Moon saw this he said, "From now on it will always be like this. This is the right way. Women should stay inside, not men. They will be shut away when the men dance the jakuí. They may not go out, they may not look. Women may not see the bull-roarer either, because it is the companion of the jakuí."

The men learned everything that the Iamuricumá women had known: the music of the jakuí, its songs and dances. At first only the women knew these things.

Stool

THE IAMURICUMÁ WOMEN:
The Women without a
Right Breast

(Kamaiurá)

The Iamuricumá women held a great festival for the ear-piercing of the boys. After the festival, one part of the village went fishing. The fishermen took along a lot of beijus to eat. The fishing area was far from the village. When they got there, they pounded some *timbó* [poisonous liana] into the water and began to catch fish. The days went by and the fishermen did not go home. It was taking them a long time. The boys whose ears had been pierced were in confinement, waiting for the fish that their fathers had gone to catch for them. More than a moon passed, and still the fishermen were gone. In the village, a man who had not gone fishing, the son of the morerequát, decided to go after the fishing party and see what had happened. He had some beijus made for the trip and went off. When he arrived at their camp, the fishermen hid their fish. They did not want him to see them. His people were making a frightful racket. They were all turning into wild pigs and other forest animals. The son of the morerequát did not like it and went home. Back at the village he said the fishermen would be a few more days fishing. But he told his mother the truth and said his father and the other people were turning into things, animals of the forest.

The chief's wife then ordered the women to prepare beijus for the festival and to cut their sons' hair, the boys whose ears had been pierced. When the beijus were ready, the women set up stools in the center of the village, where their sons would sit while their hair was cut in the ceremony. After it was over, the chief's wife told the other women that they could not stay there any longer. They had to leave that place because their husbands were not people any more, they were turning into animals. All night long, the women talked about it, repeating over and over that they could not stay there any longer. The chief's wife spoke endlessly; day and night she carried on about the need for leaving at once and for abandoning the village forever. Then they all began preparing to leave. They spent two days getting ready, gathering their things, preparing everything: ornaments, necklaces, cotton yarn to wrap around their arms, all things that their men wore.

The morerequát's wife, before anyone else, began to adorn herself with feathers, armbands, necklaces, and to paint herself with urucu and genipap. After adorning herself exactly like the men, she began to sing. By herself, she sang and sang continuously. Singing, she climbed on top of a house and there went on singing. The men who were left in the village started to complain and curse, but the singing went on. Another woman, adorned the same way, climbed on top of another house and began to sing too. After a while, still chanting their songs, the two women came down to the center of the village, where the other women, by now also adorned and painted like men, joined in the song. Then they started to spread poison over their bodies, to turn themselves into *mamaés* [spirits]. That is why today, in the place where the Iamuricumá lived, no one is allowed to remove lianas, roots, or anything else from the forest. Whoever does goes mad and gets lost, never to be seen again. They also drank the poison they rubbed on their bodies.

The songs and dances in the village lasted for two whole days. Then the Iamuricumá women, without interrupting their song, slowly began to move away. But before this, they grabbed an old man and dressed him in the shell of a *tatu-açu*. They put beiju spatulas in his hand and told him to lead the way. As he set off, the old man said, "Now I'm not a person any more. I'm an armadillo." Saying this, he took the lead. After taking a few turns around the village, the Iamuricumá women, still singing, followed behind the tatu-açu, who went ahead, burrowing. He kept taking dives into the ground. He would plunge down at one spot, only to bob up ahead of them. Farther on, the women went past their husbands, who were still fishing. The small children were being carried. The fishermen asked their wives to stop, so the boys could eat some fish. The women would not listen and went on their way. Singing, adorned with feathers, and painted with urucu and genipap, each day they traveled farther, following the armadillo,

Beiju spatulas

who went along opening tunnels in the earth. Farther on, they passed the Macão-acáp village. It was midday. The local chief asked his people not to look, so as not to be taken away by the Iamuricumá women. The women did not obey and looked, and the Iamuricumá women carried them all off. Their husbands, who went after them, were also captured. Farther ahead, they passed another village called Etapemetáp. The chief gave his people the same warning, but they would not obey either, and they too were captured.

The Iamuricumá women went on with their journey, traveling forever. They walked day and night without stopping. The small children were thrown into the lagoons, and they turned into fish. The Iamuricumá women are walking still today, ever adorned and singing. They use bows and arrows and do not have a right breast, so they can pull back their bowstrings more easily.

Mamaés (spirits of the dead)

ARAVUTARÁ:
The Fate of the Dead

(*Kamaiurá*)

Aravutará had a friend who was his inseparable companion. They hunted together, fished together, went to the gardens together, worked and took walks together. They never left each other's side for a single moment. They were great friends. The two were always talking about what they would do if one of them died. And they decided that when one of them died, the other would go after him. Aravutará said, "If I die, you search until you find me. And I'll do the same for you, if you die first."

"We cannot remain apart because we wouldn't be able to stand the loneliness."

This conversation took place daily between the two friends. And they always said that the one who went on living should make bow and arrows for the dead one, so he could fish and hunt up in the sky. One day Aravutará's friend fell ill and sent for him. "Friend," he said, "I am very ill and I'm going to die."

Aravutará, saddened by what he heard, tried to cheer his friend up, saying that his illness was nothing, he was going to get well. But the sick man was not convinced and said, "No, it's hopeless. I really am dying."

Two days later Aravutará's friend died. Just as they had planned, Aravutará went to look for his spirit everywhere he used to go when he was alive. Every day Aravutará visited these places, and he kept calling to his companion over and over. Tirelessly he went from place to place in search of his missing friend. One day there was an eclipse, and Aravutará told his mother that he was going to find his friend. "My friend asked me to look for him when one day the sun went out. That is why I am sure I will find him now." He said this and left. He walked along a trail, and there, at a spot he picked, he sat down and began to wait. Night fell, and still Aravutará was sitting and waiting. At dawn he started to talk to himself, "My friend is taking a long time. It must be very hard for him to appear." After waiting a long time, he went home.

Very early the next day he went to the trail again. When he was dropping with exhaustion, he began to whimper softly. Just then he heard the laugh of the mamaés [spirits of the dead], who were approaching. Shortly afterward, the mamaés began to pass by him. Since they can't stand the odor of living people, as they passed him, they complained about his odor and said, "There are people here that smell bad, that still have a body."

Each of them said the same thing as he went past Aravutará. They came all adorned with feathers and carrying bows and arrows. Aravutará looked for his friend among those who crossed in front of him. Since he could not find him, he said to a mamaé who was passing by, "Will my friend be along?"

"He's back there, bringing up the rear," the mamaé answered.

And the mamaés kept going by, one after another. Aravutará's friend was the last of them all. He came along laughing. Aravutará could hear him. When he got close, his friend's spirit spoke, "Well, friend, didn't wé agree that if one of us died, the other would go look for him?"

"That's why I'm here. I came to look for you."

They stood talking to each other. Then Aravutará asked his friend, "Where is this group going?"

"They are going to a festival to do battle with the birds."

"I'll go with you."

"It's very dangerous. You shouldn't come."

"I'll come anyway. We're friends, that's why I have to go with you. I must go anyway, because we always walk together."

"Come along then. Do you have any arrows?"

"No, I don't."

"Then go get some."

Then Aravutará said, "Don't leave me, friend. Wait for me here."

As Aravutará was leaving, his friend's spirit asked him to bring a lot of *tuaví* [bast mats] to keep the birds' feathers in. Aravutará went home and returned right away. When he came to the spot where he had left his friend, he started to call him, "My friend, are you here?"

"Yes, here I am, waiting for you."

Aravutará had brought bow and arrows, and a *nhumiatotó* [bamboo flute]. They began to talk to each other.

"To get where we're going, we have to sleep on the way. But you must not go to sleep," said the dead man.

After walking some distance, they came to the place where they would pass the night. The friend's spirit said to Aravutará, "Let's pass the night here, and tomorrow we'll get there early."

Aravutará was hanging up his hammock and fixing the campsite. His friend's spirit warned him again not to go to sleep. "Don't go to sleep, my friend. Lie down, but don't fall asleep."

He said that and sat at the edge of the fire. After a while he said to Aravutará, "My friend, would you like me to lie with you in the hammock?"

Aravutará said yes. The friend lay down and said, "Don't be afraid of me."

And there they lay, stretched out together. In spite of his friend's warning, Aravutará slept for a short time; then he woke up and got out of the hammock. Then he got back in and went back to sleep. A little later he roused himself and got up again, but right away he lay down and fell asleep. When he woke up for the third time, he looked at his friend and saw that he had turned into a snake. Aravutará started with fear and said, "What's this snake doing, lying here with me?"

Saying that, he turned the hammock over. The snake fell out beside the fire and said, "What's this, my friend? Are you trying to burn me up? I'm your friend. I told you not to be afraid of me."

Having said that, he went back to being a spirit. All mamaés turn into snakes when they go to sleep. After being thrown on the ground, the spirit of Aravutará's friend would not come back into the hammock with him. He remained by the fireside. Aravutará fell asleep, and when he woke up, he saw that his friend had turned into a snake again. He also saw that the rest of the mamaés had turned into snakes. The next day, the mamaés continued their journey. Along the way, they came to a sprouting *sapezal* [area overgrown with *sapé* grass] and were afraid to step on the pointed sprouts. They were afraid of injuring themselves and dying completely. This was why they didn't want to walk over it. Mamaés may not wound themselves, or they will die completely. So they came to a halt and waited for Aravutará. Aravutará arrived and asked his friend what was going on. He explained that there were prickly spines ahead.

"These spines are harmless, wait and I'll go in front of you," said Aravutará.

Leading the way, he trampled a path through the sprouting grass. The mamaés followed behind. Farther ahead they came across the *arutsãms* [frogs], who terrified them. The arutsãms carried cudgels in their hands. The mamaés retreated. Aravutará came up and asked what was going on.

"They say that there are large animals in our path," his friend's spirit answered.

"Let's have a look. That's ridiculous," he said, when he saw that it was nothing but a bunch of frogs.

He picked up a piece of wood and went about killing the frogs, till he had killed every last one. Aravutará's friend, seeing this, observed, "How about that, my friend? If you hadn't come along, we would have died once and for all at the hands of the frogs or in the grass back there."

When the trail was free of arutsãms, the mamaés marched on. Farther on, they ran into the crabs, who were armed with big clubs and lying in wait for the travelers. This brought the spirits up short.

Crabs

"What's the matter now?" asked Aravutará, when he caught up.

"There are some huge beasts ahead waiting to kill us," his friend explained.

"That's nonsense," Aravutará said, seeing the crabs.

And he stepped on them, killing them all. When the trail was clear, the mamaés went on their way, until they came to a ravine that had no bridge. The mamaés put a log across the ravine, but it was not very steady and kept rolling this way and that. Afraid to cross, they retreated a little. Aravutará caught up and asked why they had turned back. His friend explained that a fierce beast was at the root of it. Aravutará had a look and saw the log bobbing up and down in the water. He went a little farther on and made the bridge secure. When he was done, he said, "It's ready, my friends, now you can go across."

The mamaés went across and continued the journey. Farther on, they came to a fire and stopped. Aravutará put out the fire, and they went on. It was still early when they neared the birds' village. When they saw the mamaés coming, they flew toward them.

Aravutará's friend asked, "Who's going first?"

"You spirits are," answered Aravutará. "I want to see how you fight."

The mamaés went to meet the birds. In the clash, the birds started to kill off the mamaés by pecking at them. They were dying one after the other. Aravutará said to his friend, "We must spread charcoal over our bodies to scare away the birds."

So the two friends smeared themselves with charcoal and joined the fight. When the mamaés had almost given up, the friend's spirit asked Aravutará to shout. "Shout, my friend, to scare the birds away for a while. My people can't stand any more."

All kinds of birds were there: eagles, parrots, macaws, toucans, all of them. Aravutará started to shout, but he too had no strength left. He was all bitten, scratched, hairless, and wounded. The birds were pulling everyone's hair out for themselves. The charcoal was almost all gone from the friends' bodies. The friend's spirit said, "Friend, play your flute to get rid of these birds."

Aravutará started to play the nhumiatotó, running back and forth. He played on and on, because he did not want the birds to kill all the mamaés. At the sound of the flute, the birds flew off, but it wasn't long before they fell upon the spirits again. Then Aravutará's friend said that his people would fight only once more, because they couldn't stand any more. He said, "This time we will kill only the big birds."

After this battle, the chief of the birds told his tribesmen to quit fighting, because they were being killed at an alarming rate. It was Aravutará who was mainly responsible for the deaths. So the birds quit fighting and retreated. Aravutará gathered up all the birds he had killed: eagles, macaws, toucans, jabiru storks, parrots, congo kingbirds, and many others. He cleaned the feathers off all the birds and put them in between the mats. He filled all the feather holders.

His friend said to him, "How about that, my friend? If you hadn't come along, the birds would have killed all of us."

"That's exactly why I came," answered Aravutará.

The birds, whenever they killed a mamaé, would carry him off to the giant eagle to eat. He ate every one they brought. They went on killing and carrying them to him.

"Look, my friend," said the spirit, "right before our very eyes they're carrying people off to the eagle."

And the two of them watched the birds carrying off the dead.

"That's what they do. They kill people and give them to the eagle. That's what happens here to all of us."

After his friend finished explaining, Aravutará said, "Now let's leave. I looked for you because I was very lonely for you. We were friends always."

And the mamaés began to turn back. Only Aravutará was carrying feathers. The mamaés had come only to make a festival, which is their battle with the birds. The festival is always held when the sun becomes dark in the daytime. The souls that die in the battle are finished forever.

When they reached the spot where Aravutará had once gone to wait, his friend said, "Now don't look, because I'm going to disappear."

After that Aravutará could only hear the footsteps of the mamaés, but he did not look at them. When the mamaés had gone away, Aravutará, alone now, thought about them. Why had he gone with them? And he went back to his village. At midday he was nearly there, but he didn't go in until nightfall. Outside his house, he could hear his mother weeping. When he went inside, his mother stopped weeping

Toucans

and was very happy. Aravutará said to her, "I told you that when my friend died, I would have to go look for him."

He said that and started to weep over the loss of his friend. Then the weeping turned to vomiting. When he stopped vomiting, he passed out and remained senseless. The shamans brought him back to his senses, and after that he was all right. Then he told the people everything that had happened to him. His brother asked him why he had vomited. Aravutará answered, "I couldn't stand the smell of the mamaés any more. I was sick of the stench."

And he went on with his story. He told the people everything. There was one who did not believe him and said that he was lying. But Aravutará went on telling his brother everything that had happened to him from the very beginning, from the day he went to wait for his friend on the trail, up till his encounter with the spirits, their trek to the birds' village, and the battle against them. When he finished telling them everything, he drank a special liquid to make himself vomit, to cure himself completely. The next day he sorted out the eagle feathers and brought them to the center of the village to distribute them among his tribesmen. While he handed out the feathers, Aravutará kept saying that he had been a great friend of the dead man and that they had never quarreled.

"That is why I went to look for my friend," he said, "and after I found him, I went with him to the festival of the spirits."

After these words, Aravutará revealed to the people what happens to the dead, saying that in the battle with the birds, the mamaés who die are carried off to a giant eagle who eats them.

"It is he, the eagle, who finishes us off once and for all."

Then he said that whoever goes to the feast without a bow and arrow is easily killed by the birds, but those who bring these weapons don't die quite so easily. It's much more difficult for them. He said that whoever covers his head with one of his body ornaments will not die easily either. The women must take a spindle to defend themselves with.

At last Aravutará told them how he had played the nhumiatotó flute up there, and added, "When you down here shouted at the sound of the nhumiatotó, the birds backed off. From here, you helped me very much up there," Aravutará concluded.

IGARANHÃ:
The Enchanted Canoe

(Kamaiurá)

Once a man decided to make a canoe out of jatobá bark, and no sooner had he finished it than his wife had a baby. Since he could not work with a newborn baby in the house, he stayed home and could not put the canoe into the water. The canoe stayed out in the forest. Days later, when he was able to work again, he said to his wife, "I think my canoe must be spoiled by now, but I'll go see what state it's in."

He came to the place and could not find his canoe. It was not where he had left it. The man sat beside the jatobá tree and tried to imagine what could have happened to the canoe. After a while he began to hear noises coming from the forest. Then he saw that it was the canoe coming back by itself to its place.

"What's this, my canoe is turning into a spirit?"

He said this and watched. He saw that the boat had eyes, one on each side of the prow. "I think I'll climb inside," he said. As he sat inside, he said, "Can you carry me somewhere?"

The canoe stirred itself and walked off toward the lagoon. As soon as it went into the water, the fish began to jump inside it. The canoe gobbled up all the fish immediately. And that very moment, more fish jumped inside it. These the *igaranhã* gave to its master. After that the canoe came out of the water and dragged itself off to its place in the forest. When it came to the jatobá tree, the man gathered up his fish, and climbing out of the canoe, he said, "You stay here quietly and I'll be back another day."

Saying that, he went home, carrying his fish. When he got there, his wife asked him, "Wherever did you catch so many fish?"

"I found a very good place to fish."

Some days later he told his wife that he was going fishing again. He

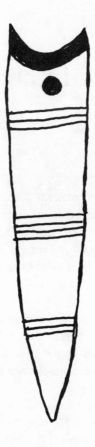

Canoe

went and could not find the boat under the jatobá. It was out traveling. After a while he heard the sound of something dragging itself. It was the canoe coming up. Its master sat down and watched it. The canoe came up, stopped, and tottered back and forth a little. The master said to himself, "When it totters like that, it's calling to me. I'll climb in." Saying this, he climbed in. The canoe then marched off toward the lagoon and plunged into the water. The fish jumped right in. The fisherman wanted to grab up all the fish. But when he started to gather the fish together, he was swallowed by the igaranhã.

The igaranhã was very angry because the first fish were supposed to be for him. The master had been in too much of a hurry, and for that reason he had been swallowed. There in his house his wife waited for him and he never came home.

ALAPÁ:
The Rejuvenating Water

(*Juruna*)

There once was an old man who wanted to get married, but no woman wanted to marry him. He was very ugly. Saddened by this, he decided to die. He went to the forest and wandered about aimlessly. He went from place to place, always thinking of death. One day, in his roving, he came to a clear part of the forest, where he found a ladder coming down from the sky to the ground. The old man stopped and looked at the ladder without understanding the reason for it. After examining it for a long time, he decided to go up, saying to himself, "I'll go up and see what it's like there." He said this and began to climb. At the top, in the sky, he found people. There were three women working, weaving straw, and one man, their husband, making a bow. Seeing the old man arriving, one of the women said to him, "Your grandfather is over there," and pointed to a path. The old man took the path and followed it. In time, he came to Alapá, who was also making a bow.

"Where did you come from?" asked Alapá.

"I came up a ladder that dropped down from here to me."

"You are very beautiful," observed Alapá, looking at the old man.

"No, I'm not beautiful. I'm rather ugly."

After talking for a while, Alapá went to his daughters. They were drying corn. They stopped work when they saw their father approaching. Alapá told them about the man who had arrived, asking his daughters to come meet him. There were four girls. Three of them went. The other, the youngest, stayed home. When they saw the old man, they said the same thing as their father had: "You are very beautiful."

The old man, hearing this, was embarrassed and did not answer. Alapá's daughters came close and asked him to sit on the ground.

When the old man sat down, the girls, one at a time, sat on top of him. The old man, out of fear, did not take advantage of any of them. The girls liked his way and repeated that he was very beautiful, taking him over to where their father was. Alapá, hearing that the old man had not tried to meddle with his daughters, told them to take him to bathe. The old man made a few dives into the water and came out transformed, with the face of a youth and clear skin. His arms, which had been thin and long, were massaged by Alapá's daughters until they filled out and became short. His hair grew longer, and they improved the shape of his face. When they were ready, the girls took the old man, now rejuvenated, to their father. There Alapá called his youngest daughter and said to the rejuvenated Juruna, "You will marry this one, because nobody else would marry you."

Woman's face

But the Juruna thought the girl was very ugly and didn't want to marry her. So Alapá sent his daughter to bathe. She went and came back transformed, with a new skin, a beautiful face, completely different from before. The Juruna did not recognize her. Now she was beautiful. With that, he became fond of her and married her.

Three moons passed and the Juruna was still up in the sky, living with Alapá. Down below, in his village, his old mother, her hair cut short in mourning, spent her days weeping over her son, whom she thought dead. Alapá, hearing her lament, said to his son-in-law, "Your mother is thinking about you and crying a lot."

The Juruna's wife said the same thing and told her husband to go see his mother. Early the next day the Juruna began the descent from the sky. At night he came to his mother's house and said from outside, "Mother, I've just come home."

His mother, who was weeping inside, did not answer. She could not believe that her son was alive, he had been gone such a long time. When he called her for the third time, she recognized him and ran to open the door, asking, "Where have you been?"

"When I was out walking, I found a ladder coming down from the sky. I went up, and there I found people. I bathed in some water and became the way I am now."

When the mother heard this, she began to weep again, she was so happy. After she stopped crying, the son asked her not to tell anyone about him. The Juruna was embarrassed to be seen, transformed as he was. He wanted to stay hidden, without having anyone find out he was there. But the next morning a friend of the house saw him. He had come to bring manioc drink to his mother. This man told the others, saying, "He's come back and is very different from what he was. I don't know how he changed so much."

The entire village, hearing this, wanted to see the rejuvenated Juruna; even the women who refused to marry him when he had been old and ugly. But the Juruna would not show himself for anybody. He stayed shut up inside his house. "How are we going to get him out of there?" the village men asked each other. They decided to organize a fishing party. They caught a lot of fish, put them in the center of the village, and called all the people to eat. The keeper of the fish sent for the Juruna in hiding. Before he came out, his mother adorned him with earrings and necklaces. In the village center, all the people went to look at him and admire him from up close. The women who before hadn't wanted to marry him all wanted to be his wife now, but the

Juruna would not take any of them, because he already had a wife up there in Alapá's village. In the center of the village he talked to everybody, but he didn't tell any of them about the ladder and the sky where he was living. Only his mother knew. When the meal of fish was over, he got ready to leave, saying to his mother that it was time to go back, because he had a wife up there. Before he left, his mother asked him to bring his wife when he returned. That woman up there was not like the women down here. She was more beautiful. Her face was red. She was very different.

After a moon had passed, the Juruna came back down, bringing his wife with him. He also brought his baby daughter, who turned into a little bird the moment she touched the ground. She turned into a bird,

Bird

but she always stayed at her parents' side. In his mother's village, the Juruna and his wife taught the people all the songs they knew. There was a Juruna who, jealous of the one who had gone up, also wanted to go to the sky to bathe in the water that had transformed the other man. This good water was almost unbearably cold. The first Juruna warned the other one about this, but he wanted to go anyway, and went up. When he arrived, he ran into Alapá, who asked him, "Where did you come from?"

Learning that the visitor had come from down below, he told him to wait and went to get his daughters. The girls came to meet the Juruna and asked him to sit down. The first one who sat in his lap, to test him, was raped by him. Standing up, the girl said, "This man will not do, he is a bad man." The girls went back to their father.

"What is he like?" Alapá asked.

"He is good for nothing. He is mean," answered his daughters.

Furious, Alapá told them, "Take him to the other water."

This other water was very ugly and dark. After the first dive, he turned into an *araraúna* [macaw] and came out of the water flying.

"You will always be like that, black and eating nothing but excrement," Alapá ordained.

The first Juruna, Alapá's son-in-law, stayed on down there in his mother's village. Every day he went with his wife to the garden and left his bird-daughter in her grandmother's care. Only at night did the child take on human shape. When the sun came up, she turned into a little bird and spent the day in the company of her grandmother. Her parents never took her with them when they went to the garden to pull up manioc. The Juruna's mother was getting bored with taking care of the bird, who to her was only a bird, an animal. One day, in annoyance, she threw the bird out of the house. The mother, there in the garden, heard her daughter scream as she fell to the ground.

When she got home, her daughter complained, saying, "Mama, my grandmother hit me."

The mother, upset by what had happened, told her husband she was leaving immediately and went out running, carrying her daughter. Her husband ran after them, but he could not catch up to his wife. She had plunged into a murky part of the woods, and finding the ladder by way of a shortcut, she climbed up and was gone. The Juruna did not want to go right up. He went home. He wanted to see his mother once more before leaving forever.

The next day he left to return to his house in the sky. Another man from the village went with him. The day before this other man had been warned that, if he wanted to go to Alapá's village, he would have to abstain from sleeping with a woman the night before. The Juruna who lived in the sky said to him, "If you mess with a woman, the ladder will break."

When they came to the bottom of the ladder, Alapá's son-in-law asked his companion to let him go up first, because he knew that the other had had relations with a woman. When he got to the top, up there in the sky, he told his companion to follow. He was almost to the top, when the ladder collapsed and he fell down. The ladder was never lowered again. The Juruna who climbed up still lives there today. Alapá had wanted to come down here to meet the Juruna. He would have liked the Juruna to visit his place when they became old, to grow young again in the good water. But the Juruna who slept with a woman when he was not supposed to made the ladder break, and it would never be lowered again.

UAIÇÁ:
The Sleep-Inducing Tree

(Juruna)

Uaiçá went out one day to hunt. At a spot in the forest, under a large tree, he saw a lot of dead animals, a great heap of them. Uaiçá stood there staring, without understanding why all this had happened. While he was looking, he walked around the tree. As he was passing under it, he got dizzy, fell down, and went to sleep. Asleep, he dreamed of many things. He dreamed of people who sang. He dreamed of tapirs and all kinds of animals. In his dreams, he also saw Sinaá, an ancestor of the Juruna, who talked to him for a long time. When he woke up, he went right home because it was already late, the sun had gone down. The next day he went back to the tree, fell down, and went to sleep, dreaming about everything as before: Sinaá, people singing, animals, his own people. For several days Uaiçá visited the tree, where, upon falling asleep, he always had the same dreams. From the first day, Uaiçá had been fasting. He ate nothing. On his last visit, Sinaá said to him in a dream, "Never come under this tree again. It's enough now."

Uaiçá, waking up, scraped some bark off the tree and went to the water's edge. There, out of the scrapings, he made a tea and drank it. He got drunk right away, and jumping into the water, he began to catch fish with his bare hands. He caught the tucunaré and several other fishes. Back at the village, Uaiçá's grandfather wanted to know why he was going into the forest every day. Uaiçá told his grandfather about finding the tree and all the dreams he had had. His grandfather wanted to see the tree, so Uaiçá took him there. The old man fell asleep but didn't dream much and did not want to go back again. He only went once. The other Juruna knew nothing about it. Uaiçá stopped going to the tree and turned to drinking what he had made out of its scrapings, acquiring thereby many powers. He began to show what he could do when, for the first time, he cured a very sick child whom the village shaman could not cure. The Juruna were surprised and asked themselves, "How could Uaiçá do that if he's not a shaman and is so young?" And intrigued with Uaiçá's sudden power, they went to ask him how he had managed to cure the boy. Uaiçá answered, "It wasn't I who cured him. It was somebody else."

After a while, after he performed other cures, the Juruna began to consider Uaiçá a great shaman. Uaiçá took disease away with a touch of his hand. All sick people—men, women, and children—were brought to him, and all of them got well.

Some time passed, and Uaiçá told them what had happened to him: the encounter with the tree, the dreams, the conversations with Sinaá, and everything. Uaiçá continued having his dreams, and in them he transported himself to Sinaá's side, to learn from him. And from there he brought back everything the Juruna wanted. Every time he went to sleep, he talked to Sinaá. On one of these occasions Sinaá said, "You must become exactly as I was, always helping our people."

Uaiçá had no wife. The Juruna wanted him to get married, but he did not want to. The only person living with him was the first child he had cured. In his dreams he went looking for everything the child wanted: necklaces and other things. Because the Juruna asked him so often, Uaiçá finally got married. Whenever he went hunting or fishing, Uaiçá would send his house ahead of him, to give his people shelter in case of rain. Because of this and all the other things he did, the Juruna liked him very much. And they always said, "Now everything is fine because another Sinaá has come to us."

But one day something very bad happened. Uaiçá, back from a fishing expedition, discovered that there was a man sleeping with his wife. Uaiçá did not say anything at the time. As usual, he called his people to eat the fish he had caught. After the distribution, he asked his wife to go to the river to get some water so he could wash. The woman went and was followed by her lover. Uaiçá waited awhile and then went off toward the water as well. When he got there, he saw his wife sitting on the lap of the man who had followed her. Uaiçá did not say a word. He just stood watching, with the eyes he had in his back. When the woman wanted to climb off her lover's lap, she could not, she was stuck there. Soon after Uaiçá's mother-in-law arrived at the water's edge. Seeing her daughter in that situation, she beat her and her lover very hard. The woman made another attempt to free herself, and when she couldn't, she dragged herself as she was to the river and fell in. At that moment, Uaiçá blew on the two of them and they turned into *botos* and went off, jumping and bobbing up in the water.

Uaiçá's father-in-law and brother-in-law got very angry at him and decided to kill him. "How are we going to kill Uaiçá?" they asked each other. Finally they decided to kill him in the center of the village when he was eating. His brother-in-law prepared everything. On a set day he brought a lot of fish to the center and called everybody over. Invited too, Uaiçá went. He sat on a stool and began to eat. His brother-in-law, taking advantage of the opportunity, came up from behind with his cudgel raised. Uaiçá, with the eyes he had in his back, was watching his movements. When the cudgel came down, he darted out from under and that very instant disappeared into the ground with all his belongings: hammock, weapons, and all the other things he owned. He went into the earth and came out far away. His house, his garden, everything moved with him.

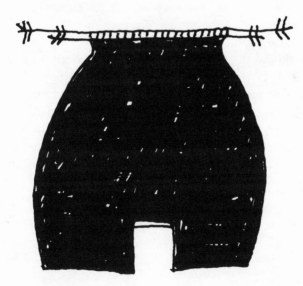

House

Time passed, and the village people went out to look for him. Far away, they found Uaiçá. He was clearing a garden. His brother-in-law spoke to him, saying, "We wanted to kill you, on account of my sister, whom you turned into an animal. But now we don't want to harm you any more. We've forgotten everything."

His brother-in-law was lying. What he wanted was to catch Uaiçá. But Uaiçá believed him and returned to the village with all of his belongings. His brother-in-law went out fishing again. When he arrived with the fish, he took counsel with his companions. "How shall we do it? I think it would be better to take the fish over to the rock, so he can't slip through."

The fish were carried over to the rocks. They called Uaiçá and gave him a stool to sit on. Uaiçá sat down and started to eat with the others. His brother-in-law, as before, came slowly from behind with his cudgel. Uaiçá, with the eyes in his back, was watching and left the place just at the moment the blow fell. The cudgel hit the ground and split the rock open. Uaiçá, with all his people and his belongings, dived into the crack opened by the cudgel; and before he disappeared forever, he said, "Now I will never come back to live with you again. You will be like this forever, using arrows and cudgels only. I wanted to teach you many more things that Sinaá asked me to teach you. But now I'm leaving, and I'll never come back."

Uaiçá still lives there at the Pedra Seca [dry rock], the rocky island in the middle of the Xingu River. All his belongings are still there. They have all turned into stone. If anyone touches any of it, pots, house poles, he falls ill and dies. If he should make a garden there, the wind will carry everything away. A long time ago the Juruna went by and saw Uaiçá's hand, open and stretched upward, on top of a stone. That is where his house is. He wanted the Juruna to come inside, but they couldn't find the door, and in any case they were frightened.

UUATSIM:
The Ear-Piercing Ceremony
in the Village of the Birds

(*Kamaiurá*)

Uuatsim invited his brothers to go fishing. Four people went out, seated inside a single canoe. When the sun was sinking, they passed a village called Tsariuaparrét. Uuatsim stopped there and asked the owner of the house for manioc drink, but he only had cauim [manioc bread dissolved in water]. Uuatsim and his brothers did not want any. They really wanted *morrét* [manioc flour mixed with water]. They refused it and went on their way.

Farther ahead they passed by Kamaiuté, another village. The local people greeted them, saying, "What are you doing here?"

"We stopped for manioc drink," said Uuatsim, answering their greeting.

Then the inhabitants asked where they were going. Learning that they were planning to fish at night, by torchlight, they observed, "Be careful, or you will get lost."

Uuatsim and his companions drank the manioc drink and went on their way. Farther on, they passed by another village, Uruemetáp. As before, the inhabitants wanted to know where they were going. When they found out, they warned the fishermen, "Be very careful, or you really will get lost."

Uuatsim and his brothers drank the manioc drink that was served to them and sent off again upriver. At night they reached the fishing area. They lit the torches and went along, shining them on the river bank. They began to kill all kinds of fish. At a certain spot, one of the fishermen came across a fish, a *pintado,* and called Uuatsim to shoot it with an arrow. Uuatsim drew his bow, and the pintado ran away with the arrow. The brothers went in pursuit, paddling upriver in the canoe. The pintado raced upstream, with the men following behind. But at the top the wounded fish left the river and went into a lake. The fishermen abandoned their canoe and continued the pursuit by land, circling the water. They went laughing and shouting after the fish. The jakuí, who were playing their flutes underwater, heard the shouts and laughter. They looked up and saw the fishermen walking along the *ivacacapé* [the Milky Way]. The jakuí put their flutes away in the tapãim and came out of the water to call the fishermen back. They yelled, but the men did not hear. But when the jakuí blew on the flutes, the fishermen heard and realized they had lost their way. They put out their torches of fire and turned to go back, but a giant snake appeared in the path and blocked their retreat. So Uuatsim and his brothers began to accuse each other.

"Who told you to shoot an arrow?" said one.

"You told me to," answered another.

And there they stood, putting the blame on each other for a long time. When the argument subsided, one of the brothers asked Uuatsim, "Wasn't it you in our house who raised parrots, ibises, and parakeets?"

"Yes, it was I."

"Well then, let us go find the birds."

And they went to look for the village of the birds. After a short while, they found a little *socó* [heron], who was fishing.

"What are you doing here?" asked the heron.

"We're just here," answered Uuatsim.

The socó told them that the birds were having a festival and that he had gone to fish for it. He explained that it was an ear-piercing festival for the parakeets. Uuatsim said that he had come to take part in the festival, which was for his son. It was the spirit of the little parakeet that he had brought up. The fishermen lost in the sky said goodbye to the little socó and went on their way.

Farther on, they came to another heron, who also was fishing. He said that the festival was to pierce the ear of Uuatsim's son. Uuatsim said he knew, he had come to take part in the festival. A little farther, the brothers met the jabiru stork, who was fishing with a *tatorí* [fish trap]; and then they walked on and on. "How long it's taking to get to the village of the birds!" one of them cried. With the sun at its zenith, the brothers were nearing the village they were looking for. From a distance the village people saw them.

"Who's that coming there?" the birds asked one another.

"It's my father, who's come to take part in my festival," said the parakeet in their midst.

When the travelers came into the village, the parakeet took Uuatsim by the hand and led him to his house. He hung up a hammock for him and asked his father to stretch out, saying, "How about that, Father? They're making this feast to pierce my ears."

"I know, my son. I came to take part."

In the afternoon the birds all emerged from their houses to sing the namim, the festival song. They sang in the center of the village. The main singer was the *ueravapirum* [stork]. The parakeet told Uuatsim it was the song of the ueravapirum. "Listen carefully to the way he is singing, so that you can learn. When the people sing, you have to give the singers some fish."

The next day the birds sang the same song again. They sang for several days in a row, day and night, without stopping. Two days before the ear-piercing, the people began to prepare the manioc, pulling it up, carrying it to the village, making the dough. When everything was ready to make beijus, the parakeet asked Uuatsim to make *jequis* [funnel-shaped devices made of woven splints used as fish traps], saying, "I know you know how, Father. When I was crying at your feet, there in our house, I was always watching you make them."

Uuatsim answered that he certainly did know how, and took his brothers to make the traps. As Uuatsim went into the forest, the parakeet said, "It's very good that you're going, because there's a lot of fish where my people go fishing."

Uuatsim made two jequis, and each of his brothers made one. They made five all together. That night, the chief of the birds said that the beijus could be made the next day. The villagers spent the whole night singing. After the sun rose the following day, the birds went fishing. Coming to the place, they set up their camp and began to fish. Uuatsim ordered the first catch to be cooked for the fishermen. Then he told them to close off the mouth of the lake to set up the traps, and to crush the timbó. A number of platforms were erected in the middle of the lake so that the children could shoot the fish with their arrows. Almost all the fish died, poisoned by the timbó. The ones that were not killed by the sap of the timbó were speared by arrows or grabbed when they floated up. The jequis, too, filled with fish. The catch was given to

Uuatsim, who was the chief of the fishermen. It was early when the people reached their village with the fish, piles of them. In the village, the birds decked themselves out, and started up their songs and dances again. They sang the rest of the day and all night long. The parakeet again begged his father Uuatsim to listen to the songs to learn everything.

When the day began to break, the singers, who were singing inside the houses, going from one to another, came out to the center of the village where this first phase of the festival of the namim ended. Then the preparations for the ear-piercing ceremony began. First, the hair-cutting ceremony, to the accompaniment of new songs. Then, the piercing of the ears, together with other songs, took place. When this was over, the children were brought inside the houses, where they stretched out in the hammocks and began to fast.

Two days later, Uuatsim went out to fish for the parakeets. It was midday when he came back with the fish, already prepared on the *moquém* grill, and gave it out among them. The boys were kept inside for several days, and Uuatsim stayed beside his son, the parakeet that he had raised. Uuatsim left again to fish, so that his parakeet could come out of confinement. Uuatsim was tired of living there, in the village of the birds. Coming back from fishing, he started to prepare his son. Before cutting his hair again, he dressed him in a necklace and smeared charcoal on his arms. After the haircut, Uuatsim told the parakeet that he was leaving, explaining that he had come only to take part in the festival. The parakeet begged him to stay just one more day, while he went to ask for the vulture's canoe, so that Uuatsim and his brothers could go back down. Saying that, he went to the vulture's house to make the request. "I came to ask for your canoe so my father can go down, because he's already tired of staying with me."

"All right, I'll take him," answered the vulture.

The next day, very early, the vulture began to carry them. First he took the youngest of the four brothers down. When they were almost there, the canoe still in the air, the youth jumped to the ground and died. Seeing this, the vulture said to himself, "It won't work that way. They have to wait to come farther down. It was still too far up." He said that and went back to get another one. This second brother did the same thing as the first. He jumped out of the canoe before he should have and died. The third one went the same route: he jumped before the vulture landed on the ground and was dashed to pieces. When it was Uuatsim's turn, the parakeet explained that he had to wait for the vulture to land on the ground and not jump out before. The parakeet said, "My father, don't jump out before the canoe reaches the ground, otherwise you'll die. Your brothers are all dead."

The parakeet had not taught the others, because they had been mean to him when he was growing up. They would not feed him, they kicked him, they threw him out of the house, and they made all kinds of trouble for him. That is why the parakeet let them die and did not show them how to get out of the vulture's canoe. Uuatsim got off near the village of the Kuikúru. After teaching the villagers the songs of the namim, *mavurauá, pequeiatsin, tauarauanã,* and jakuí, Uuatsim went to the Kalapalo village and then to Arapatsiuatáp, and there too he taught everyone the songs. He stayed a long time in these places. From these villages, Uuatsim went to the village of the Auetí, and all the people there learned to sing with him. From the Auetí, he went to the village of the Iaualapití. As in the other places, he taught everybody all the songs: tauarauanã, mavurauá, the song to ask for food, and still others. He left the village of the Iaualapití and went over to the Kamaiurá village, where he spent less time, only ten moons. When Uuatsim's brother, who was from the village of the Waurá, found out that he was staying with the Kamaiurá, he went to find him. Uuatsim asked his brother to wait, saying, "Let's stay here awhile longer; I want to teach these people something."

"I'll wait."

Uuatsim then started to sing day and night, so that the people of the village could learn. Before leaving, he told his whole story to the Kamaiurá. The people all listened to him.

"We lit torches to kill fish. There before us we saw a pintado fish. I shot an arrow, he ran off, and we followed behind. After walking a long way, chasing the fish on foot around the lake shore, we heard the flutes playing down below. Then we realized we were lost and we wanted to turn back, but a giant snake in the path would not let us. We could only go on. That's how we got lost. Then we started to look for the village of the birds. We found the little socó, another heron, and the jabiru stork, all fishing."

The Kamaiurá listened attentively to the story that was being told. And Uuatsim went on telling it all: the arrival at the village of the birds, the festival of the namim, the songs that he had heard, the return to earth in the vulture's canoe. After finishing the story, which the Kamaiurá listened to crowded around him, Uuatsim said he was going to stay only two more days in the village.

"I would like to stay longer," said Uuatsim, "but I must go, because my brother came to get me."

Early the next day he departed.

Ever since this happened, the Kamaiurá have said, "If Uuatsim had come to our village first, today we would know all the songs better than anybody else. But since he first came down among the Kuikúru, the Kalapalo, and others, they know more than we do. We also don't know much because Uuatsim did not stay long in our village."

IAMULUMULU:
The Formation of the Rivers

(*Kamaiurá*)

Iamulumulu lived on the Tuatuarí, a tributary on the left bank of the Kuluene River. The giant otters worked for her. Every day the otters fished for Iamulumulu. They fished a great deal, but they themselves did not fish. They would catch a lot of fish with the púa, but they never kept any for themselves and brought it all to Iamulumulu.

The Sun and Moon had heard tell of Iamulumulu. Her husband, Savuru, had two wives, Iamulumulu and one more. Every morning at dawn, Savuru went to bathe with them. They would always build a fire to dry themselves after their bath. The Sun and Moon wanted to meet Iamulumulu. They made up their minds and left.

Iamulumulu was raising a large frog near her village's beach. The Sun, on arrival, gave the frog a cigar to smoke. The frog smoked the cigar right down to the butt. Then the Sun gave him pepper to eat. The frog ate it and died. The Sun and the Moon then dug a hole and buried the frog. But since the place he was buried made a loud noise when stepped on, the Sun exhumed the frog and turned it over, belly up, pointing its head the way the day breaks. They wanted the frog to be able to see the sun rise. The Sun and Moon were still at the beach when the otters began to come back from fishing. The Sun stood there waiting. The otters swam up slowly, saying to one another, "There seems to be people here." One otter went ahead of the others and swam toward the Sun.

"Where did you all come from?" the Sun asked.

"We're coming home from fishing."

The Sun called together all the otters. "Come closer, so we can talk a little. And you mustn't be afraid of me."

When the otters came around, the Sun asked, "Do you eat fish?"

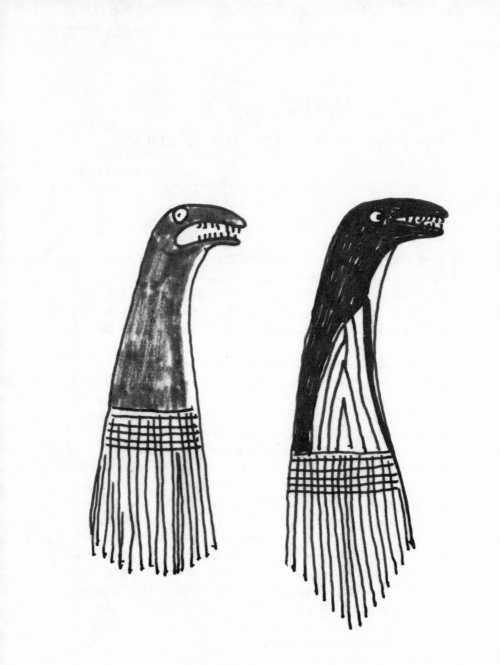

Otter masks

"No."

"Why do you go fishing then? Why do you fish only for others and not for yourselves?"

"Iamulumulu doesn't give us fish, boiled or roasted. That's why we don't eat it."

"This can't go on. You might eat half the fish you catch. What is it that you eat, then?"

"We eat earthworms and things like that."

"No! You must eat the fish you catch."

Having said that, he distributed the roasted fish among the otters and went on talking. "You must kill fish and eat fish. Not just catch for others to eat. That's not right."

When the otters finished eating the fish he had given them, the Sun said, "Now you must kill Savuru. You must really kill him."

"We're afraid," the otters answered. And they began to whisper to each other, "Can it be that we can actually kill?"

The Moon, seeing that they couldn't make up their minds, prodded them. "You must kill Savuru, so you can eat fish always."

The Sun, after handing out more fish, gave them a big net to capture Savuru. The otters asked the Moon how they were meant to put up the net. The Sun stepped forward and explained, "This afternoon you put up the net here at the beach. When Savuru comes to bathe and jumps in the water, he'll fall into the net."

That afternoon, as the Sun had suggested, the otters went to the beach without making a sound, not even talking to each other, and put up the net. They brought no fish that day to Savuru's house. That night when they came to the village, Savuru asked why they had arrived in such a sneaky way that he hadn't seen them. "What is this? Why didn't you bring any fish? I never hurt you. What's the matter with you?"

At dawn Savuru went out alone to bathe, and coming to the beach, he sat down and washed himself. Then he jumped in the water and fell into the net. He was trapped. He twisted to one side and to the other, wanting to get out, but he could not. He drowned inside the net. At home, his wives, thinking Savuru was taking much too long, went down to the beach after him. There they found their husband already dead in the net. They went back to the village and asked the otters, "Why did you do that to your uncle?"

And, infuriated, they set fire to the otters' house, but the otters dug a hole in the floor and all of them escaped. After some time they returned to mourn Savuru, who had already been taken home. The otters, after weeping at his side, dug a hole and buried him. The Sun and Moon also went to Savuru's house to mourn his death. They cried over his grave. The dead man's wives took the visitors to their house. The next day they were given the ceremonial bath which ends mourning.

Two days later the widows began to prepare themselves to go with the Sun and Moon. When they were about to leave, they were still vacillating, and one widow said to the other, "Well, are we going with them or not?" The Moon, seeing that they hadn't made up their minds, told them that they could not stay there alone. So they decided to go with the two of them, and they left by canoe for the village of the Sun. The Moon rode in the prow and the Sun in the stern, steering. The women were still weeping. The Sun and Moon tried to distract them by doing funny things. They made faces, splashed water on each other, and did a number of tricks, but the women would not laugh. They went on weeping. At a certain point in the journey, the women tried to catch some small fish that were swimming alongside the canoe, and when these began to jump, the women thought it was funny and laughed. Seeing this, the Moon said, "That's good. If you kept crying forever, you'd die of sadness."

After a day of traveling, they came to the Morená, where the Sun's village was.

A long time passed. The Sun and the Moon had married the widows of Savuru. The Sun married the older woman, the Moon the younger. But they were not able to have relations with their wives. They could only caress them. They were impotent. The women asked if they didn't know about Iamururú's remedy for impotence. The Sun said, "Let's go get this medicine."

As they came closer to Iamururú's house, they already felt better, but they kept on going anyway. They went into Iamururú's house and said, "We came to take your cure."

Iamururú said that it wasn't necessary, since the cure had already taken hold of them. But the Moon wanted it anyway. So Iamururú gave them the remedy to take with them. When they were halfway home, seeing that their members would no longer be impotent, they went back to Iamururú's house and returned the medicine to him. From then on they began to live normally.

The only thing missing was jealousy. The Sun and the Moon were not jealous of their wives, who resented this and said that Ierẽp had a remedy to make jealousy. And so all of them went to get the remedy. They came to Ierẽp's house, but he was not home. He had gone to the garden. When he came back from the garden, he began to beat his wife. The wives of the Sun and Moon asked the old man for his remedy. He said it was not going to be necessary, because the remedy had already taken hold of their husbands. But the women wanted it anyway. So Ierẽp gave it to them. Halfway home, the Sun and the Moon began to beat their wives. This jealousy was too much. They turned back and handed the remedy over to Ierẽp. Their jealousy abated a little, but when they got back to the village, they began to beat their wives again. And the women said, "This is what the people like. It's fine now."

They couldn't sleep, husbands or wives. Night after night they spent sleepless. The women said that Uiaó had the remedy to bring sleep. They went to Uiaó's house.

"Grandfather, are you here?"

"Yes, I am."

"We came to get the remedy that brings sleep."

"You don't need it. Sleep has already taken hold of you."

And they fell sound asleep. They only woke up when the owner of the house arrived. But they wanted the remedy anyway, and so Uiaó gave it to them.

On the way home, the Sun said, "This is too much." They would walk a few steps and stop to go to sleep. They even fell asleep while they were walking. Since they couldn't even walk without falling asleep, they decided to turn around and give the remedy back to Uiaó. Back in their village, they slept very well, the whole night through.

The women said, "That's how we like it. It's been a long time since we slept. Everything is fine now."

Water was another thing they lacked. The women asked the Sun to get it for them. Only Canutsipém had water that was good to drink.

"Let's go have a look at Canutsipém's water," said the Moon.

For that, they went to his house.

"Are you here, Grandfather?"

"Yes, I am."

"We are looking for water to drink," the Sun said. "We don't have good water."

They asked for it and waited. They had arrived at noon. In the afternoon Canutsipém invited the two of them, the Sun and Moon, to bathe. The water was very dirty where they went. The Moon asked, "Is this his water?"

The Sun answered that that was not the real water; it was only to fool them. "Canutsipém has good water, but it's hidden."

The two came back from bathing, and one of them said to the other that that had not been the real water and the good water was hidden inside the tapãim. So the Moon turned himself into a hummingbird and went to look at the water inside the tapãim. He saw all the water kept in there and came back, saying to the Sun, "There is water in there. He has a great many pots brimful of water. The other water really was meant to fool us."

They spent the whole day in Canutsipém's house, and the night too. The next day Canutsipém told the visitors that his people had been fishing. They had fished at night with the püa net, right inside the tapãim itself, and had caught a lot of fish. Canutsipém told the Sun and the Moon to wait, so that they might eat the fish that his people were roasting at that very moment. They fried poraquê and peixe-cachorro for the visitors. The Sun went to the socó's house to ask for water to be able to eat the fish, which had a lot of spines. The socó gave him two ladlefuls. The Sun and Moon, after eating and drinking water, went to tell Canutsipém that they were going. As they were leaving, Canutsipém gave them two gourds full of water to take with them. When they reached their village, the women drank the water and said it was excellent. "That really is drinking water," the women said. Then all the people in the village of the Sun and their neighbors decided to take possession of Canutsipém's water. They all decided to go: the Sun, the Moon, Vanivaní, Ianamá, Kanaratê, and others.

Beforehand, however, they made many things representing angry spirits: *turuá* [image of a forest spirit that lives at the top of the jatobá tree], horí-horí and masks: *jakuí-katu, mearatsim, ivát, jakuiaép,* and

Masks of water spirits

Masks of land spirits

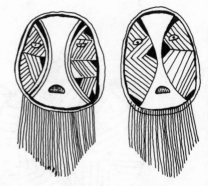

Masks of water spirits

Masks of tree spirits

tavarí, which represent spirits that live in the depths of the waters. After everything was ready, they danced for a great while with the masks, and set out for Canutsipém's village to take his water from him. They wanted to break his pots to make a big body of water in the Morená. The one who reached Canutsipém's village first was mearatsim's mask. He went in singing.

Terrified, Canutsipém said, "Now they are going to finish us off."

Just then the village was invaded by Ianamá, Vanivaní, the Sun, the Moon, and all the rest. They kept charging into the tapãim, smashing the pots and breaking them all. The Moon was the last to invade the tapãim, and he broke the last pot. A huge animal came out of it and devoured him. Canutsipém's village turned into a great lagoon, and the people began to go down with the waters, forming the rivers. The Sun came, bringing the Ronuro River and calling to the Moon. He did not answer. The first to answer was Vanivaní, who was going down with the Maritsauá River. Then came Ianamá, who was bringing a tributary of the Ronuro. Kanaratê answered from the Paranajuva River. The Kuluene River was brought by the *tracajá* turtle. The Sun

Turtles

went on shouting for the Moon, but he did not answer. He was inside the animal's belly, there in Canutsipém's tapãim.

The Sun wanted to make a big lagoon at the Morená, but was annoyed because the waters would not all flow together in that direction. Then he got to thinking about how to find his brother. I have to find my brother. At this point there was only a thread of water coming down, very little. So the Sun took a termite hill, broke it into pieces, and made a dam to keep the water back. And the fish started to go by. The Sun proceeded to kill them and open their bellies to see if he could find his brother. He killed tucunarés, *matrinxãs,* and many others. Then came an *acará-açu.* He was taking his time.

The Sun drew back his bow and said, "I'm going to kill this acará."

"What's that, Grandpa, you can't do that to me. I was going to tell you where your brother is."

The Sun, hearing this, loosened his bowstring and paid attention.

"Your brother," said the acará, "is inside the *jacunâum's* belly. You had better go find him."

"What should I do?"

"Roll a cigar to bring to the jacunâum."

The Sun went first to the house of the *taperá* [field swallow], to ask for a hook. The taperá gave him a tiny hook.

"You'd better give me a bigger one. This little one won't work," said the Sun.

The taperá gave him a big hook. The Sun made a line and went to the place where he had been fishing. He rolled a cigar, put the hook through one end, and gave it to the acará. The acará swam upstream with the cigar, while the Sun stood holding the line. Before leaving, the acará said, "When the jacunâum sticks the cigar in his mouth, I'll give a tug on the line to let you know."

The acará took his time going upstream, smoking a little himself. When the jacunâum saw the acará going past, he asked to have the cigar, saying that his belly was full and he wanted to empty it. The acará handed him the cigar. The moment the jacunâum put the cigar into his mouth, the acará gave the signal. The Sun, at the other end, yanked the line and hooked the jacunâum, who ran around inside the tapãim, caught on the line. When he came out, the acará ran to tell the Sun. The Sun started to pull in the line, until he had dragged the jacunâum in front of him. He hauled him out of the water and imme-diately opened his belly. All he found was the bones of the Moon, and he began to grieve, saying, "Oh, my poor brother, you're dead!" After taking the remains out of the jacunâum's belly, he let him go in the water. But he did not leave then. He stayed right there in the Morená.

Then the Sun drew an outline of a person on the ground and put the bones on top of the drawing. Every bone went in the right place. He saw that only the thumbs were missing. After he had arranged the skeleton on top of the drawing, he covered it all with fragrant enemeóp leaves. At once he began to utter supplications to bring his brother back to life. Meanwhile, the flesh was forming on top of the bones. When the skeleton was all covered with flesh, the Moon's body rebuilt, the Sun called the *jaó* [tinamou] and said, "Come and do something to wake my brother up."

The jaó came, flew close by, and the Moon stirred a little. Then he called the *rolinha* [dove], who flew right over and caused the Moon to move again. The Sun wondered what he could try next. He grabbed a tiny mosquito and stuck it up his brother's nose. The mosquito stayed inside, flying around. The Moon started to sneeze and woke up. He got up and said that he had fallen asleep.

"You weren't asleep at all, you were in the jacunâum's belly," said the Sun.

He told his brother to sit down. He lit a cigar and began to sing and blow smoke all over the Moon, to make him completely well again. Then he told the Moon to breathe deeply. The Moon took sev-eral breaths, and when he got up from the stool, he was much better. The Sun sent for a shaman whose name was Caapaié and asked him to take care of his brother, so he would be even healthier. Then he sent for the birds that are called *atsim-aum* to perform a curing cere-mony. They did the job, and the Moon got up and walked around. He was completely cured.

"There's nothing wrong with me any more. I'm just the way I used to be," said the Moon.

The art of the shamans was begun by the Sun. He was the first shaman.

VITI-VITÍ:
The Origin of the Ditches

(*Kuikúru*)

Viti-Vití was a person. He had a nose. He had a mouth. He had ears. He had eyes. He had everything that people have.

Viti-Vití was married to a woman of his own tribe. He had a brother-in-law, a mother-in-law, and a father-in-law. Viti-Vití decided to go get honey out of the hive. He went as it was getting dark, because the bees were very fierce. Viti-Vití took his wife and brother-in-law. They went into the forest. When they got there, Viti-Vití said, "Brother-in-law, who's going to climb the tree, you or I?"

"I'd rather you went," answered the brother-in-law.

The wife had brought a large clay pot for the honey. Viti-Vití climbed up in the tree, carrying a shell to bore holes in the hive, to pull out the honeycombs. From up in the tree, Viti-Vití told them to bring the pot close to the tree to catch the honey in, but he was doing nothing of the kind. Viti-Vití was using the shell to turn his right leg into an animal's leg. With the shell he was cutting his leg, or rather scraping it to make it thin and end in a point. On the ground, his wife and brother-in-law kept asking him to throw down honey. Viti-Vití threw honey down to them. But what was falling into the pot was blood from Viti-Vití's leg. As it was dark, they could not see that it was blood. The two of them, wife and brother-in-law, ate up all the blood Viti-Vití had thrown down to them. Suddenly Viti-Vití's brother-in-law began to smell blood. He became suspicious and went to check the pot. Discovering that it was actually blood, he said to his sister, "This is blood. What can he be doing up there? He must be going crazy. We'd better get out of here and leave him alone. You go ahead and I'll be along shortly."

Viti-Vití's wife went off. Up there in the treetop, Viti-Vití continued

Zoömorphic clay pot in the form of a bat

to work on his foot. He asked his brother-in-law, "Well, have we got enough honey yet?"

"We have half a pot."

The brother-in-law knew that the half a pot was Viti-Vití's blood and said, "I'm moving just a few steps away. The bees are getting ferocious and biting us. We can't take any more."

He was talking and waving his hand in front of his face at the same time. Saying that, he began to move away slowly. When he was a little way off, he started to run. That left Viti-Vití all by himself, but he thought his wife and brother-in-law were down there, waiting for him. Meanwhile, he had given his leg the shape he wanted. From up there, Viti-Vití shouted, "Brother-in-law, oh, brother-in-law!"

Since he got no answer, he said to himself, "Where could they have gone?" As no one answered, he climbed out of the tree and on the ground continued calling to the two of them. Before she left, Viti-Vití's wife had dumped all the blood out of the pot. Viti-Vití kept calling, but no one answered. He decided to go home to get the two of them. When he reached home, he found everything shut up. Out of fear, his brother-in-law had closed the entire house. Viti-Vití from outside ordered them to open up. His brother-in-law did not want to open, because he knew if he did, Viti-Vití would kill him with his pointed foot. Viti-Vití's leg had become very long and pointed. It was his weapon. Viti-Vití peered in from outside, but he could not see his brother-in-law, who was hidden.

"Where are you, brother-in-law?" he asked.

The brother-in-law did not answer and would not let his sister, Viti-Vití's wife, answer. Viti-Vití got tired of calling to his brother-in-law and his wife. As nobody had answered him, he decided to leave that very hour for the forest, taking with him all his people. Everywhere he went that seemed like a nice place to stay, Viti-Vití would make long, deep ditches and leave part of his people there, and he himself would continue traveling. He advised all of them to build their village outside the ditch, within the semicircle described by it. The ditches were almost always arc-shaped, and one end always led to or away from water. The ditches, Viti-Vití recommended, should be used when it became necessary to protect themselves against cold winds. In almost every habitable place he found, Viti-Vití left a few of his people and a deep ditch for shelter. Viti-Vití still lives today with some of his people on the shores of the great Kuikúru-Ípa lagoon, at one end of a ditch, where it meets the water.

At night Viti-Vití's footsteps can be heard. They make a dry sound when he steps on the ground with his pointed leg: toc, tim, toc, tim. That is the sound.

Curassow

THE CURASSOW:
Work, Plant, in Order to Eat

(Kamaiurá)

The curassow was married to two women, but neither of them could stand him. They thought their husband was very ugly. Everything about him seemed ugly to them, but the worst thing was his hair, which was all curled up. And that is why they would do nothing for their husband. They would not bake beiju, they would not make manioc drink, they would not cook fish. Every day the curassow's mother begged her daughters-in-law to take care of their husband, but they paid no attention and wouldn't move a muscle. The two were sisters, daughters of the parakeet. The curassow, in spite of it all, went on living in his house, completely ignored by his wives. Whenever he went hunting or fishing, he would invite his wives, and they would refuse to go with him. The curassow's mother, sick of doing all the work herself, one day called her son and said, "My son, you must leave these women and marry the daughters of the *coeme* [roseate spoonbill].

The curassow agreed and said that he would go to the coeme the next day. The following day, as he left, he said to his mother, "If my uncle should say anything to me, if he wants me to get married, I'll have to stay there for a while."

Along the way he passed the house of the dung beetle. The beetle was playing a flute, and the curassow stopped to watch. When the beetle saw the curassow coming up, he quickly hid his flute, because he did not want the bird to see it. So the curassow pretended to leave. He walked off, turned around, and hid behind the dung beetle's house. This one, after a while, took up his flute again and began to play. The curassow charged into the beetle's house and after a furious struggle grabbed the flute away from him. When the curassow was leaving his house, the dung beetle said, "The reason you came by was to marry the coeme's daughters, because your wives can't stand you."

The curassow went on his way, and walked along the path, examining the stolen flute. At first he thought it was very beautiful, but farther along, looking it over carefully, it dawned on him that the flute looked very suspicious, and he said, "This is a piece of dung." And to prove the point, he poked a hole in the flute with a stick and took a whiff. Seeing that it actually was made of dung, he threw the flute away. At midday, the curassow came to the coeme's village. When he arrived, the people wanted to know where he was going. He answered that he was looking for his uncle. The coeme appeared, took the visitor's bow and hammock, and led him to his house. After asking the curassow to sit down, he called his daughters and asked them, "Which of you wants to marry this young man?"

Both of them wanted to, the older as well as the younger. And right away the two women went to make food for the curassow. One made manioc drink, the other beiju. That afternoon they took the curassow to bathe. They were already married to him.

When they came back from the lagoon, the coeme called his daughters and said, "You must like your husband, because his first wives did not like him. You also have to do something to make him better looking."

The next day the women began to improve their husband's appearance. The first thing they did was to comb his hair; then they straightened his legs, arms, and everything. Already settled in the village, the curassow began to get up at dawn to talk to his brothers-in-law, with all of the coeme people. He told them that they had to work very hard, to clear big gardens, because without gardens they could not live. Work, work, every day, to be able to live better. Every sunset and sunrise the curassow and his father-in-law went to the center of the village to advise and instruct the people. The curassow was a hard worker; he had many gardens and planted all kinds of things: corn, manioc, yams, potatoes, tobacco, cotton; he raised everything. After spending several days in the coeme's village, the curassow told his father-in-law that he had to go to his own village but that he would be back soon. He said he was going only to serve his people manioc drink.

"When I come back," said the curassow, "I'll never leave here again."

The next morning he again informed his father-in-law that he had to go to his own village. The coeme told his daughters that they could not stay. They had to go with their husband. The following day the curassow, accompanied by his two wives, took off. Along the way, passing the dung beetle's house, he stopped for a while to chat, and the beetle said to him jokingly, "How is it that you are so beautiful now? I'll bet your wives fixed you up to look like this."

In the afternoon the curassow reached his village. All the people came to greet him. His mother was pounding corn. When he came to his house, his former wives, jealous of the others, tried to give the old woman a hand at the pestle, but she wouldn't let them. Ashamed and jealous, the two wives took down their hammocks and left. But they could still hear their former mother-in-law say, "You did it to yourselves. You didn't like my son, and so he had to marry somebody else."

When the curassow went into his house, his mother, overjoyed, said, "What are you doing here, my son? Why did you bring these girls along? You don't have a thing and they'll go hungry here."

His mother was only joking, because she was so happy. The curassow and his wives sat down to rest for a while. Minutes later the two women jumped up and begged their mother-in-law to let them serve.

"Let us do that," they said.

The curassow's mother, pleased with the manners of her daughters-in-law, said, "I like people like you, hard-working people."

The women pounded all the corn and made the beijus. That afternoon the two of them went to bathe with their husband in the lagoon. Five days later the curassow told his wives to make beijus and manioc drink, so he could offer it to the people of the village. A large amount of the two things was prepared. The curassow took it all to the center of the village and distributed it to everybody. At nightfall he went outside and told his people that the next day he was going to his father-in-law's house and he would never return. "Now you can eat all my corn and manioc, because I'm never coming back."

The next day, along the way to his father-in-law's house, the curassow was teaching and sharing his things with the people he found on the way. When he passed by the wasp, he said, "You, look for ant eggs to eat. That will be your flour, your food."

The wasp said all right, he would do that from now on. To another wasp that he met farther ahead, he said the same thing. And he, too, took his advice. To the dung beetle, the curassow said, as he passed by his house, "You can eat some of the manioc I left."

"All right. Is it dung?"

"Yes. That's exactly what it is," said the curassow.

From that day on, the beetle eats only filth. The curassow tried to get him to eat manioc, but since he asked that question, he wound up eating nothing but dung. In the fox's village, the curassow told her to go get the fire he had left in the canebrake. Late in the afternoon the curassow, with his wives and mother, came to the village of his father-in-law.

Back there, he started to teach his brothers-in-law and the people of the village. He taught them everything. Every day he talked to them all. Among other things the coeme people learned that the fire lived inside the sugarcane stalk. The curassow never went back to his former village. He spent the rest of his life with his father-in-law. He had eight children by his two wives: three men and five women.

THE TAPIR:
The Anta and the Stars

(*Kamaiurá*)

There was a genipap tree that the children visited every day. They climbed the tree, picked the ripe fruit, and ate it up there. The *anta* or tapir was also in the habit of going there daily to get genipap, but he always failed. The boys not only picked the fruit on the tree, they also gathered what had fallen on the ground. The tapir wasted a trip every time. One morning the boys went on foot to the genipap tree. They went quite early. As always they ate the fruit on the ground and then climbed up to eat what was still on the tree. As soon as they were all up there, the tapir appeared. As he was coming along, one of the boys said, "Here comes the old man."

The oldest of them, seeing the tapir coming, warned his companions, "We'd better give a little genipap to the tapir, otherwise he'll be furious at us."

When the tapir got there, from down below he eyed the tree and said to the children, "Have you got a lot up there?"

"There's plenty up here."

"Well then, throw some down to me," said the tapir.

The boys tossed a few genipaps down, and the tapir began to eat. After dropping whole genipaps, the boys took to throwing down only the peel. This annoyed the tapir, and he kicked the trunk of the tree hard with his hoof, causing the boys to fall to the ground. There was only one boy left up in the tree. He did not fall when the tree shook with the tapir's kick. From up there he said to the ones who had fallen, "Why did you throw peels to the tapir?"

When the boys fell, the tapir went around stepping on them and burying them with his foot. The tapir, after killing and burying the boys, left and went a long way away. After a while the boys in the ground began to be born, some in the form of little turtles, others as real people. The one up in the tree said to the others down below, "How are you doing down there?"

"We're all right. Did you see which way the tapir went?"

After the one in the tree showed them the direction, the ones below said, "Now it's our turn, we must kill the tapir."

They all marched off in the direction the tapir had taken. After walking awhile, they came to a pile of excrement and asked it, "Where did your master go?"

"He went this way, but it's been a long time since he passed by here."

The boys kept walking and found more piles of excrement ahead. They asked the same question and got the same answer: their master had passed by a long time ago. Thus, from pile to pile, the boys went after the tapir, for days and days on end. After a trek many moons long, they began to find fresher excrement.

"When did your master pass by here?"

"Five days ago" was the answer.

Tapir

This cheered the boys up, and they went forward in a livelier mood. A pile of excrement they found some days later had not even dried yet. The next was still smoking. On questioning it, the boys were told that its master had passed by that very day. They went on and found, just ahead, a pile of excrement that had been left minutes earlier. The boys took a few steps, and there was the tapir, stretched out in front of them, asleep. They killed him on the spot with spears and cudgels. They cut the tapir into pieces, set up a large wooden rack, and roasted all the meat. They roasted everything, head, legs, ribs, everything. Then they ate. Afterward, seeing that they had come a long way, the boys decided to climb up to the sky. They first sent up their roasting rack, and then they all followed behind. There, in the sky, they all stayed together, gathered in one place. They are the group of stars that, in the cold season, appear in the south, and in the hot season, in the north.

AVATSIU:
The Language of the Birds

(*Kamaiurá*)

O nce a woman had a fight with her husband. The young man, dis-
gusted, decided to go off alone. He rolled a couple of cigars
and went into the forest. There, in the middle of the forest, he leaned
against a camioá tree and said, "Tamãi, I would like to become just
like you."

"You wouldn't be able to stand it, my grandson. To be a tree is
very difficult. You have to stay awake all the time. If you fall asleep,
you'll die, and that's that," the camioá answered.

So the young man went on wandering and said the same thing when
he came to the ivurapaputã. "Tamãi, I want to become just like you."

"No, you can't, my grandson. You wouldn't last very long. Everybody that wants to make a bow will come and cut you up. We live a
very short time," answered the ivurapaputã.

The young man listened to him and went on his way. Farther ahead,
he passed a small column of smoke that was floating up right beside
him. After walking awhile longer, he decided to come back and see
whom the smoke belonged to. He turned around, saying to himself,
"I wonder who lives here?" Close up he saw that the birds were burning grass, and he walked over to where they were. When he came up
to them, the birds asked him, "What are you up to, Grandpa?"

"Nothing. I was out walking and I stopped to watch you."

"Then let's sit down," the birds invited him.

They all sat down. They rolled cigars and started to talk. After their
chat, the birds said, "You must come with us over to our village. This
is our garden. We are clearing it a little."

The young man accepted their invitation and followed the birds.
The birds were all pleased at the arrival of a new person, somebody
from the village of Avatsiú, whom they wanted to kill. The birds did

174

not like Avatsiú, because Avatsiú was always killing their people: eagles, macaws, parrots, toucans, and many others.

The next day the chief of the birds said to his people, "Tomorrow we must make our visitor look just like us."

The chief said this several times. He said it in the morning and also in the afternoon. The birds who had found the young man and brought him back with them warned him, "Don't fall asleep, at night or during the day, because it is very dangerous."

The next day, bright and early, all the birds got feathers and went to put them on the young man. They first spread a glue-like tree milk over his body, and then they began to stick the feathers on. First they glued the ones on his chest and legs. Next they put the big ones on, for the tail and wings. All the feathers came from the giant eagle. When the young man was covered with feathers, they told him to shake his plumage to see if any feathers would fall out. He shook and not a single one fell. They told him to shake again. This time, one fell. Seeing this, the birds exclaimed, "This young man is not going to live. He will fall into the hands of Avatsiú."

Saying this, they took the man to the place where they trained young birds. They came to a tree that had a termite high up on it. They asked the young man to fly up and pluck off the termite. The man flew up but missed the termite completely, so he flew back to the ground. They told him to try again. He took off, flew once around the tree, and got stuck as he was trying to snatch the termite. So the birds told him to fly down from the top of the tree, pick up a rock that had been placed on the ground, and hover with it. The young man flew down, missing the rock entirely. They told him to try again, and he missed again. Finally the birds said, "It's no use trying to teach him. He's no good at all."

Saying this, they went back to the village. The birds who had found the man warned him again, "Listen, don't go to sleep. You have to stay awake all night long."

The following morning the birds left with the young man to try and catch Avatsiú. Avatsiú was singing when the birds arrived at his village. The birds landed where they usually perched. From there they could hear Avatsiú singing inside his house. The young man was with the birds, perched in the trees. They sat there waiting for Avatsiú to come outside. The birds said, "We have to wait for him to come outside."

"Wait. Wait," they kept telling the young man, who kept threatening to fly. Avatsiú stopped playing and appeared at the door, ready to come out. The young man dived down toward him, but he missed and instead was caught by Avatsiú. Avatsiú grabbed him, pulled him into the house, and killed him. The birds went back to their village, sad and ashamed because they had let the young man die.

That afternoon the birds gathered together for a discussion. They asked the birds who had brought the young man to the village if he had any children. They informed the others that he had a son. They were all happy to hear this and said that they would have to go and get the boy. The araraúna [ox blood: a red bird] was entrusted with the mission. The next day the araraúna went to the village of Avatsiú where the boy lived. When he arrived there, he sat on the food rack on the terrace, right in front of the house.

When the boy's mother came out to dump waste, she saw the little bird on the food rack and called to her son, "There's a little red bird out here. Come see."

The little boy charged out of the house with his bow and arrow. As he got close to the food rack, the araraúna flew to a nearby tree. When the boy approached the tree, the bird flew to another one farther off. Thus, the bird, from one place to the next, led the boy away from the village. When the araraúna saw that they were far enough from the houses, he took his feathers off, became a person, and approached the boy, saying, "I came to get you, to kill Avatsiú."

"I'll be glad to," said the boy. "But first let me talk to my mother."

"Go ahead. I'll stay here waiting for you."

The boy went and told his mother that they had come to get him to kill Avatsiú. When she heard what the boy was saying, the mother started to cry. When she stopped crying, she said to him, "You may go, my son. But listen to me; when you go to kill Avatsiú, don't attack him from the front, your father died doing that. Come from behind, so you can kill him."

Before leaving, the boy asked for three mats to keep feathers in. His mother gave them to him, and he went out to find the araraúna. The araraúna dressed the boy with feathers he had brought for the occasion, and from there they flew back to the birds' village. Reaching their destination, the araraúna brought the boy to his own house. All the birds came to see him. They came one by one to greet him. "*Parecó piá. Parecó piá.* [How are you, my son?]"

After the greetings, the chief of the birds said, "Now, my son, you must avenge the death of your father by killing Avatsiú.

"How do you have in mind killing Avatsiú? If you meet him face to face, it'll be he who will grab you," said the boy. And he concluded, "We must come up from behind. That way is easier and more certain."

The next morning the birds went to dress the boy. They spread tree milk over his body and right away began to glue the feathers of the *uirapê,* the harpy or giant crested eagle, on him. When they had covered the boy's body with down, the birds proceeded to put the larger feathers on, for the tail and the wings. When it was all ready, they told the boy to shake his plumage to see if any feathers would fall out. None did. They told him to shake again, and not a one came unglued. They were stuck fast. That afternoon the birds took the boy to the training ground. There, as they had done with his father, they told him to fly to the top of the tree and snatch the termite off. The boy flew up and knocked the termite off. Then they told him that, from the top of the tree, he should fly down, pick up the rock, and hold it up. The boy flew down like an arrow, picked up the rock, and when he was hovering with it, three giant eagles came to help him. Among them they carried the rock high in the air, and from up there they let it drop. The rock smashed against the ground. At that moment the birds began to rejoice and said, "This boy really will be able to kill Avatsiú."

Before they left for Avatsiú's village, the birds kept warning the boy, telling him over and over to watch out for Avatsiú, who was exceedingly dangerous. When they came to the village, Avatsiú was singing and dancing, he and his sons, and while they danced, they were breaking up their house pots, for they had a premonition that they were going to die. In his song Avatsiú was saying, "I have an enemy with great talons who is going to kill me." As soon as he arrived, the boy asked his companions where he was supposed to wait. The eagles showed him the place, and he thought it was no good. "I'm not staying there. I'll wait behind the house." He flew to the spot he had chosen, and the birds went with him. Avatsiú, inside his house, was

Gourd rattle

still singing, singing without stop. Meanwhile, the birds perched in the trees waited for the moment he would leave his house. When Avatsiú, gourd rattle in hand, emerged from his house, the boy swooped down on him, grabbing him hard with his talons and lifting him a little from the ground. The eagles who were watching, realizing that the boy was not going to be able to lift Avatsiú all by himself, rushed to help him. Avatsiú, thus carried by a number of them, was lifted into the sky, higher and higher. At the same time, the other birds grabbed his wife and sons, and did the same thing to them. When the boy and the eagles were very far up, they let go of Avatsiú, and he fell, till he smashed on the ground below.

Having accomplished this, the birds circled down to the ground, to the spot where Avatsiú had fallen. There the chief of the birds chose two of his tribesmen and sent them to invite another village of their relatives to produce something from Avatsiú's blood. The pariáts were

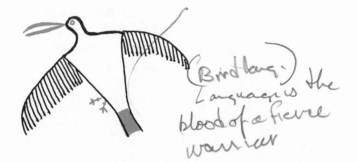

(Bird lang:)
Language is the
blood of a fierce
warrior

Hummingbird

the dove and the hummingbird. The two left to carry the invitation and came back right away, saying that the people from the other village were on their way. Soon afterward the guests arrived, speaking the language of people. None of them had their own language, the language of birds. With Avatsiú's blood, they were going to make new languages for all of them. The first to get their own language, drawn from the blood of Avatsiú, were the *iapacaní* and the *uapaní* eagles. Before, like all the others, they had spoken the language of people. The guests kept coming, taking some of the blood, and using it to produce new languages. The hummingbird started to speak in the language he had composed, as did the *anhuma* [horned screamer], but then both of them realized that their languages did not suit them very well. The hummingbird's speech was too deep and the anhuma's too shrill. So they decided to trade. The anhuma took the hummingbird's language, and he kept the anhuma's. And the dove traded his with the curassow. The dove's was too loud and that of the curassow too feeble. Both of them were very pleased with the exchange.

Afterward the curassow said, "Now, when the day breaks, we will sing, and it will be beautiful."

After the preparation of their languages, the birds flew back to their village. When they got there, they said, "Now, let's take our friend home." But before that they plucked many feathers from themselves and gave them to the boy. When they came to his village, they said to the boy's mother, "We came to bring your son. Now he's back again. He killed Avatsiú to avenge his father's death." They handed the boy over to his mother and went back to their village. In his own village, the boy told all of his story to his people. He told them everything that had happened, even the creation of languages with Avatsiú's blood.

TAMACAVÍ:
The Killing of the Jaguars

(Kamaiurá)

Every day Tamacaví went to his garden. Whenever he went out, he would always tell his wife not to mess with his images of the jaguar, which he took great care of. Every time he went out of the house he would give her this warning. One day, as soon as he left, his wife felt an urge to look at the images. She felt the urge, and she couldn't contain herself. She took his carrying bag down from the storage rack, pulled the images out of it, and began to look at them. And while she looked, she spoke softly to herself, admiring the claws in the pictures, "These images are good enough for a person to make a necklace." No sooner had she said these words than the images began to grow and turn into live animals. That same moment they killed the woman and charged out of the house roaring. Tamacaví, who was in his garden, heard the roars and immediately realized what had happened. The jaguars, coming out of the house, ate all the people in the village. Tamacaví ran back to his house. He made a cigar and began to lure the jaguars. The jaguars came forward little by little until they were touching Tamacaví. Then he gave them the cigar and said, "You can go to other villages and eat other people too."

Those of Tamacaví's people who had escaped the jaguars because they had been away sent a warning to the neighboring village that there were jaguars scouring the countryside and finishing everybody off.

The jaguars, still wandering around, came to the village that had been forewarned and on arrival ate five people. The rest of them had gone into hiding. They came out of their hiding places and went to warn the next village about the jaguars. They were going from village to village and devouring people. The news traveled from place to place, always brought by those who survived the raids. The jaguars were very

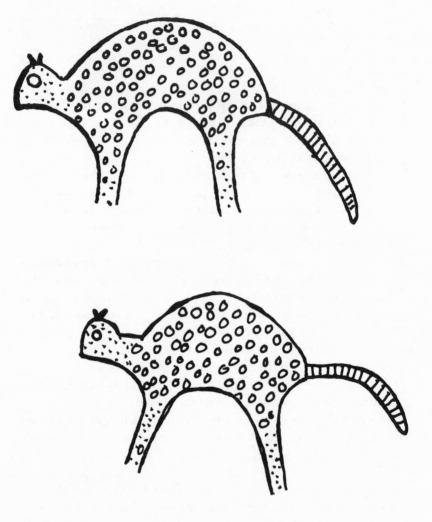

Jaguars

big and growing steadily. From the very beginning they had been taller than a man. When they invaded a village, the inhabitants climbed on top of their houses or hid in holes.

The village of the Bakirí was also warned. Two of its men climbed a pole and waited there for the jaguars. The others went to the trail to warn everybody when they appeared. It wasn't long before the jaguars showed up and began to approach the village. The female led the way and was followed by the male. The two Bakirís still on top of the tree were alerted that the animals were getting nearer. When the lead jaguar passed by them, she was shot with an arrow and killed. The other turned back. The Bakirís skinned the jaguar and divided strips of it among all of them. Each of them got a leather band.

The chief of the Bakirí sent a warning to Tamacaví that the jaguar had turned back to his village. Tamacaví had already moved to the Itavununo lagoon. Before the jaguars came, he had lived on the banks of the Kurizêvo River. The jaguar had gotten very large. He was already the size of a house. When Tamacaví heard that the jaguar was coming back in his direction, he began to train two boys, whose job it would be to face the animal. First he had medicine rubbed on their bodies to make them great archers. Then he had the chosen ones put into confinement, so they would develop well and grow in body and strength. The next day their father asked them what they had dreamed of. They answered that they had dreamed of shooting arrows into a great termite hill. The father concluded from this that they would doubtless become great archers. In confinement, every day the young men grew in body and became stronger.

After they had achieved their full growth and had turned into mature men, Tamacaví had two wooden platforms built on the path, one on each side, facing each other, so the young men could wait for the jaguar. Right in front of the platforms, in the middle of the road, Tamacaví had a deep hole dug for the jaguar to fall into, when he was shot. The jaguar was wandering among the other villages, always killing and eating the inhabitants. The young men, each with two arrows, went to their platforms and stayed there waiting. The jaguar came along roaring, closer each time. The *uirapareáts* [archers], perched on their platforms, could already hear him. The people, to trick the animal and get him to come faster, began to make a great racket in the village, shouting, whistling, and doing all kinds of things to attract the jaguar. He came closer and closer, until he came into sight on the path. He came with a cigar in his mouth. The people could see the cigar light up in the distance whenever the jaguar drew on it. They were all happy because they knew that this time the animal was going to die. And each time he got closer, still on the path, the cigar glowing and dimming. As he passed between the platforms, he was shot with four arrows, fell in the hole, and died.

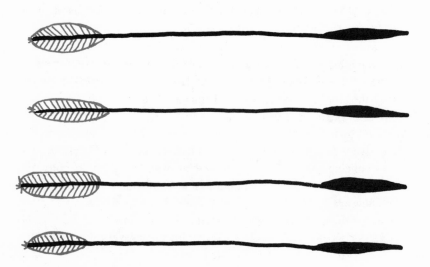

Arrows

All the people, when they saw this, shouted with joy and ran to drag him out of the hole. But no one was strong enough to lift the enormous animal. Not even all together were they able to do it. They tied him to a pole, but that did not work either. They tied a thick vine around the jaguar's neck and pulled, but nothing happened. Finally they managed to lift the jaguar with the help of all the men in the village at one time, tying an enormous vine around his belly.

When the jaguar was pulled out of the hole, Tamacaví ordered the people to sing for him. Then they all started to sing, and the words of the song said that the jaguar had died at the Itavununo. The men sang so that Tamacaví, their chief and master of the jaguar, would not die because of the jaguar's death. They were afraid that their chief would fall ill and die too. When the song was over, Tamacaví told them to remove the hide. The men, intoning new chants, began to remove the hide. They began early, worked all day long, that night, and all the next day, to finish the job. The jaguar was much bigger than a house.

There was a village nearby that had been listening to the chants at the Itavununo. Their chief sent some of his people to see what Tamacaví's people were doing. The men went, but did not go as far as the village. They watched from a distance, in hiding. Back in their village they said, lying, that the people of the Itavununo were singing and dancing the mavurauá. The neighboring chief did not believe them and sent others. These never got to the village either. They watched from a distance and came back, saying that Tamacaví's people were just singing. The neighboring chief again did not believe his scouts and went to see for himself what was happening at the Itavununo. When he arrived at the village, the people told him that the jaguar had been slain. The neighboring chief arrived when Tamacaví's men were still singing and finishing the skinning of the animal. He could hear a little of the song that the people of the Itavununo had been singing for days. The hide, after removal, was stretched and put in the sun to dry.

The neighboring chief, when he returned to his village, berated his scouts for having lied to him. He was furious because, on account of them, he had come too late to the Itavununo, and could not hear and learn all the songs sung by the people there. Tamacaví, after the work was done and the hide was stretched and dry, cut the whole thing in strips and shared it with his people. What was left over, he sent as gifts to the neighboring villages. All of the neighbors received bands of jaguar leather, even those who had run away and come back after his death.

ARUTSÃM:
The Clever Frog

(*Kamaiurá*)

A rutsãm, the frog, went to the jaguar's house to ask for a bow. The jaguar was his brother-in-law. When Arutsãm, or Minorí, as he was also called, was crossing the plaza of the village in the direction of the jaguar's house, the people who were around teased him, saying he was going to be eaten by his brother-in-law. Minorí kept on walking and went into the jaguar's house, greeting him, "How are you doing, brother-in-law?"

The jaguar replied that he was just fine, and everything was going well. He asked Minorí to have a seat. And they sat there talking. As he was taking a long time to leave the house, the people outside began to say that Minorí wanted to die. That afternoon the jaguar invited Minorí to go bathe. "Brother-in-law," he said, "now we should go bathe."

And they went. Along the path, the jaguar, who had gone out ahead of Minorí, kept trying to find a way to get behind him, but Minorí, aware of his brother-in-law's wiles, kept his place at the rear.

As they were coming back from bathing and crossing the center of the village, the people remarked, "Either the jaguar is getting soft, or he doesn't want to eat Minorí. They went to bathe, and he didn't do a thing."

When it was getting dark, the jaguar said, "Brother-in-law, it's time for us to turn in."

Before stretching out, Minorí went outside to get a firefly. He found one and caught it. He opened the firefly, took out the little lantern it has inside, and rubbed it over his eyelids, to make them shine and give the jaguar the impression he was awake when, in fact, he was sleeping. Then he stretched out and went to sleep. Late at night the jaguar went to grab Minorí, but when he saw his bright eyes, he left him alone, thinking that his brother-in-law was awake. When day began to break, the jaguar yelled out, "Brother-in-law!"

Minorí didn't answer. The jaguar shouted louder. Finally Minorí woke up and said, "I'm sleeping too much."

The jaguar then said to himself, "Ahah! He was asleep and I thought he was awake." And the two of them went to bathe in the lagoon. This time Minorí did not go into the water. He stayed out, and only washed his face and head. On the way back, the jaguar again tried to get behind him, but Minorí, ever alert, followed all his movements and wouldn't let him do it.

As they crossed the center of the village, the people remarked again, "Well, well, the jaguar really is getting soft. Why didn't he eat Minorí?"

As soon as he returned from bathing, Minorí said to the jaguar, "I'm off, brother-in-law."

The jaguar asked Minorí before he left, "Well, brother-in-law, what exactly did you come here for?"

"Oh, yes! I came to ask you for a bow and a nhumiatotó."

The jaguar told him to wait. He went to the back of the house, picked up the two things, and gave them to Minorí. Minorí took the objects and left. The jaguar came right behind him, in secret, without letting Minorí see him. Minorí walked for a while, then stopped and made a lot of army ants appear on both sides of the path. He made the ants and then divided them between the two sides, to find out if the jaguar was coming after him. As soon as he had done this, he heard the jaguar stamp his foot. He went over to where the jaguar was and asked, "What are you doing here, brother-in-law?"

The jaguar said he had been following Minorí because the children might harm him. Minorí went back to the path, kept walking, and, after a while, scattered some more ants. The jaguar, who was still following him, stamped his foot again. And Minorí again went over to him, asking once more, "What are you doing here, brother-in-law?"

The answer was the same: "I'm watching out for you, so the children will leave you alone."

Minorí went back to the path, and kept creating and spreading ants in every direction. And the jaguar kept following him and stamping his foot on the ground to get rid of the ants. Then he came close and stamped his foot right beside him, so Minorí put an arrow in his bow and went to talk to his brother-in-law. "What are you doing here, brother-in-law?"

The jaguar gave the same reply: "I'm here watching out for you, because of the people."

This time Minorí spoke in a different tone, "What people! It's you who want to eat me."

He said that and shot an arrow at him, but missed. The jaguar ran away. Minorí kept walking. But the jaguar got ahead of him and went to advise the snakes, asking them to kill Minorí when he passed by there. The snakes got ready to do what the jaguar had asked, saying to each other, "Let's kill him. As soon as he gets here, we'll grab him and kill him."

When Minorí appeared on the path, the snakes said, "There he comes. Let's get him."

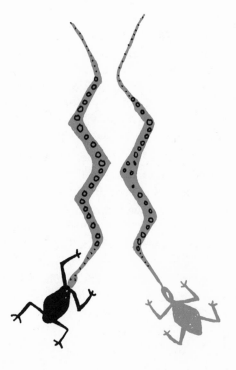

Snakes and frogs

Minorí, when he came to the village of the snakes, where they brought him, asked for a stool to sit on, saying that he wanted to talk for a while. The snakes brought the stool. Minorí sat down and said, "I know that you want to kill me, but it's better to do this on the shore of the lagoon. If you kill me here, my blood will fill your village and swamp everything. It must be on the shores of the lagoon."

So the snakes took hold of Minorí and started to run to the shore and brought him right to the edge of the water.

"Now," said Minorí, "you sit me here, stand off over there, and run from there with your cudgels and beat me over the head till I die."

When the snakes began to move off toward the spot he had pointed to, Minorí jumped into the water. The snakes saw this and jumped in after him, to recapture him. The anaconda, the salamanta, the *muçurana* [large blue-black snake], the boa, and all the snakes plunged in after Minorí. They were swimming every which way, down at the bottom. They searched and searched, but couldn't find a trace of him. Finally they all crawled out where it was dry and sat down to wait on the shore.

Not much later Minorí stuck his hand out of the water, palm out, and said, "With this hand I felt your wives."

The snakes, from the shore where they were, shot arrows, but none of them stuck in Minorí's hand, they flew right through it to the other side. So the snakes plunged into the water again, searched it in every direction, but they couldn't find a sign of Minorí. They crawled out on the shore again and waited, staring at the water. Minorí let some time go by, and then he stuck his hand out again, saying that with it he had messed with their women. The snakes again shot arrows at his hand, but as before none of them took hold. Minorí's hand was very thin, and so the arrow would pass right through and get lost in the water. While on the shore the snakes were waiting for another opportunity to shoot, Minorí sneaked out of the water and, singing, went off to the snakes' village. He came into the village singing and began to break all the pots he found inside the houses. In the village were only the women who had tiny children. The others were at the lagoon trying to catch Minorí. Seeing Minorí, the village women started to scream for their husbands, saying that Minorí was wrecking everything. "Hey, people, Minorí is here, breaking all our pots," they screamed. He had

The decorated base of a large clay pot

only one house left, when the snakes heard the screams. As they came running up to the village, Minorí hid in the tapãim. After searching all the houses, the snakes went into the tapãim and began to turn over all the straw in the roof. Minorí had hidden himself well and nobody found him. When the snakes crawled down to the ground, Minorí went up to the moon, singing. Up there he began to play the nhumiatotó.

The jaguar, on hearing the sound of the flute, got very angry at the snakes and said, "I told you to kill Minorí, and you didn't kill him. You're too soft."

Minorí is on the moon still today.

VANIVANÍ:
The Master of the Red Macaws

(Kamaiurá)

The red macaw was always flying over the Sun's village at the Morená. In the afternoon, when the Sun was sitting in his doorway, the macaw would pass over the village. He showed up every day. He would circle the village and then head back in the direction he had come from.

"Did you see the beautiful bird that's always flying over here?" the Sun asked his brother the Moon.

The next day, when the macaw appeared, the sun called his brother to see. The Moon immediately recognized him as Vanivaní's macaw. Wanting to see the macaw close up, the two agreed to go to Vanivaní's village the following day. The next morning they set off. When they arrived, Vanivaní asked, "What did you come here for? Do you want something?"

"We're just out for a walk," answered the Sun.

Seeing Vanivaní's macaws, the Moon commented, "Our friend here makes a lot of macaws."

Vanivaní again asked his visitors what they wanted. The Sun, under persistent questioning, answered that they had come to ask for a macaw. Vanivaní right away gave them one of his birds. And then he said, "Now I will have to scrape [bleed] you."

He performed the scarification on the Sun first, and with the blood he got from it, he made five tiny spheres. Then he called the Moon and scarified him too, making another five balls out of the blood he had drawn. After this Vanivaní put the blood away in the same place he made macaws. He left it there for safekeeping. Then he told the Sun and the Moon to stay in his village till the next day, so they might have the macaws he was going to make. At daybreak the macaws that were being made began to scream. Vanivaní woke up the Sun and the Moon to watch. He showed them and said, "That is how I make macaws. I always do it this way."

After this remark, he gave his guests five macaws each, made with their own blood. The Sun and the Moon were delighted with Vanivaní's gift. Vanivaní had in his village two houses full of macaws. The houses were for them alone.

When the Sun and the Moon left, Ianamá arrived. Vanivaní asked him what he had come for. Ianamá replied that he was there only to visit.

The Sun went back to his village in the Morená and began to make macaws himself. He and the Moon did it together. They made them with their own blood and that of their wives. When there were enough of these manufactured macaws, they decided to build a deep ravine, to serve as dwelling place for them. They set to work, raising the river banks. While they were laboring, Vanivaní arrived in their village. Mavutsinim was alone there with the wives of the masters of the house. As he was leaving, Vanivaní invited the two women to come with him. They accepted the invitation and left with Vanivaní. Before leaving, Vanivaní rounded up all the macaws in the Sun's village: the ones he had given them, as well as any others he could find. And he went back to his village. When they arrived there, Mavutsinim, who had come along, asked him why he had taken the wives of the masters of the village in the Morená. Vanivaní answered, "They wanted to take my macaws. That is why I brought their women here."

There in the Morená, the village of the Sun, only the parrot was left. He belonged to the Moon. The Sun and all his people were still out building the ravine. When Vanivaní left, the parrot started calling for his masters, shouting that their wives had been stolen. This is what he shouted: *"Paicã! Vanivaní Werahá né remerikó."* [My uncle, Vanivaní took your wife.]

He shouted this over and over. The Sun heard it and said to the Moon, "Listen to what he is saying."

When the two had heard and understood what the parrot was shouting, they stopped work and went back to the village. Only the parrot was there. When they arrived, the parrot said to them, "Your friend was here and took your wives. I don't know why they went with him."

The Sun and the Moon sat down to think and talk about what to do.

One of them said, "We have to go get our wives. They belong to us, so we must go."

The following day they went off to Vanivaní's village. They crept up on it slowly, and from hiding they saw their wives sitting in Vanivaní's doorway. The Moon picked up a piece of wax, molded some motuca flies, and sent them to sit on his own wife's breast and on the leg of the Sun's wife. The motucas flew off and sat down to suck blood. As soon as they felt them, the women shooed the motucas away. They flew off and were caught by the Sun. Then the Sun and the Moon milked the blood they had sucked and deposited it in the fork of the *aputereóp* tree. They covered the blood carefully and spent the night there waiting. The next day the blood was already turning into people. They were laughing in the crotch of the tree.

"Listen," said the Moon, "our women are laughing up there."

Vanivaní, there in the village, said to himself, "I'm going to take these women that I have brought farther downstream." He got a canoe and went down the river with them. The Sun and the Moon were in the Morená. Vanivaní was going much farther down. He rested along the way and continued the journey the next day. He traveled without stopping, going down the river day after day. He stopped only when he came to the big river. There he settled in. Back in his village, the only person left was Mavutsinim, the old man. He stayed there, all by himself. After some time, the old man went downriver after Vanivaní. He traveled and traveled until he caught up with him, camping at the same place, on the opposite bank of the river. There he stood, shouting for a canoe, so he could come across. Vanivaní sent over a tiny canoe to get the old man. The canoe was very small and seated only one person. Mavutsinim did not want to cross in it, because he thought it wasn't safe. Vanivaní sent another one the same size as the first. Mavutsinim again refused to get into it. Again he thought it was too small. Vanivaní then sent the cayman to get the old man. The cayman leaned up against the steep bank and called to Mavutsinim to get on board. Mavutsinim said, "Now, I'll go with you."

And he went across on the cayman. On the other bank he found Vanivaní's house and went inside. Vanivaní told the old man to have a seat and gave him a tiny gourd of cauim. Mavutsinim wanted to drink the whole thing, but he couldn't. The gourd kept filling up with cauim, and never ran out. Afterward, Vanivaní gave him a beiju, also very tiny. Mavutsinim tried to eat the whole thing, but there was no end to it. The beiju kept replenishing itself every time he took a bite.

If Vanivaní had not left, the red macaws would still be living up here. There are no macaws here, because he took them all downstream.

NATEICÁ and VAITSAUÊ: The Origin of the Pequi

(Kamaiurá)

The *jacaré* cayman was wooing the wives of Vaitsauê. Every day they made manioc drink and beiju for him. The beiju was excellent, made only with manioc flour. For their husband, they made it quite differently. His beiju was made of a coarse manioc dough, with no special care. The cayman lived on the edge of Vaitsauê's garden. The beiju and manioc drink were brought to him when the women went to pull up manioc. They came to the field and shouted for their lover. addressing him as Nateicá, to fool their husband. They shouted, "Nateicá! Nateicá!" until the cayman showed up. He came, ate the beiju, drank the manioc drink, and then made love to the women. This went on every day. Vaitsauê didn't know a thing. He was generally in the forest hunting. He always went by himself, and then his wives would run to meet the cayman at the garden.

One day, as Vaitsauê was coming back from the forest, he was walking slowly to see if he could find any animal and he saw an agouti right nearby. As he was about to let his arrows fly, the agouti said, "Why do you want to do this to me, my grandson? Don't you know who is fooling around with your wives? And who they take beiju and manioc drink to every day?"

"Show me where they are doing this."

"Let's go. I'll show you the place where they carry on."

When they reached the place, the agouti said, "Here is where they drink manioc drink and make love. They come here every day. Your wives bring beautiful beijus and morrét to the cayman. Your beiju they make with *teparatê* [squeezed dough]. They use only manioc flour for the cayman's."

And then he said, "Build yourself a high platform to sit on, and wait till they show up."

Jacaré cayman

After building the platform, Vaitsauê cut buriti palm to make arrow points, and then he went home. There he began to make arrows. His wives asked him, "Why are you doing that?"

"To kill the man who is carrying on with you."

"Who told you that?"

"I know you've been fooling around."

The next day Vaitsauê went out earlier than the women. He went straight to the platform. He climbed up and stayed there, quiet and ready. When it began to get light, the women, thinking their husband had gone hunting as usual, headed toward the field. When they got there, they began to call the cayman as they always did: "Nateicá! Nateicá! Come and get your beiju!" The cayman didn't answer, and they kept on calling: "Nateicá! Nateicá! Come and eat beiju!" They called and called till their lover answered and came. Vaitsauê was up on top of the platform, listening. The cayman came, ate the beiju, drank the manioc drink, and then took the women to the spot under the platform where they always went to make love. He did not know that his mistresses' husband was right above them. Vaitsauê shot two arrows and killed the cayman. The women looked up and asked, "Why did you kill this young man?"

"I had to kill this 'husband' of yours!"

He climbed down from the platform and beat his wives in anger. Then he went back to the village. They stayed there crying over the dead cayman. Vaitsauê had killed him early in the morning. That afternoon he went to find his wives. But they refused to go home with their husband. They stayed there in the garden, crying. One of them said to the other, "What shall we do, bury him or burn him?" They decided to burn their lover's body. They made a great fire and put the dead cayman on top of it. The body burned for a long time before it turned to ashes. The women were still there. Since they would not leave the place, Vaitsauê's people built a house where they were, near the cayman's ashes. When the rains came and soaked the ashes, a plant sprang up on the spot. The women went to look, but they did not recognize the plant. The next day they went again to where the fire had been and saw that two more plants had appeared, which they did not recognize either.

After some time had passed, the Sun and the Moon showed up in the women's village. They went to pay them a visit. They came early in the morning. That afternoon the women asked them to come see what kind of plants had sprouted from the ashes of the cayman, saying that they went to look at them every day but they didn't recognize them and wanted to know what they were. They led the Sun and the Moon to the spot. They examined the plants and revealed their names. The women asked and the men answered.

"What's that?"

"Pepper."

"And that?"

"Gourd."

"And that over there?"

"Pequi. In a while, when this one grows up, it will bloom. When the flowers fall off, it will bear a lot of fruit," explained the Moon.

And so it was. The pequi grew and bloomed, and after the flowers, it bore a lot of fruit. Before they were ripe, the Sun and the Moon went back to their own village, telling the women as they left that they would return when the pequis started to fall. They left, and the women waited for their return, so that they could learn more about the pequi.

Some time went by, and the Sun and the Moon came back when the pequis were beginning to fall from the tree. They asked the women if they had tried the fruit. They said no, they hadn't tried it. The Sun went over to the tree, picked a fruit off the ground, opened it, took out the stone, and sniffed. It had no aroma at all.

"This pequi has no smell. That's no good. Let's make it fragrant."

Saying this, he opened some pequis and made them fragrant. Then the Moon told them to gather a lot of pequi, so they could make a drink. The Sun advised the women not to eat the pequis right away because they would make them sick. He was just frightening them, so they would finish their task. While they were working, opening the fruit and boiling the pits, the Sun and the Moon were playing the *aviraré* [jew's-harp] inside the tapãim. They were playing and shouting with joy. All the people were waiting for the pequis the women were preparing. When it was ready, they filled large gourds with pequi paste and handed them to the Sun, together with beijus, to share with the people. Before everybody served themselves, the Sun sang a chant to keep them from catching a disease. After the meal, the Sun scarified everybody. First he scraped those who were outside the houses, and then those who were inside. Then the Sun said it was necessary to do this always, whenever they ate pequi, so as not to become ill.

The Sun and the Moon stayed for many days in the village of the women. More and more pequis fell. The women went to tell the Sun that there were a lot of pequis on the ground. The Sun told them to gather them all up to make a dough, and then keep them in water. And they did what he told them to. The pequi dough was stored in long wicker baskets and kept in water. A few days later the Sun told them to try it. The drink was mixed and everybody liked it very much. The pequis kept on falling. More and more fell, and the women continued preparing the dough and storing it in water inside the wicker baskets. The Sun told them to make *tucumaiá* [another pequi drink], which also pleased everybody. The Sun told the women that he was going to play the aviraré to celebrate the pequi. That afternoon he and the Moon went inside all the houses, dancing and playing the aviraré. They were all very happy, men, women, and children.

When the rejoicing was over, the Moon told the women that their husband would be coming in a few days and that they should receive him well. They answered that they did not like him and they would rather not have him come. The Moon insisted, saying that they had to begin to like their husband again, because living alone like that was very bad. In the company of their husband, they would be better off. And Vaitsauê actually did come. He arrived all dressed up, with necklaces, armbands, and earrings. When the women saw their husband coming up the path, they began to cry, because they could not stand him. The Moon stood up and said, "I don't like this. You're doing everything wrong. Prepare a drink for your husband. Talk to him. That's what you should do."

Vaitsauê's wives prepared the drink, because the Moon had ordered them to, but they made it out of the skin of the pequi. The Sun saw this and said that the skin was no good for that. "Anybody who drinks this will be sick for the rest of his life. He'll never get well," he said. So the women made a real drink from the pequi pulp. They made it and offered it to their husband. Seeing this, the Sun said, "It will be all right now."

After Vaitsauê drank a gourdful, his wives began talking with him. The Sun and the Moon were pleased that they had been able to make peace. And the pequis kept on falling. Every morning the ground was covered with fruit. The women went to the Sun and told him that they were sick and tired of cooking pequi. So the Sun and Moon climbed the tree, shook the branches, and made all the pequis drop. When he came down, the Sun said, "The tree from now on will bear fruit only when the rains come. It will always be that way. If it bore fruit all the time, everybody would get very sick of it."

Then the Sun and the Moon said that they were going to leave and would come back only at the time of the pequi. Before they left, they advised the women to treat their husband well and not to fight any more.

UVAIACÁ:
Why the Fish Have
Colored Spots

(Kamaiurá)

Uvaiacá was taking a medicine to make himself strong. Every day he drank it, in the morning, at midday, and in the afternoon. A dove he was raising inside the house would always take a sip out of the gourd of medicine. First he would drink, then the dove would sneak a little too. One day Uvaiacá's mother saw this and showed her son. Uvaiacá, who was near the gourd, kicked the dove, sending him flying out of the house. Out in the open air, the dove started to circle low over the village. The Sun and the Moon, who were watching, said, "You can fly higher." And the dove went up. "Higher still," the Sun urged. And the dove flew even higher. Seeing the dove fly way up, the Sun thought, That's the way it should be. It's all right now.

Then the dove, from way up where he was circling, threw up on the village all the water he had drunk. And a huge lagoon formed below, where Uvaiacá's village had once been. His house was surrounded by water. All the wild animals that the dove had in his stomach— piranha-*aruiáp*,[1] tucunaré-aruiáp, *taiaú-aruiáp* [wild pig], *moinrucú* [large snake], and others—came out with the water that he vomited. Uvaiacá and his family and all his relatives were eaten up by the animals. The only person who escaped was a brother who had been at the field. When he came back, he made the lagoon shrink, so that he could look for Uvaiacá and the others more easily. After looking every which way, exhausted, he decided to give up and said to himself, "It wasn't I who told you to drink that medicine and raise a dove so he could fly away afterward. You didn't have to do that. You yourself wanted to."

---

[1] The word "aruiáp" after the name of an animal adds the characteristic of supernatural monstrosity.

Dove

After muttering this to himself, he decided to search a little more. He went around the shore of the lagoon, shouting for his brother. He went back and forth, always shouting and calling to his relatives. Finally he realized that he could never find anyone alive. But now what he wanted was to find their bones, to put their skeletons on top of outlines of people and bring them back to life. He looked and looked, but found nothing. When he saw that the search was getting him nowhere, he gave it up once and for all and thought, Let it stay this way and become only a story. And then he said, "I can't stay here, where my brother lived." He said this and went out wandering. He walked and walked, now in one direction, now in another, till he came out at the *Itaperum* [black water] lagoon. There he cut wood, and in the middle of the lagoon, he built a very tall platform to wait on. When it was ready, he climbed up and sat on top of it.

The Sun and the Moon spotted the structure in the distance and went over to get a closer look. When they got there, they asked Uvaiacá's brother, "What are you doing there in the middle of the lagoon, sitting on top of that platform?"

"I'm here because the animals ate my brother and his wife and sons, everything. Now I want them to eat me too, because I too am Uvaiacá."

The Sun and Moon, thinking that was all wrong, told Uvaiacá's brother to come down from there, and then they dismantled the platform, saying that it had not been the animals in the Itaperum lagoon who had eaten his relatives but the ones in the Ipavú lagoon, the one belonging to the Kamaiurá.

"You ought to leave Itaperum and go over to Ipavú, to be eaten there," said the Sun finally.

So Uvaiacá's brother went back to Ipavú. When they got there, the Sun and Moon built a huge platform in the middle of the lagoon and told him to climb up. He went up and there on top started to shoot arrows at the fish. He killed all the fish that passed under him: piranhas, pintados, *jaraquís,* tucunarés, *piraputsiús,* all sorts of fish. He shot them with his bow. When Uvaiacá's brother shot the peixe-cachorro, his father, the chief of the fish, got very angry and told the others, "We must kill Uvaiacá because he killed my son."

All the fish were upset at the death of their chief's son, and they went to the Iaualapití's lagoon to get the *uetsimós,* the fish who know how to jump high up, to kill Uvaiacá's brother. Two uetsimós came, man and wife. When they came to the Ipavú, the male leaped first. He died in the air, shot by the arrow of Uvaiacá's brother. The female jumped right after him and died too, before she could get to the top. All the fish were saddened by the death of the uetsimós and wondered whom they might ask to do the job now. Uvaiacá's brother went on killing fish, and the fish were getting angrier each time. After discussing it, the Ipavú fish decided to ask the uetsimós from the Kuikúru's lagoon. They were sent for, and they came in great numbers. Their chief, on arrival, ordered them all to stay far away from Uvaiacá's brother. Only the one who was jumping should come close. This is what they

Pacu

Pirarara

did. The people stayed clustered together at a distance. One headed by himself toward the platform and jumped on Uvaiacá's brother, but was pierced by the arrow before he could succeed. The second one who jumped, the first one's wife, also died in the air. The people from the Kuikúru's lagoon were ashamed of their uetsimós and deeply saddened by their death. This left only the fish from the Itavununo lagoon to ask. They went to make the request, telling the tribesmen there that in the Ipavú somebody was trying to wipe them out. The uetsimós from the Itavununo asked the messengers from Ipavú which side the others had jumped on. Learning that it was in front of the archer, they said, "That won't work. You have to pounce on him from behind and from the side at the same time, so he can't see." The uetsimós headed toward the Ipavú in the company of the others. As soon as they got there, they asked, "Where is this fellow who's killing all of you?"

"There he is," the fish said, pointing at the platform.

The uetsimós sat thinking for a while which position to take. Then the man said to his wife, "You jump from the side and I'll jump from behind."

The husband jumped first and hit Uvaiacá's brother in the ear. Almost at the same moment, his wife jumped, hitting the other ear. Uvaiacá's brother fell, taking with him the uetsimós, who were holding on to him from both sides. The fish who were watching shouted for joy and joined forces to carry the enemy's body. All the fishes from the lagoon were there: the piranha, the pintado, the tucunaré, the *curimatá*, the jaraquí, the *pirarara,* and many others. After dragging Uvaiacá's brother from under the platform, they started to eat him. As they ate, they began to be stained with the urucu and genipap juice that the dead man had on his body. The piranha's head was stained with urucu; the pirarara stained his tail; the tucunaré got a little on his neck; the *pacu,* his ribs and head; the jaraquí got spots on his head and tail; the *piau* got urucu only on the tip of his tail, while the rest of his body was covered with genipap. The pintado never touched the urucu, but was completely stained by the genipap. The body of Uvaiacá's brother was entirely eaten. The piraputsiú ate much more than the rest of them, and that is why he is the fattest of the lot, the one with the most blubber.

KALUANÁ:
The Training of the Wrestler

(*Kamaiurá*)

Kaluaná always wrestled *huca-huca* style with his companions, but he would lose every time. He lost to everybody. He never won. His father, vexed because his son was so weak, put him in confinement to see if he would get stronger and stop losing in all the competitions against the wrestlers of the nearby villages, as always happened. After a few months of confinement, in which Kaluaná received special treatment, with lots of choice food and medicine meant to make him strong, his father told him to come out and wrestle with his companions. He wanted to see what shape he was in. Kaluaná wrestled, but again he lost to one and all, strong and weak. Seeing his son's weakness, the father was very sad and told him he would not have to wrestle again. He was never going to wrestle, not with anyone, neither in the village nor elsewhere.

After some time, Kaluaná's people were invited to the festival of a nearby village. His father, who was the village chief, left the house and went to talk with the pariáts, who had already made themselves comfortable on the little stools in the center of the village. After talking with them, the chief told the messengers that his own son Kaluaná was too weak to wrestle and so they did not have to be afraid of him.

"My son," he said, "is fat, tall, and strong, but he doesn't know how to wrestle; he is soft and loses all the matches."

Kaluaná, dancing in the center of the village, was listening to his father's conversation. Finally the village chief asked the pariáts what day he could leave with his people for the festival. The messengers said the next day. When the pariáts had left, the father said to Kaluaná, "You may not go to the festival. You stay here in the village."

Kaluaná was not pleased and mumbled, "I'll go later. Let the people go first." The next day, when everyone had left, Kaluaná prepared a little pot of pepper and went into the forest. Passing by a tree, he stopped next to it. He placed the pot of pepper at the foot of the tree and said, "Tamãi, make me into a great wrestler."

The master of the *tavariri,* the spirit of the tree, explained that he couldn't help, because he himself got dizzy spells, burned easily with fire, and fell down for no special reason. "I am weak," he said. And he advised Kaluaná to look for another tree, the *manucaiá.*

"The manucaiá is good, my grandson. Go look for him."

Kaluaná left and found the manucaiá. He put the pot of pepper at the foot of the tree and said, "Tamãi, would you like to make me into a wrestler?"

The master of the manucaiá accepted the pepper and said he would. He tasted the pepper and said, "Let's go to my house. I want to see what is wrong with you."

The two of them went to the manucaiá's house. There the manucaiá examined Kaluaná's arms, neck, legs, and every part of his body, explaining that he was weak because he used women's things: tameóp, *maraucá* [woman's fiber belt], and aputereóp. The manucaiá, after telling Kaluaná to stop using these things, told him to lie in the hammock. At midday he told him to get up and go wrestle with his people. Kaluaná lost the first fight. He won the second. And he never lost again. He won all the rest.

The manucaiá then said, "You are all right now. Now that you know how to wrestle, you'll never lose again."

After this Kaluaná headed toward the village where the festival was taking place. He went along shouting, his new, invisible friends keeping him company, the manucaiás, whom only he could see. Late in the afternoon he arrived at the village of the festival and camped far from his father's people. The wrestling bouts were set to begin the following day. Kaluaná's father, seeing his son arrive and put up camp so far away, yelled out to him, "Come over here, closer." Before Kaluaná could move, the manucaiás warned him, "We must stay right here." As he wasn't coming over, Kaluaná's wife brought him some manioc drink, but the manucaiás would not let him drink it, saying that if he did, he would get sick. They, the manucaiás, drank a different drink, which they made themselves. Kaluaná adorned himself and went to dance the uruá with a companion. He played and danced all night long. The manucaiás warned him not to go to sleep. And so Kaluaná spent the whole night awake, playing the uruá. When it began to get light, everybody began to paint himself to enter the village. When they were done with the painting, Kaluaná took off to play and dance again. The people of his father's village rejoiced with Kaluaná and shouted when they saw him come out of the house playing the uruá.

The manucaiás, always at Kaluaná's side, commented, "See how happy the people are about you?" Kaluaná and his flute partner, still dancing, headed toward the center of the village and took a turn around the kuarups, tree trunks that symbolize the dead honored by the festival. All the people in the village were saying how strong Kaluaná was, discussing it with the visitors. They agreed, but said that he didn't know how to wrestle: he was slow and he always lost.

The manucaiás, who were listening to these remarks, said to Kaluaná, "Can you hear what they're saying about you? They're saying you are weak and don't know how to wrestle."

When it came time for the wrestling, Kaluaná, before anyone else, headed toward the center of the circle formed by the wrestlers and stood waiting for his opponent. It is always the strongest who wrestles first. That was why his father wanted to stop him from wrestling before the others, saying that he was too weak to fight in first place, that he would lose. But Kaluaná would not come out of the ring. He waited there for his opponent. The first to appear was thrown immediately. The same thing happened with the second: he came forward and fell in the first clash. Kaluaná's father began to be happy to see his son win.

His men, also ecstatic, asked each other, "How come he's winning today? He's not like that. He always loses. Why is he winning now?"

And Kaluaná kept throwing them down, one after the other, his father more and more delighted with each victory. The matches went on till midday, without Kaluaná losing a single one. He beat them all. When he finished wrestling with the last one, the host of the festival ordered the matches to stop. The festival was over. After dancing the uruá for a while, Kaluaná told his father he was leaving. And he got ready to leave with his companions, whom only he could see. His father wanted Kaluaná to take beiju and manioc drink to eat on the way, but Kaluaná didn't want to, saying that he had a little of both.

The manucaiás were always telling him not to eat fish, beiju, or manioc drink that was not theirs.

As he was leaving, Kaluaná's wife wanted to go with him, but he would not let her, saying, "You go later with my father." He said that, and went ahead of everybody. After walking for a while, seeing that he was out of sight of the people coming behind, he began to fly with the manucaiás toward their village. As soon as they got there, the manucaiás gave him liquid to make him vomit. After he had vomited, he was sent to his hammock, where he stayed for two days without eating anything. After this rest period, the manucaiás gave him fish and manioc drink, and immediately called him out to fight. Kaluaná defeated everybody. He never fell once. The chief of the manucaiás then said to Kaluaná, "Now you are a truly fine wrestler. Very good indeed."

Kaluaná continued living with his mamaé friends. He stayed with them for a long time. In his village everybody thought he was dead, eaten by the jaguars. His wife had already cut her hair, thinking she was a widow. After this sojourn, the manucaiás told Kaluaná that they had nothing left to teach him. They had shown him everything, and he could go back to his relatives. The next day, after giving Kaluaná fish, they went out flying with him in the direction of his village. They did not go that far. They left Kaluaná on the trail, so he could go in by himself. Before leaving, the manucaiás said, "Listen, you must not lie with women. If you do that, you'll die. Nor should you tell anyone that we were the ones to make a great fighter of you."

After giving Kaluaná these warnings, they asked him, "How many children do you have?"

"Two sons and two daughters."

"Then you may lie with a woman again after you have a grandchild. When you are really old, then it'll be all right."

They said this and disappeared flying. A long time went by. Kaluaná grew old, and his grandchildren increased around him. In the end there were many, twelve all told. His sons had given him three and four children, respectively. His daughters, two and three. Kaluaná, now very old, lived in his hammock; he hardly walked any more. Only in the morning would he go out to warm himself in the sun at the door of the house. His grandchildren never left his side. They were always playing nearby. One day, when his sons had all gone to the field, he asked his grandchildren to remove the bugs he had on his feet. "These bugs that are growing on my feet used to be my strength. Don't throw them away. Pass the scraper over your bodies and then rub these bugs on top. If you do this, you'll become very strong. Now I shall tell you where the medicine I took is."

He said this and pointed in its direction. His grandchildren asked what was the name of the medicine. Kaluaná replied that it was manucaiá and explained how to get there: "You go in this direction, into the forest, and cross a stream that runs there. On the other side you'll begin to hear the manucaiás wrestling."

When he had finished telling them this, Kaluaná died, sitting on the stool where he was. His grandchildren were all very sad. Weeping, they put their grandfather into his hammock and went on crying beside him. Then they went out to tell their parents that their grandfather had died. They stopped work and came home quickly. The daughters of Kaluaná, after weeping for a long time beside his hammock, painted their father's body with urucu, so he could be buried. In the afternoon the children dug a hole and, weeping, buried their grandfather. A moon after Kaluaná's death, the boys took off in search of the medicine their grandfather had told them about. They went into the forest, crossed the stream, and as their grandfather had said, they began hearing the manucaiás wrestling. They came closer and saw the gourds of medicine. These had all turned to stone. Kaluaná's grandchildren stood there for a long time, watching and examining the medicine inside the gourds. Finally one of them said, "Well, shall we carry the medicine away?"

"We'll carry it away and drink it, to see what will happen."

For a while they couldn't make up their minds, but finally they took the stone gourds home with them. There, when they went into confinement, they took the medicine for two moons. When they came out to wrestle, they threw all the other fighters. They became just like their grandfather, and they took his place in the wrestling contests with the nearby villages. Kaluaná's grandchildren, after they got married, told the people of the village that they were strong wrestlers because they had taken the medicine of the manucaiás. They told where the medicine was. All the youths in the village took the manucaiá medicine and they all became great wrestlers.

AVINHOCÁ:
The Origin of the Bow

(Kuikúru)

O n the banks of the Kuluene River, above the mouth of the Turuine River, Avinhocá decided to gather together all the Indians, peaceful and wild, to distribute weapons. The first to appear was the Kuikúru, who took the white bow. From then on, all the Kuikúru and their relatives used bows of this kind. Afterward another Indian appeared, who took a bow made of dark wood. Finally another one came and took the firearm. After doing this, Avinhocá showed them a small lagoon and told them all to bathe there. Since the lagoon had a lot of piranhas, caymans, snakes, etc., the Indians were frightened, which made Avinhocá very angry. The Indians got only their hands wet and ran to dry them on a tree trunk. The tree came to have white bark— it is the pau-de-leite. A braver one obeyed Avinhocá and plunged into the lagoon, and that made him white. That is the civilized one who took the firearm. Just then a tree shouted from inside the forest and the Indians answered. Avinhocá predicted, "The trees will die one day and the Indians will also disappear." Another shout was heard, this time coming from a stone. The civilized one answered, and then Avinhocá said, "The stone will never die, and therefore, the *caraíbas* [Europeans] will never disappear."

After all of this, Avinhocá decided that they would all go away, each in a different direction. Avinhocá was still there when his sons, Tivári and Torrôngo, arrived. At that moment, Rit-Taurinha appeared. He gave pequi oil to one of Avinhocá's sons and told him to rub it on his body. Avinhocá would not let him, saying that the oil brought on old age. To prove it, he rubbed the oil on his own body and became very old. Right after this, Rit-Taurinha gave Avinhocá's other son a bit of tobacco and told the young man to smoke it. Avinhocá intervened again, saying that tobacco was only for the old. A young man smoking it becomes old too soon. That is why only old Indians smoke it. Rit-Taurinha went away, leaving Avinhocá with his sons. One of them, Tivári, decided to get married, and for that purpose he gathered all the female birds and animals together and went with them to the bank of the river. When they got there, he said that the woman who went with him would become his wife. Saying this, he plunged into the water. They all were frightened, and even the capybaras ran away. The swallow, however, lacking prudence, kept swooping over the water, and once when she grazed the surface, Tivári grabbed her and carried her to his village at the bottom of the river. Everybody believes that at the bottom of the river there is a big village with beautiful gardens.

KANARATÊ AND KARANAVARÊ:
Jealousy and Fratricide

(Kamaiurá)

Karanavarê called Kanaratê, his younger brother.
"What do you want?" asked Kanaratê.
"Come here so we can talk for a while."
Kanaratê went to his brother's house.
"I want you to go get some camioá wood that I cut and left in the woods."
"All right," said Kanaratê.
Kanaratê went home. There his grandfather asked what Karanavarê had wanted. After hearing it, Kanaratê's grandfather said, "That's a very heavy wood. You can't carry it all by yourself. You must take three companions. You should take a termite, a little palm-fiber rope, and a forked stick, to help you carry it."
Kanaratê left, taking with him the companions his grandfather had suggested. The termite got there and gobbled up the heart of the wood. He hollowed the whole thing out. Only the bark was left. This they lifted to their backs and began to carry the camioá over to Karanavarê's house. When they were nearby, Kanaratê put two stones in the hollow, so it would weigh more and give the appearance of being whole. Unloading the wood, they piled it up in a hole that Karanavarê had opened. The two stones teetered inside and would not let the wood stand upright. Karanavarê tried a number of times to set it up straight. When he saw that it would not stand up straight, he left it crooked as it was.
Three days later he called his brother again and asked him to get a baby macaw he had found out of a hollow tree in the forest.
"I'll do it," Kanaratê said. And he went home.
"What does your brother want now?" his grandfather asked.
"He asked me to get a baby macaw out of a hollow tree trunk in the forest."

"Take a piece of buriti."

Karanavarê had told him that he had made a sign at the place where the baby macaw was, saying, "You go because the wood is marked."

Kanaratê went and searched until he found it. He climbed the tree and slipped the piece of buriti in the hole. A snake that was inside bit the stalk, and Kanaratê pulled it out. When the snake's head appeared, he grabbed it by the neck. He held it tight and climbed down from the tree. He didn't kill the snake. He took it to his brother. Karanavarê's wives, aware of the whole thing, accused their husband of fooling his brother. Karanavarê answered them by saying that the snake was actually a baby macaw. He wanted to kill Kanaratê because he kept messing around with Karanavarê's wives. He was very angry for that reason. He had wanted the snake to bite Kanaratê, but as it hadn't, he pulled out its teeth and made them into a scraper for drawing blood, the *iaiáp*.

Early the next day Kanaratê went out to bathe. His sisters-in-law followed to bathe with him. In the middle of the day Karanavarê called his brother again. He went and asked what he wanted. Karanavarê said that he had made a scraper and wanted to try it. Kanaratê went home to take off his armbands, for the scarification. Before he returned to his brother's house, his grandfather taught him several things. He told him to put tree bark on his body, so that he would not feel the scraper. Kanaratê dressed himself up in tree bark and went over to his brother's house. There his body was scratched from head to foot. When the bloodletting was over, Kanaratê said he was going to the lagoon to wash off the blood. His grandfather was there at the shore waiting for him. The old man pulled off the tree bark he had on and passed a real scraper over his skin, to leave his body marked. After this, Kanaratê said, "My brother isn't clever enough to kill me. I'm still alive."

The following day he rose early and went to bathe, whistling. His sisters-in-law heard him and followed behind. When they came back, their husband said, "So you think Kanaratê is still alive? He should be stiff in his hammock by now."

"He's not dead at all. In fact, he was just bathing."

Karanavarê, astonished, called his brother to examine the scarification. When he saw it, he thought to himself, I really did a job on him, so why does it look like this?

Three days later he called Kanaratê again. This time Karanavarê asked him to fetch some tobacco in the village of the *pitoarrã* [flycatcher], saying he didn't have any and wanted very much to have a smoke.

"All right, I'll go," said Kanaratê.

When he got home, his grandfather asked him what his brother wanted this time. Kanaratê said that it was for him to get tobacco in the village of the pitoarrã. His grandfather wept, and then told him to take three companions: hummingbirds, both large and small. Kanaratê called his companions and went off to get the tobacco. When they were almost there, the hummingbirds told him to wait. They didn't

Hummingbird spirits

want him to get too close. The birds went the rest of the way by themselves. The pitoarrã was singing. Kanaratê could hear him from where he was. His companions picked the tobacco leaves and brought them to Kanaratê, asking him to wait while they went to play a little with the pitoarrã. Kanaratê busied himself sorting the tobacco leaves, putting the good ones aside for himself. The hummingbirds, back at the pitoarrã's garden, began to pull off leaves, making a lot of noise. The pitoarrã, thinking it was being done by people, went out to look around. The hummingbirds flew back to where they had left their companion and from there headed home to the village. Kanaratê found his grandfather weeping. "I can't understand why your brother is angry with you." Kanaratê gave his brother the tobacco leaves that had spoiled and kept the good ones. When he got the tobacco, Karanavarê said, "I asked you to go get tobacco, because people can't do without it."

Days later he called Kanaratê again. "Come here so we can talk for a while."

Kanaratê went to see what his brother wanted. This time he wanted some cane to make arrows. Kanaratê agreed to get it and went home.

"What does your brother want now?" asked his grandfather.

"He wants some arrows," said Kanaratê.

His grandfather told him to take five companions, finches and doves. Kanaratê went out with his companions. At a certain point on the trail, far from where there was anything to make arrows with, his companions told Kanaratê to wait, and they went by themselves. There they cut a lot of arrow canes. Handing them to Kanaratê, they asked him to wait while they went off to play. When they began to make a lot of noise in the canebrake, it woke up a wild beast. This was the *tataruiáp* [a monstrous armadillo]. The birds started to make fun of him, watching him looking all around for people. When they had had enough fun, they rejoined Kanaratê, who was sorting the good stalks from the bad. Back in his village, Kanaratê found his grandfather weeping because he had taken so long.

"Tamãi, open the door so I can come in."

"I don't know why your brother is so angry with you."

Bright and early the next day Kanaratê went to bathe, whistling. His sisters-in-law, hearing the whistle, went after him. "Have you come back?"

"Yes, I have."

Returning to the village, the women told their husband that his brother was back.

"Of course he's not back," said Karanavarê. "At this very moment he is burned to a crisp. What's left of him is ashes."

No sooner had he said that than his brother appeared to give him the arrows.

Karanavarê said, as he took them, "It's a good thing you brought them. People can't be without arrows for long because they're very important."

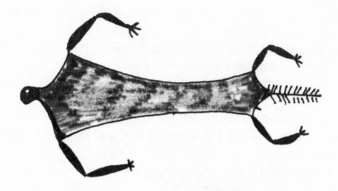

Squirrel

And three days later he called his brother again and asked him to go pick some genipap. Kanaratê, after saying that he would go the following day, went back to his house, and his grandfather asked what his brother wanted. Learning that it was genipap, he advised his grandson to take three companions: the spider, the squirrel, and the opossum. The day after, Kanaratê, with his chosen companions, went out looking for genipap. Coming to the lagoon where there was some, the spider spun three threads over to the genipap tree and, with his companions, carried a lot of fruit down to the ground. After making the transfer, they told Kanaratê that they were going to play a little with the master of the genipap tree. The spider picked a fruit and threw it way out in the water. When the genipap fell, a swarm of ferocious animals popped to the surface of the lagoon. The spider made a house in a leaf and hid inside. The squirrel and the opossum also hid themselves, but they left their tails out, hanging in the water. The little fish converged on them, eating off the tip of the squirrel's tail and peeling the opossum's.

After they were done playing, Kanaratê and his companions went back to the village. Along the trail they talked about their game, remembering the little fish who skinned off the opossum's tail and the animals that had popped out of the water. Kanaratê asked his companions if they wanted some genipap. They said yes, and painted themselves with the dye from this fruit. Kanaratê kept the green genipap for himself and saved the ripe ones for his brother.

In the village Karanavarê kept fooling his grandfather by pulling his door open all the time, so the old man would think that Kanaratê was back. Kanaratê arrived when it was almost night and from outside asked the old man to open the door.

The next morning, as was his habit, Kanaratê left whistling for his bath. His sisters-in-law said to one another, "Let's go and bathe with Kanaratê. We must bathe with him."

Coming back from bathing, they told their husband that his brother was back.

"Nonsense," said Karanavarê, "my brother is nowhere around. He is inside the belly of a wild animal."

After bathing, Kanaratê went to give the genipap to his brother. Karanavarê, taking it, said it was good that Kanaratê had gone to get genipap, so that now the people could paint themselves. That same day all the men in the village painted themselves.

A few days went by, and Karanavarê called his brother again and asked him to go to the village of *Tupã* to get an ax. When he found out that it was Tupã's ax that Karanavarê wanted, the old man told Kanaratê to invite six companions: three *arapavás* and three *javariás* [two different kinds of woodpecker]. Accompanied by them, Kanaratê headed for Tupã's village. He came to his house and went right in. The only person home was Tupã's wife, who greeted Kanaratê, saying, "What are you doing here, grandson? Wait awhile; your grandfather went to chop wood and will be back soon."

Woodpecker

Then she asked what Kanaratê wanted. He said that he had come to get an ax. So the old woman showed him her husband's new axes. As Tupã was coming home, his wife grabbed Kanaratê and shut him in a room that had no cracks. The rest of the house was all split from lightning.

"You stay here," the old woman said.

Tupã came in, exploding.

"Your grandson is here," said his wife.

Tupã went on thundering. His wife spoke again, "You must stop for a while because your grandson is here."

"Which grandson?" asked Tupã.

And he said when he saw Kanaratê, "Oh! It's you? Where are you going?"

"I came to ask you for an ax. My brother says you're chopping wood for your girl friend. That's why we came to ask you for an ax. We heard you had a few."

At that moment Tupã's wife started to tickle her husband kidding him because Karanavarê had said that he was chopping wood for his girl friend. She tickled Tupã until "he died a little." When he was himself again, laughing, he asked Kanaratê, "Is that what your brother is saying about me?"

Kanaratê said it was, and Tupã's wife started to tickle her husband to make him "die" again. When Tupã passed out for the second time, the old woman told Kanaratê to get the axes. He grabbed the five axes he found there and ran. Tupã was still unconscious. When he came to, he had another fit of laughter and asked again, "Is that really what your brother is saying about me?"

"Kanaratê has already left," said his wife.

Furious, Tupã began to shoot fire at Kanaratê. The javariás and the arapavás shot arrows at Tupã. This frightened him and he almost fell down. He stopped throwing lightning and hid inside his house. Kanaratê reached his village that night.

Early the next day he left whistling, to bathe. His sisters-in-law as usual followed him. The two of them, coming back from the lagoon, where they had been with Kanaratê, told their husband that his brother was back. Karanavarê did not believe them and said to the women, "You think my brother is back? He is never coming back. At this very moment he is only a heap of bones in Tupã's house."

"Not at all," the women said. "He really is back. We've seen him."

Karanavarê still would not believe them. Only when Kanaratê came to deliver the axes did he believe his brother had returned. Taking the tools, Karanavarê defended himself, saying, "I sent you to get axes at Tupã's house because we didn't have a single one to chop wood with and we needed one badly. Now we're all set."

Kanaratê gave his brother the used axes, keeping the new ones for himself.

Three days after the trip to Tupã's house, Karanavarê sent for his brother again. He said, "It would be nice if you went to Aicaconí's house to get some necklaces and belts for us."

"Tomorrow I'll go," said Kanaratê.

When he got home, his grandfather asked him, "Now what does your brother want?"

"He asked me to go to Aicaconí's house for necklaces and belts."

"That is very dangerous," reflected the old man.

And saying this, he told Kanaratê to take as companions: muscle cramps, stumps, and mud. Kanaratê assembled his companions and left. Aicaconí lived near the place where the Auetí live today. Kanaratê walked along praying, till he came to Aicaconí's village. He said to Aicaconí, "Are you there, tamãi? I came to ask you for necklaces and belts."

Aicaconí sent Kanaratê to his brother's house, saying that he had more necklaces. The brother's name was Iaricó. He was younger. Kanaratê knew that he was going to the house of wild people. Kanaratê walked along singing, and he was singing when he came to the village of Iaricó. The people there wanted to kill Kanaratê the minute he arrived. Kanaratê asked them not to do this, to wait awhile. He wanted to talk first. And he said, "I know that you want to kill me and eat me. Do this: those of you who want to eat my arm, tie a belt around it; those who want to eat my neck, hang a necklace on it."

The people of the village did what Kanaratê suggested, tying necklaces and belts where he said to. Then Kanaratê said, "Now walk a few steps away, and then one of you come running and hit me with a cudgel to kill me."

When the people walked away from him, Kanaratê ran. The people from the village went after him, but the mud, the stumps, and the cramps would not let them. The pursuers slipped in the mud, tripped over the stumps, and were immobilized by cramps. Kanaratê ran all the way to the other end of the trail. When he thought he was far enough away, he sorted the belts and necklaces—the perfect ones for himself, the spoiled ones for his brother—and then he set off for home, coming to his village by night.

Early the next day he went to deliver the necklaces and belts to Karanavarê. He gave him the bad ones and kept the good ones.

Three days later Karanavarê called him again and said, "I found an eaglet on top of a tree and I want you to get it down for me."

"I'll go tomorrow," answered Kanaratê.

When he got home, he told his grandfather what Karanavarê had asked him. The old man advised him to take some mice. The next day, as soon as it began to get light, Kanaratê went into the forest with his brother. This time Karanavarê wanted to keep him company. When they came to the tree, Karanavarê, seeing him carrying the mice, asked, "Why are you carrying mice?"

"For the eagle to eat," answered the other, as he began the climb.

When he got to the top of the tree, Karanavarê took away the ladder that his brother had used to climb. Kanaratê asked from up on top, "Why did you take away the ladder I used to climb?"

His brother answered from down below, "So you can spend the rest of your life up there, till you die of hunger."

Karanavarê said that and went back to the village. But before he left, he kicked the trunk of the tree to make it grow more. And it grew and grew, becoming very tall. Kanaratê was up at the top, without a ladder to get back down. At the end of the day he got very thirsty and drank his own urine. He urinated in his hand and drank. Then the bees began to arrive, and they enveloped Kanaratê's face. That night the dead mice started to stink. By the middle of the following day, the vultures were beginning to circle above. They circled down till they were perched in the tree. Then Kanaratê asked the vulture who was perched beside him to get him down from there. "Tamãi, get me out of here and put me down over there."

The vulture said that her own canoe was too small, but her husband had one big enough for three people. Saying this, she flew off to find her mate. When the couple came back, Kanaratê asked again, "Tamãi, would you like to take me down and put me over there on the ground?"

The vulture said he would. Kanaratê was delighted and wanted to give him the mice, but the vulture wouldn't take them till he had got Kanaratê down. He told Kanaratê to get into the canoe. Kanaratê got in and sat down. The vultures flew off. During the flight, the vulture said, "You must do something about your brother, because he is being very mean to you. You ought to get even with him."

The vultures flew and flew, and then they slowly descended. They were bringing Kanaratê to their own village. When they alighted there, Kanaratê gave the mice to the vultures and said, "Only you could have gotten me down out of that tree."

In the vultures' village, Kanaratê was put in confinement. He was very weak and thin. To cure him quickly, every day his hosts went fishing for him. Kanaratê began to get fatter and look well again. At that time the parakeets showed up at the vultures' house. They did not like other birds to visit them, because their guests went around saying that their house smelled bad. The parakeets on arrival remarked to one another that there was a fine-looking person staying in the vultures' house. Some said it was the vulture himself; others said no, they had already had a look, and it was a different sort of people. They wanted to meet Kanaratê, and they went inside the enclosure where he was being confined. The vulture, master of the house, told Kanaratê to pull out the tail feathers of all the birds who came in, to take home when it was time to leave. Kanaratê spent the rest of his confinement pulling out the tail feathers of the birds who came to visit him.

When, one day, he pulled out the feathers of the daughter of the morerequát, her father was furious. And all the birds wished Kanaratê would become like them, a bird too, so he wouldn't pull out feathers any more. Then the vulture warned Kanaratê that the people were all mad at him. The following day they painted and adorned Kanaratê, and went outside to dance the mavurauá with him. The orange parrots came and took part in the dance. And all the women went to dance with the parrots, but when they saw Kanaratê sing and dance, they went over beside him. That left the parrots without any women. Everybody danced and sang all night long. The vulture told Kanaratê to listen carefully to the songs, so that he could sing them afterward, in his village.

The following morning, the vultures told Kanaratê that they were going to take him back to his village. "If you stay here any longer, the people will end by killing you. They might even kill you to eat, because they are very hungry and angry."

They also said, "When you get back to your village, you must do something to your brother. You have to get even with him."

After saying that, they told Kanaratê to get into the canoe. He climbed in, and the vultures took off, flying slowly. During the trip, they told Kanaratê that they were not going to come down in the village. "We'll put you down somewhere on the path, and from there you can walk back by yourself."

When they landed, they warned Kanaratê that his brother was making a huge beast to kill him with. Before flying home, they asked Kanaratê to leave all the animals he killed out of the water, so that they would have something to eat. That afternoon Kanaratê came to his own house and asked his grandfather to open the door. He found the old man weeping because he thought his grandson had died. When he stopped weeping, the grandfather said, "You must do the same thing to your brother."

At dawn the next day, Kanaratê, as he had always done, left whistling for his bath in the lagoon. Karanavarê's wives heard him and said to each other, "Kanaratê has come back. Let's go bathe with him."

Saying this, they ran out to catch up with him. When they returned from bathing, they told their husband that his brother had come home.

"It can't be him. My brother is all dried up at the top of that tree," he answered.

But later Karanavarê went over to his brother's house to see if it was true that he had come home. When he came into the house, his brother said to him, "I'm back, all right. Why are you so angry with me? I haven't done a thing. It's you who are doing all these things to me."

Karanavarê defended himself by saying, "The rope that I had fastened the ladder with was rotten and broke. That's why the ladder fell down."

Kanaratê replied, "I wasn't blind, I saw you cut it."

It didn't do any good for Karanavarê to defend himself. His brother did not believe any of his excuses.

Five days after this conversation, Karanavarê called his brother again, inviting him to go hunting, saying that he had nobody else to go with him.

"All right, tomorrow morning we'll leave," answered Kanaratê.

Back in his house, Kanaratê's grandfather warned him that Karanavarê had made a huge animal that was very dangerous. Kanaratê went out that day to wrestle, saying, "I'm going wrestling, because there's a wild animal that wants to eat me."

At dawn the next day Karanavarê went to call his brother for the hunt they had planned. Before Kanaratê left, his grandfather told him he had to go to the hunt adorned with feathers, earrings, and necklaces. Kanaratê dressed himself up and went off with his brother. In the first thicket they came to, they saw nothing. They went to another place, another thicket, where the beast Karanavarê had made was hiding. They started looking for game. Kanaratê already knew that the wild animal was in there. He took off his ornaments, laid them on the ground, and went on hunting. Karanavarê, a little way ahead of him, said, "There's a huge animal here, which you will see."

Just as he said that, the beast got up and began to charge. First he went after Kanaratê, attacking him. Kanaratê hid behind a thick tree and stood waiting. When the animal came close, Kanaratê poked him with his bow, saying, "Your master is over there," and pointed to his brother.

That very moment the animal wheeled around, ran after Karanavarê, and grabbed him by the chest between his horns, charging off like a shot. Karanavarê shouted to it, "Pass in front of my house, so that my wives can see this."

The animal ran through the center of the village, right in front of Karanavarê's house. The women, seeing their husband hanging from the animal's head, were very grieved and wept for him. Weeping, they said, "Why were you so mean to your brother?"

When Kanaratê came back home, his grandfather asked, "Did you do your job?"

"Yes. He enjoyed doing mean things to me. This time I did the same to him."

The grandfather, weeping, said to him, "I don't know why you were so angry with each other. You are brothers. I don't know why you do these things."

He said this and went on crying over Karanavarê. Karanavarê's wives moved into their brother-in-law's house and married him, but they still cried about their husband. The old man told them to stop crying: "Now you are married again and you must not go on crying."

Nobody knew which way the animal had gone, with Karanavarê caught between his horns. Later on the old man called Kanaratê to tell him that no one was angry at him. Kanaratê had no relative other than his grandfather. When everything was past, the old man delivered this judgment:

"Now it will always be this way. Husband will be jealous of wife and brother will fight with brother."

Spirit mask of the wild dog, wolf, fox

UARAIM AND TACUAVECÊ:
The Mother Who Gives Her Daughter to the Animal

(*Kamaiurá*)

There was a little girl who cried a lot. She was always crying. Day and night she cried. The father would go fishing and leave the child crying. When he came home, she was still crying. Her father was a great fisherman. He went fishing every day, and every time he came home he found his daughter crying. The child who cried was so tiny she could barely walk. Her father would say to her, "Don't cry, my daughter. We're going to eat fish now." But this did not stop the daughter from crying. Every day the same thing happened.

One day, the mother, fed up with her daughter's crying, said to her husband when he came home, "Put this girl out there and let the *uaraim* [dog of the woods, wild dog] take her away."

The child's father did not want to do that. He did not want to give his daughter to the mamaé, to have an animal carry her off. So the mother decided to do it herself. She dragged her daughter along the path far from their house and left her there for the uaraim to take. When she put the child down on the ground, she said, "Take her, uaraim, and bring her up. When she's a grown woman, make her your wife."

The child stayed there in the path crying. The uaraim appeared and spoke to the child, "Don't cry, little girl. Come and eat fish with me."

The child thought it was her father. And the animal took her away.

As soon as she got home, the mother regretted what she had done. She went back to the path, but her daughter was nowhere to be found. The husband, when he found out, said that the child must have been taken in by her aunt. They went to see, but could not find her. They went through all the houses in the village, to no avail. No one had seen the child. They next went to the closest village, with no result. They went to another, farther away, but again found nothing. They visited all the neighboring villages, and none of them had any news of their daughter. Seeing that they were not going to find her, they quit looking. The girl grew up in the house of the uaraim. She became a young woman while living with him.

One day a youth from her parents' village went out to hunt monkeys. He walked far into the forest. A long way from his village he killed a monkey, who stayed curled up around the branch. From up in the tree where he had climbed to get his catch, he heard a pestle pounding ahead of where he was. After listening for a while, he came down from the tree and climbed a taller one. There, from its highest branch, he saw a house, far in the distance. As it was already late, he went back to his village. It was dark when he got there.

Five days later he told his mother he was going hunting again. He explained, "I'm going to look for my arrow and make the path longer, go far ahead."

After saying this to his mother, he went out. He came to the place where he had climbed the tree. From there he went in the direction of the house he had seen. He walked for a while and began to hear the pestle. When he realized, by the sound of the blows, that he was close by, he walked slower to avoid making noise. Cautiously, he came very close. At that moment he saw a girl coming out of a house to dump waste. The youth whistled, and when the girl turned her face toward him, he asked, "Who are you?"

She did not answer. Then he asked, "Where is your husband?"

"I'm all by myself."

And saying this, she invited the youth inside, adding, "There's no one here. You can come in."

The youth went in, and the mistress of the house gave him manioc drink. After talking for a while, the girl pointed to a flute hanging up, asking the guest not to mess with it, otherwise its master, the uaraim, would hear it and come home.

"He's fishing now and you can stay."

In the youth's village, his mother was weeping because she thought that the jaguars had eaten her son. In the uaraim's house, the youth, after drinking the manioc drink, again asked the girl who she was. "Who are you?"

The girl laughed and said, "Don't you know me? Don't you remember me?" And she then explained, "I'm that child who cried a lot and whose mother left her in the path for the uaraim to take."

"Oh! It's you?" And then he recognized her. And he said, "I'm enjoying it here. I'm not going to leave now."

The youth was already making love to the young woman. Later, when the uaraim came home, seeing urucu on his wife's arm, he asked her, "Who spread urucu on you?"

"It was you yourself."

The uaraim believed her and said, "That's right. It was I."

Every day the uaraim would go fishing and, when he came home, wanted to know who had rubbed urucu on his wife, and Tacuavecé always said that it had been he himself. Tacuavecé was the name that the uaraim had given his wife. The uaraim was always telling his wife to cook fish to give to his flute players. One day, seeing that his wife's belly had grown, the uaraim asked, "Who's making a child in you?"

"It's you yourself."

And the uaraim believed her. When the child was born, he asked, "Is it man or woman? Does it look like me?"

Tacuavecé answered that the boy was exactly like him: hair, ears, nose, all the same. The uaraim was very pleased to hear that the child looked like him.

"It *is* my child," he said.

In fact, it was not. The boy was the son of the youth, who lived in his house, hidden on top of a storage rack. One day the uaraim was fishing and he heard his own flute. He ran home and asked his wife who was playing. She answered, "It's you yourself." And the uaraim agreed. When Tacuavecé's son learned to walk, the uaraim said that he was going to do something to make him look more like his father. The child's real father was hidden on top of the storage rack. At night the uaraim again spoke with Tacuavecé about their son. "Tomorrow I'll make my son look just like me."

He wanted the child to have a tail, head, ears, nose, hair, everything just like his own. The next day he grabbed the child and began to squeeze his hand, to give it the shape of his own. Tacuavecé had already warned the child's father, asking him not to let the uaraim do it. She had said, "When our child screams, you jump down and take the boy out of the uaraim's hands." And that's what the youth did.

The minute the uaraim grabbed the child and began to squeeze his hand, Tacuavecé's *cupatsim* [lover] jumped on top of him and said, "What are you doing to my son?"

The uaraim ran away, but when he remembered that he had forgotten his flute, he came back to get it and then ran away again. Not far off, he stopped and stamped his foot on the ground, turning the place where he lived into a forest with a thick growth of lianas. Tacuavecé, her companion, and their son slept in the forest, where the uaraim's house had once been.

The following morning the youth said to Tacuavecé, "We must leave here now."

"I'm embarrassed to go back to the village."

"But didn't you live there?"

"Yes, but now I'm ashamed."

Finally they decided to return to the village. They gathered up the fish that the uaraim had left and took off. They came to the village by night.

"Mother, open the door," the young man said.

"Who's that?" his mother asked from inside.

And to herself she mumbled, "It sounds like my son." She opened the door and cried out when she recognized him. The old woman had already cut her hair, thinking that her son was dead.

"Where have you been?" asked his mother, in tears.

"I was in another village, and there I got married."

At first the young man would not tell his mother what had happened to him. The next morning the old woman, seeing her grandson, lifted him up and started to dance around. Then she turned to her son and asked, "Whom did you marry?"

She wanted to know who her daughter-in-law's father was. The young man answered, laughing, "Look at her face and you'll know her. Now that we are alone, I'll tell you everything."

He then told his mother that his wife was the little girl who used to cry a lot and was left on the path for the uaraim to take. He told her the whole story.

Days later, Tacuavecé's mother found out too. They told her "Look," they said, "here is your daughter whom you gave to the uaraim. Aputuié was the one who found her in the woods, living with the uaraim."

Hearing this, the girl's mother wanted to see her daughter. She went up to her and said, "So you've come home, my daughter?"

"You're not my mother. You gave me to the uaraim when I was a baby. And so I can't be fond of you."

The mother stayed at her daughter's side, but the girl wouldn't look at her. Tacuavecé asked her husband not to tell anyone else the story. "If they all find out, they will begin to say things that will embarrass me."

Tacuavecé did not live very long. She died soon afterward and was carried away again by the uaraim.

SINAÁ:
Flood and the End of the World

(Juruna)

I

Sinaá lived with the Juruna. He was a Juruna himself. His father was an enormous jaguar who lived on top of a storage platform inside the house. The jaguar was called *ducá*. Sinaá's mother was a person. The jaguar had not slept with the woman to bring forth Sinaá. The jaguar had stuck his penis in the hole where he had seen the woman urinate. That was how Sinaá was born. The jaguar was extremely fierce and never came down from the platform. He drooled a lot. There was always a gourd next to him to hold the drool. If the drool were to fall to the ground, other Indians would come and kill the Juruna. When the jaguar's drool filled the gourd, it had to be dumped into a deep hole. When a small quantity of drool was spilled, the wind would scatter it and turn it into little birds.

The jaguar would not look forward. He always had his head turned aside. He could not see anyone. If he were to see, other Indians would come and kill the Juruna. He could see the people only with the eyes he had in his back. Sinaá was also that way. He had eyes in his back. If Sinaá or his father the jaguar stepped in the river, its water would dry up. Sinaá had three sons. He bathed in a separate water. His sons also used this water, which was set off and hidden. It was very cold. In the very beginning there was no water. Only the bird had it. He was the *juriti* [dove]. Only he brought water for his people to drink. He brought it down from a huge tank up there. The juriti one day stopped bringing water, and the sons of Sinaá began to cry with thirst. They said, crying, "Our grandfather is not bringing us any more water."

Sinaá's oldest son decided to break the tank of water up there. He went first to talk with his father. Sinaá said, "Be careful, some big fish might eat all of you."

"There's no danger. We'll just break it and jump out of the way."

Since Sinaá did not want them to, his sons went without his knowledge, saying, "Let the fish eat us." There were a great many fish inside the tank. All the fish were there. The tank was very far away and very big. When the boys came near it, they were frightened. They stood looking at it, fearful of breaking it. The oldest brother said to the youngest, "Now you smash it with a club and then jump out of the way. Don't stand there or the fish will grab you."

The boy smashed it, but did not jump away soon enough. The fish came out of the tank and ate him. The oldest and the middle brothers jumped out of the way in time, and the fish did not catch them. Sinaá was in his house and heard the sound of the water as it began to come down. It was a very big noise, like a thunderclap. A lot of water was beginning to flow. Sinaá said to himself, "The boys have broken the tank." He said that and went out to look for his sons, but could not find them. The youngest was in the belly of the big fish. Only his feet were sticking out. The waters were coming down. The other two boys were running ahead of it. They wanted to dam the water with stones farther down, to save their brother and drag him out of the fish's mouth. The water reached the first dam they made and passed right over it. They made another farther down, and the water passed over that one too. They built another, and the same thing happened. They built many, to no avail. Finally, way ahead they built a very tall weir and stood on top of it, waiting. When the fish appeared with his head up, carrying the boy in his mouth, climbing with the water, Sinaá's oldest son grabbed his brother by the foot and yanked him out. The fish swam to the other side in the water that poured over the dam. After coming to dry land, Sinaá's oldest son said, "Let's make this river wider."

And he widened the river so much that the other bank disappeared. Then he cut a leaf from the wild banana tree and put it over his brother, the one who had been in the fish's mouth. He was dead. The oldest brother cut off the youngest one's legs and arms and blew on the blood that came out. Instantly the brother came back to life. Alive again, he did not know anything any more. He didn't even remember his brothers. The oldest had to teach him everything all over again. Finally he told his brother that he had been swallowed by the big fish, adding, "You were swallowed by the fish because you are not really our father's son."

Their mother, when she was carrying him, had coupled with an animal. That was why he had been born of mixed breed.

The boys went back home. Their mother thought that the fish had devoured all her sons and she was weeping. Sinaá said to her, "I hope they were eaten by the fish. Why did they go up to break the water tank? I told them not to."

When the brothers reached home, the oldest ordered the youngest to tell his father that the fish had not really eaten him. He went and said, "We broke the tank, and everything is fine now. There's plenty of water for people to drink."

Sinaá had seen the jabiru stork in a dream and said to his sons, "There is a jabiru around. Be careful of him."

"Where is he?"

"He's right around here, but watch out because he is very dangerous."

Jabiru stork

The boys went off searching and found the jabiru. He was fishing in shallow water. The oldest told the youngest to grab the jabiru by the bill, warning him, "Be careful, because he is very dangerous."

The boy went. When he was near the jabiru, he plunged into the water and turned into a fish. As he passed in front of the jabiru, he was swallowed. The jabiru's bill was stained with blood. The oldest thought awhile how to recover his brother, and turned himself into a wasp, flying over to sit on the jabiru's bill to gather some blood. After this he flew to a remote spot and blew on the blood and shaped his brother anew. And when he had come back to life, the oldest said to him, "What made you pull that trick? That's why our father doesn't like you. You are not his son. You're the son of an animal."

"Then you go and break the jabiru's beak," said the youngest brother.

Just as his brother had done, the oldest plunged into the water and turned into a fish. He swam toward the jabiru, offering himself. When the jabiru pecked at him, the oldest brother came up from the bottom and, regaining his human form, grabbed him and broke his bill off. Then the boys went home and handed the jabiru's bill to their father, saying, "You said it was dangerous, but it wasn't."

Sinaá took the beak, put it away, and said to his sons, "There's something much more dangerous around here that could cut you in half. Don't go looking for it."

"Where does this animal live?" the boys asked.

Sinaá would not tell them. The oldest said to his brothers, "I'll find out. Our father thinks that we are not his sons."

He said that and went to sleep, and in his dream he saw where the animal lived.

The next day, they went there. The dangerous beast was sweeping his house, and when he saw the boys coming over, he asked, "Where did you come from?"

He asked this and went on sweeping. After he finished cleaning the house, he held his foot out to the boys and asked them to pick out his fleas. "I have too many fleas on my foot. Come, take them off for me." His foot was shaped like a hoe. As soon as the youngest brother came over to do as he was asked, the oldest warned him, "Watch out. He's going to cut you up."

When the boy, to pick the fleas, raised the animal's foot to his stomach, the latter gave him a kick and cut him in half. There he was, split in two. Again the oldest brother turned himself into a wasp. He gathered a little of the blood and, blowing on it, rebuilt his brother. He said then, "Now I'm going to break this animal's leg right off."

"Watch out or he'll cut you up too," said the middle brother.

The animal stuck out his foot again and asked, "Pick my fleas, will you?"

When he kicked out his leg, the boy grabbed his foot and broke it off. After this, they went home. There they gave their father the leg. The youngest of the three said to him, "You said that the animal was going to cut us up, but he didn't at all."

Sinaá, after putting the leg in a safe place, said to his sons, "There are wild Indians around here. Be careful or they might kill you. It's better not to go looking for them."

The oldest brother told the youngest to go sleep and see if he could dream about the Indians and find out where they were. The boy slept, but he did not dream at all. Then the oldest went to sleep and saw where the Indians were. The next day they set off and found the Indians fishing with a hook. First the youngest went to see if he could get the hook away from the fishermen.

"Be very careful, or they'll catch you, pull you out, and kill you," said the oldest.

The boy jumped into the water and became a pirarara fish. He swam to the spot where the Indians were casting their line. When he caught the bait with his mouth, he was hooked. Since he did not turn himself back into a person at that moment to cut the line, he was pulled out and killed with blows. Seeing this, the oldest said, "They killed our brother again. That's why I didn't want him to go cut the line."

The boy in the shape of a fish was cut into pieces, fried, and eaten. Only his blood remained on the ground. The oldest became a wasp, gathered a little of the blood, and blew on it until his brother was remade. Then he said to the others, "You wait here while I go over to take their hook away from them."

He plunged into the water, became a piranha, and swam off. When he was being pulled in by the line, he cut it and kept the hook. At home, he asked his youngest brother to show the hook to their father. He went over and said, as he handed him the hook, "You told us that the Indians were going to kill us, but they didn't kill us at all."

II

In the beginning there was no night. It was always day.

Only where Sinaá slept was it dark. This was a closed place, the location of which only he knew. He slept there by himself. One day his sons saw him leave with his hammock and asked him, "Where are you going?"

"To where it's night for me," answered the old man.

"Where's that?"

Sinaá wouldn't tell. He would not tell anyone about it. The youngest son went to sleep to see if he could dream of the place, but he didn't dream at all. The oldest went to sleep and saw the place in his dream. When he woke up, he said to the others, "I saw the night. It's over there. Let's go look for it, so we can have night too. We don't sleep. It's always day for us."

The three of them took off in the direction of their father's night. They found it. The place was very dark.

"Let's hang up our hammocks and go to sleep," one of them said.

And so they did. They hung up their hammocks and slept for a while. Then they went to see their father and said to him, "We know where the night is, we've been sleeping there."

"Be careful when you open the door," said Sinaá, "or everything will get dark."

"That's exactly what we're going to do, because the night is good."

"Don't open it, or everything will get dark," Sinaá repeated.

The boys went and broke into the house; and night darkened everything.

Sinaá, back in his house, lamented, "They broke up the house of the night. They'll all get lost."

In the dark, Sinaá's youngest son got lost. He didn't know where he was any more, and he shouted, "Where did the trail go?"

"Here it is," answered the oldest brother.

They went back to their father and said, "We broke up the night's house. Now it's all right to go to sleep. It's wrong to sleep during the day."

"All right. Let's leave it that way," said Sinaá.

III

One day the sons of Sinaá saw that his back was all eaten up. The youngest asked, "What bit you?"

"The mosquito."

"Where is this mosquito?"

"Around here."

The boy went to tell his brothers. "The mosquito ate up our father's back."

"Go ask him where this mosquito is," said the middle brother.

"I already did, but he won't tell."

"I know where it is. I saw it in a dream," said the oldest of the three. They had a talk and then went to speak with their father. "We like mosquitoes, and we want to tear down their house. We've already seen where it is."

"No, mosquitoes are no good at all. Don't tear down their house. They are very mean."

After talking with their father, the boys went out without his knowledge to tear down the house of the mosquitoes. There were three houses. Their door was just a tiny hole. When they got there, each of the brothers tore one down. Sinaá, who at that hour was sitting outside his house, began to feel the mosquitoes on his back, and he went inside, already knowing that his sons had done what they had set out to do. The youngest son, right where he stood, was bitten all over by the mosquitoes: in the eyes, nose, and all over his body. The others were not bitten. Seeing what had happened to their brother, they said to him, "You really aren't our father's son. That is why the mosquitoes like to bite you."

Back home, the boys began to play at shooting arrows at the leaves in the trees. The leaves that fell were turning into birds. As soon as the birds fell, they were roasted and eaten. All three of them were shooting, but not a single leaf shot by the youngest fell, only those that had been shot by the others.

Sinaá would not teach his sons everything, because he didn't think they were his real sons. He thought that they had something else mixed in. He thought this because he had once seen his wife with an animal. One day, when he was angry, Sinaá sent his wife to the garden by herself, so that a wild Indian would kill her and eat her. He knew that there were Indians around. His wife went off, and the Indians killed her and ate her. Only Sinaá knew how his wife had disappeared. His sons knew nothing of this. They thought that it had been a jaguar or some other animal who had killed their mother. One day they went hunting and the youngest one shot a guan. When the guan fell, he said, "Why do you want to kill me? It wasn't I who killed and ate your mother. It was the Indian who did this."

The boy, frightened, ran to his brothers to tell them what the guan had said. They went home immediately to find out from their father where those Indians were. They asked, "Where are the wild Indians who killed and ate our mother?"

"They're around here some place. But be careful of them, they are very dangerous and might kill you," answered Sinaá.

Leaving their father, the youngest brother went to sleep, to dream about the Indians and find out where they were. He slept for a long time, but dreamed of nothing. Then the oldest went to sleep and dreamed about the Indians and saw where they were. Then they went to talk to their father, saying that they knew where the Indians were who had killed their mother.

The following day they smeared a fragrant dye over their bodies to keep them from being killed and went to find the Indians. They came to the place where they were camping and saw that they had no anus. Everything they ate was vomited afterward. The youngest brother defecated so the Indians would see, saying that was a better way to do it than to pass feces through the mouth. The oldest brother quickly asked the Indians if they would like them to make a hole for them exactly like the one they had. The Indians said they would like that. So the boys set about opening up their rear ends. It was the youngest who started the job, but since he wasn't cutting deep enough, the oldest took over and began to cut more deeply and to slip, without the Indians seeing, a pointed stick into each one of them. He would cut the pike and then slip it in right away. The Indians, their backs all turned, died one after the other. When the boys saw that the Indians realized what they were up to, they ran off, taking three children with them. After they were out of the Indians' reach, they roasted the children, ate a little of their flesh, and took the rest to their grandfather, the jaguar. When they reached home, they gave him the basket of meat. The jaguar swallowed it all right down. But the meat the boys had kept never ended. It replenished itself as they ate. When the meat placed in the jaguar's lair was gone, they took more from the pot that was always full. They ate the meat with the toasted manioc flour that Sinaá's wife made, at his request.

In spite of everything the boys did, Sinaá still didn't believe they were his real sons. Saying that there were no stones for the hearth, he told the three to sit on the ground and hold up the grill. Sinaá thought, If they are not my sons, they will be consumed by the fire. When the grill was removed from on top of the boys, they got up the color of fire. The youngest was almost burned to a crisp. Sinaá sent them out to the water. When they plunged in the river, they sizzled like embers. Sinaá was happy. Now the boys were given names: the oldest became Dubata, the second Panharima, and the youngest Urubiatá. Sinaá gave his sons hammocks and never scolded them again. He taught them many things and said to them, "You are really my sons. No wild animal will ever do you any harm because you are my real sons."

IV

Sinaá did not have a canoe. Only the otter had one. The otter was just like people. Sinaá asked him for a canoe, but he didn't want to give it to him, saying, "You're a great shaman, why don't you make yourself a canoe? There's a lot of wood around here."

Sinaá then asked the otter to show him how to make a canoe, but even that the otter wouldn't do. Sinaá, getting nothing out of him, cut down a dry tree and began to roam about the river with his people. The otter was in front, in his canoe, going downstream too. When the sun was high, the otter stopped to eat fish. He fried the fish with the eagle's fire. Sinaá also stopped to eat fish. He ate it raw because he had no fire. He asked the otter for fire, but the otter wouldn't give it to him and kept repeating that Sinaá was a great shaman and ought to know how to do everything. All the children of Sinaá's group had bellyaches all the time, because of the raw fish they were eating. Even Sinaá's sons were constantly evacuating and feeling sick. Sinaá thought to himself, I may be a great shaman, but I don't know how to make fire or a canoe. Angered by this, he said to his people, "I'm going to take the otter's canoe away from him. I've asked him for it again and again, and he won't give it to me. Now I'll just take it."

At the camp the otter had made, Sinaá asked him for a paddle, and he wouldn't give him that either. Sinaá insisted, saying he wanted only to look at it. Just then he grabbed the paddle and with it struck the otter on the buttocks. When he fell into the water, the otter began to catch piranhas with his teeth and turned into an animal. The paddle he had owned became his tail. From out in the middle of the river he said to Sinaá, "Why did you do this to me?"

"I asked you for a canoe, a paddle, and fire, and you would not give them to me. Now you will always be this way: an animal."

"Well, you don't have fire yet. You go and get it."

But the eagle had already flown down and taken up his fire stones. That left Sinaá with only the otter's canoe and paddle. The otter, still swimming around, asked Sinaá, "Make it so that no animal will eat me or attack me."

That is why the otter is not attacked by fish or any other animal. Sinaá, in possession of the canoe and paddle, went off to see if he could get fire from the eagle. He transformed himself into a dead tapir and lay there, waiting. The first who saw him was the vulture, who told the others. Sinaá, now in the shape of a tapir, stuck one of his legs in the air. The eagle came down and hung his carrying bag, where he kept his fire, on it. But seeing the eyes of the tapir move, he flew off right away, saying that it was a fraud and no tapir. Sinaá then plunged his arm into the earth, poking his hand out a little way off, in the shape of a dry branch. After a while the eagle came back. After breaking a twig off the dry branch (one of Sinaá's fingers), he hung his carrying bag on it. That very moment Sinaá stood up with the carrying bag in his hand. Just before, the eagle, at the vulture's request, had lit the fire with his stone, to roast the tapir. When he saw Sinaá seizing his carrying bag, he said, "You're some shaman, if you can't make fire; without fire, you don't have anything."

"Now I do, because I'm taking yours," answered Sinaá, adding, "I'm a person and you're an animal."

Sinaá said this and then blew on the eagle, causing him to become nothing but an animal, just an eagle. The eagle then wept at the loss of his fire. And this lament turned into his song: *pinhéé,* he still cries today when he flies over burning fires. Before going away once and for all, the eagle who had lost the fire asked Sinaá always to leave him some cooked fish or other meat on the racks outside. To this day, when the Juruna hunt or fish, they leave the remains of those things for the eagles.

V

A long time ago Sinaá and his people did not know about manioc and other plants. All they ate was meal made from wood scrapings. They also ate the *sucuri* snake. This was a very large kind of sucuri that lived under the earth. Sinaá would order them to dig in a certain place till they found the snake, which was pulled up, killed, and then eaten. Once, the Juruna unearthed one of these snakes and sat down on it to rest. When they wanted to get up, they couldn't, they were stuck to it. The sucuri, with all those people on top, dragged itself off and crawled into the river. There, down at the bottom, it swallowed them all. Those who escaped this fate were puzzled and couldn't understand why the sucuri had become so wild. Before it had been tame. Every day the Juruna went to see if the sucuri had returned to its place at the foot of the hill. After some time, it came out of the water

Sucuri, anaconda tails that are worn hanging from the back of the head during certain Xingu rituals

and returned to its dwelling on dry land. Then the people decided to burn it. First they cleared a wide space around it. The sucuri stayed in the middle of the felled trees. When the clearing was very dry, Sinaá ordered them to set fire to the whole thing. The sucuri went jumping around in the fire till at last it died. Then it began to rain. The death of the sucuri left Sinaá's people without their principal food, and now they ate only *jabutis* [turtles] and meal made of tree bark.

Out of the burned sucuri all kinds of plants began to spring up: manioc, potato, yam, corn, pumpkin, pepper, everything was bursting forth from the ashes of the sucuri. When it had all sprouted and grown a little, the rains stopped. The people went to see and were astonished at all that had come forth out of the burned snake. The people could only look; they did not know anything and had no idea whether it was good for anything. Once in a while those who went to look at the field ate a little raw corn or tasted the pepper. Sinaá, one day, went to see too. A little bird appeared and said, "What are you staring at? This is all food, it's good to eat."

Gaviota bird

The bird said that and began to point to the plants, one by one. "This is corn—it's good roasted; this is papaya—you can eat it when it's ripe, very yellow; this is manioc—you can make meal, dough, and a drink with it; this is pepper, it's good with fish; that is potato—you can eat it fried or baked; that's sugarcane, it should be sucked, it's very sweet."

The people didn't know that and had been roasting the sugarcane. They had no idea it was supposed to be sucked. The bird spoke about the other plants: "That's banana; when it gets yellow and the tassel is dry, you can take the bunch down and also cut down the trunk, so another one will grow in its place. That one is yam; it can be cooked, baked, or made into a drink."

The bird, after showing them all of the plants that had grown up out of the ashes of the sucuri, said that it was necessary to make new gardens at the end of the rains. He also taught how to replant each of those things. He taught all this to Sinaá and his people. Then he flew away. The Juruna even today never scare away this bird when he eats their papaya or the other things in their fields, because it was he who taught them how to plant and to harvest.

The Juruna had everything when the waters began to grow with the rains. Sinaá warned his people right away that the water of the rivers would invade and cover the forests, the fields, and the hills. He said, "The rains will not stop until it's all filled up and covered by the waters. We must make a huge canoe to plant inside."

Sinaá made the canoe. A great canoe, with room for lots of people. He filled the front half with earth and planted manioc, corn, potato, and all the other things. The waters got higher and higher. The rivers overflowed and covered the forests. Only the upper parts of the hills were still out of the water. Everything was water. The tapirs, the pigs, all the animals were swimming back and forth, trying to find earth to stand on and drowning in the end. The birds flew across the sky in all directions in search of a place to land but couldn't find one. Sinaá, with part of his people on board the canoe, now steered one way, now another. Others had gone up into the hills. Sinaá, with the produce of his floating garden, which renewed itself every day, went from hill to hill, distributing food to his people. Those who had gone far away, past the nearest hills, got lost and turned into wild people. Sinaá kept urging everybody, "Don't go far. Stay close by. The ones who go too far away will get lost."

When the rains started to diminish, Sinaá tried to reach and reunite the ones who had scattered, but he couldn't do it. They had gotten lost. The ones who didn't believe what he had said had gone down in all directions and strayed away. When the rains finally stopped, Sinaá said, "Now it will dry up, but none of you must go away. Stay near me. Whoever goes out looking for land is going to get lost."

The waters went down a little more each day, and Sinaá, in his boat, was going down with them, steering toward the main valley. He knew where the river was. His people were constantly asking him, "Where is the river?"

"It's still far away."

And the waters kept going down, and Sinaá kept steering in the direction of the river.

"Is it still far away?"

"No. We're getting closer. We'll be there in a little while."

From treetop to treetop, the boat was getting closer and closer to the river, and finally it got there.

"We're here. This is our river," said Sinaá.

The others stayed in the hills. When they saw that it was all dry, they started to come down toward the valley. They didn't come down all at once. Some remained in the hills. The wives of the ones who had gone ahead would bear children and leave the afterbirth on top of banana leaves, along the trail. The ones that came behind, thinking that it was the viscera of game, ate what they found. When they reached the river bank, in waves, one after the other, they said to those already there, "We were hungry and ate the guts you left for us along the trail."

When they found out what they had been eating, they got angry and decided to turn back. They did not want to stay in the company of the others. Sinaá, vexed, let them go, saying that they could go into the forest and become wild people. At the time of the separation, Sinaá gave each group that was leaving a different language and a piece of string, which he went along cutting and handing out.

Sinaá went downriver with the people who had stayed by him. After traveling for many days, he stopped and built his village. The people began to increase. They were many once again. The Juruna at that time ate the flesh of people. They would kill other Indians and eat them. One day Sinaá asked his granddaughter to go get meat next door. It was the flesh of people that they were roasting. The girl went over, but the master of the house didn't want to give it to her. Sinaá sent his granddaughter over to ask again. "Go ask again, and he'll give it to you this time."

The girl went again, and there at the other people's house, she was grabbed and raped. She went back home crying. Sinaá did not ask questions because he already knew what had happened. Sinaá was very upset and told his people that he was leaving. "We can't stay here any longer. We're going to another place."

The other people, when they saw Sinaá getting ready to leave, said to one another, "Let's kill our chief. He's angry and does not want to stay here." When Sinaá began to go downriver, the people went after him, shooting arrows, but the arrows didn't pierce his body or his sons'. Sinaá had shut all their bodies off against arrows. The arrows would strike against them and fall. They did not pierce them. Farther downriver, his sons began to complain about their bruised flesh and asked their father to force the other people to turn back. Sinaá then started to make a thunderous racket by clapping his arms against his sides. This terrified their pursuers, who turned back. Sinaá proceeded downriver. Much later he came to a halt, cleared gardens, built houses, and began to live there.

After some time, the Juruna came down to find him. They were not coming to fight. They wanted to know why their arrows had not pierced his body or those of his sons. When they were told what they wanted to know, they asked Sinaá to make their bodies hard too. Sinaá explained that what they would have to do was abstain from having relations with women. The day after he had made this recommendation, Sinaá, after taking certain precautions, shot each of the Juruna in the chest. Only one died, because he hadn't paid any attention to Sinaá's warning. When he died, he turned into stone and still stands today in the place where he was shot.

Later on Sinaá moved again. He went downriver and founded another village. The Juruna whose bodies had become hardened against arrows went with him.

After a time, the ones who had stayed behind took off again in search of Sinaá. They lived reunited for a long while, till Sinaá again moved farther downriver, this time with only his own group. Not much later, the rest of his people rejoined him. And again they lived all together in a single village.

Still once more Sinaá and his group moved to a new site. This time he went much farther though—near the big water. There, after a while, all the Juruna will come to live, all of Sinaá's people. Sinaá made them each presents of necklaces and anything else they wanted. After a short stay with him, half of the Juruna went back. The other half stayed with Sinaá. The chief cut the hair of all the men who stayed, and with that all of them were transformed into another people, speaking another language. These grew greatly in numbers and became today's caraíbas.

One day, a long time after that, the Juruna showed up in Sinaá's village looking for presents. They asked for what they wanted, but nobody could understand their language any more. As they couldn't make themselves understood, the Juruna went back. On the way home, they passed through another, smaller place, also occupied by people that were the same as those into which the Juruna had transformed themselves. The Juruna landed in their canoes and asked for the tools they needed: knives, machetes, axes, and other things, but they were not understood. Vexed by this, they pushed off in their canoes and from a distance shot arrows at the people who lived there. These responded to the attack by shooting darts by means of another thing that was not a bow. From then on the Juruna began to attack and take by force what they wanted and needed.

Epilogue

Sinaá goes on living there downstream where he had gone. A long time ago a Juruna visited him. Sinaá was married to a huge spider that made dresses. Sinaá was very old, all white, but he became young again each time he took a bath, pulling his skin off over his head like a sack. After Sinaá asked how his people were, he took his guest up to the top of a large rock, from which the Juruna could be seen down below, fishing in their canoes. Finally Sinaá showed the Juruna visitor an enormous forked stick that supported the sky and said, "The day our people die out entirely, I will pull this down, and the sky will collapse, and all people will disappear. That will be the end of everything."

GLOSSARY

The glossary has been indexed for the convenience of the reader. Page numbers will be found in brackets.

ACARÁ, ACARÁ-AÇU *Geophagus, Acara, Astronatus, Cichlasoma,* etc. Spiny-finned fish whose most common species, *G. brasiliensis,* feeds off what it finds at the river bottom. [161]

ACARÍ *Plecostomus, Rhinelepis.* A mailed fish, of which there are more than 260 species in Brazil. [68, 69, 117]

ANHUMA *Palamedea cornuta.* A large herbivorous bird, comparable to both the horned screamer and the turkey, found along the riverbanks and known for its distinctive call, enormous feet, and the horn-like protuberance on its head. [6, 179]

ANITSUCÚ A type of small pot once made by the Trumái. [27]

ANTA *Tapirus americanus.* The largest terrestrial mammal in the Amazon region. Related to the rhinoceros and having a short flexible proboscis, it is an excellent swimmer and is primarily nocturnal. ANTA has been translated throughout as "tapir." [171]

ANUM *Crotophaga ani.* A gregarious black bird of the cuckoo family. [60]

APÍ The penis sheath (male genital ornament), originally used by the Trumái; a string of vegetal fiber wrapped around the penis and sometimes continuing upward to encircle the neck, then returning to its point of departure. [27]

APUTEREÓP A tree; also a fiber pad used during menstruation. [193, 207]

ARAÇARI *Pteroglossus.* A bird of green and yellow plumage, smaller than the toucan (whose predominant color is black), with whom it is frequently grouped. [9]

ARAPAVÁ *Xiphocolaptes, Picolaptes.* A kind of woodpecker which uses its strong tail feathers as support when positioned on a vertical tree trunk in search of insects. [218, 219]

ARARAPIRÁ A small red fish whose eyes have been noted for their open gaze. [67]

ARARAÚNA *Anodorhynchus, Ara.* A large macaw or parrot the color of ox blood. The colloquial use of the name ARARAÚNA may also refer to the blue macaw. [141, 176, 177]

ARAVIRÍ   An armband. [92]

ARIRANHA   *Pteroneura brasiliensis.* The giant river otter of Brazil which attains an over-all length of six feet or more and travels in large boisterous groups through rivers and lagoons. ARIRANHA also refers to the common otter, and whenever the English word "otter" appears in the myths, it is the translation of ARIRANHA. [4, 67]

ARRAIA   *Hipotremados.* A batoid fish (ray, skate, etc.) of one of more than thirty species that have adapted themselves to fresh water in Brazil. [107, 108]

-ARUIÁP   A suffix word that lends to the animal to whose name it is appended the qualities of the supernatural, with an emphasis on those aspects which are monstrous or larger-than-life. [67, 68, 91, 201, 216]

ARUTSÃM   Frog or toad in the Tupi language of the Kamaiurá. [130, 186]

ATSIM-AUM   *Piaya cayana.* A long-tailed, chestnut-colored bird frequently found in the MANIOC gardens. It is commonly called the *alma-de-gato* (cat's soul). In myth this bird is an important PAJÉ. [162]

AUARATSIM   A wolf or wild canine in Kamaiurá. [60–2]

AVIRARÉ   A jew's-harp. [198, 199]

BACURAU   Common name of the birds of the family Caprimulgidae. [9]

BACURAU DE COLEIRA BRANCA   A white-collared BACURAU. [8, 9]

BANZEIRO   A large wave or swell. [106, 107, 110]

BARBADO   A fresh-water fish of the family Siluridae (catfishes). [6]

BEIJU   A thin white bread or pancake made from MANIOC flour. [33, 41, 55, 61, 62, 67, 81, 85, 110, 117, 123, 124, 149, 167, 169, 194, 195, 197, 198, 208, 209]

BEM-TE-VI   Any of the numerous, widely distributed Brazilian birds of the tyrant-flycatcher family, such as the BEM-TE-VI of Amazonia (*Pitangus sulphuratus*); see PITOARRÃ.

BICUDA   *Sphyraena picudilla, barracuda.* The elongated fish, more often found in the sea, which is also commonly known as the needle-fish. [113]

BIGUÁ *Carbo vigna.* A long-necked, large-beaked black cormorant which lives exclusively on fish. [6]

BORRACHUDO *Simulium pertinax.* A variety of buffalo gnat. [6]

BOTOS *Inia geoffrensis.* An aquatic mammal, the white dolphin, found in Amazonian waters. [145]

BRUMA SECA A "dry mist" or ground fog. [6, 8, 10]

BURITI, BURITIZEIRO *Mauritia vinifera.* A palm with an edible fruit from whose shoots a flexible bast is removed and used in the manufacture of rope, hammocks, basketry, and ritual ornaments. [4, 41, 58, 60, 75, 77, 197, 214]

CABAÇA A water dipper or other vessel made from the dried shell of a calabash or gourd; the gourd itself. [60]

CÁGADO-CABEÇA-TORTA *Hydraspis, Hydromedusa, Platemys.* A common turtle whose eggs are eaten by the Xinguanos. [6]

CALANGO *Tropidurus torquatus.* A popular designation for several of the smaller lizards. [63, 65]

CAMIOÁ, CAMIUÁ One of a group of hardwood trees of great importance to the Xingu culture. It is used for the central posts supporting the ridge pole of the house, as the trunk symbolizing the dead individual being commemorated at a KUARUP, and is regarded as the wood from which certain ancestors were made. See also MANUCAIÁ. [58, 174, 213]

CANASTRA See TATU-AÇU. [85]

CANINDÉ *Ara ararauna.* The large blue and yellow macaw or parrot. [92]

CARAÍBAS The name used by Xinguanos for non-Indians (European Brazilians). It may possibly be derived from "Cuiabá," the capital of the Mato Grosso, from which city many of the earliest expeditions into Indian lands originated. [211, 248]

CARATÚ A fish that might be grouped with the "leather fish," or *carataí (Pseudauchenipterus nodosus).* [67, 68, 69]

CARÍ, CARÍCARÍ *Doras, Oxydoras, Hemidoras.* A general term for various species of fish characterized by a highly articulated lateral bone structure. [67, 69, 115, 117]

CASCUDO Any of the mailed catfish of the family Loricariidae. [68]

CATSINIM *Cavia aperea.* Probably the rodent commonly known as the *preá,* which lives on the edge of the forest and is characterized by its distinctive voice (a series of shrill squeaks); in the Kamaiurá language this animal is sometimes called *kanuatsin*. [67–70]

CAUIM   A drink prepared from fermented MANIOC or from BEIJU dissolved in water. [99, 116, 147, 193, 194]

CAXIRI   A drink prepared from fermented MANIOC or sometimes corn. It is usually associated by the Alto-Xingu tribes with the Juruna and Caiabí tribesmen. [37]

CERRADO   Scrublands or clearings with a scattered assortment of small trees and shrubs. The bush as differentiated from the forest. [3, 4, 18]

CERVO   *Hippocamelus* or *Dorcelaphus dichotomus*. The major species of deer in South America. The largest of the Brazilian deer, with branched antlers, frequently found in swamps. [108]

COEME   See COLHEREIRO. [167–70]

COLHEREIRO   *Ajaja ajaja*. The roseate spoonbill, called COEME in Kamaiurá. [6, 8]

CORVINA   *Plagioscion, Pachypops, Pachyurus*. More commonly regarded as an ocean fish, but various species are found in the Amazonian waters. [6, 113]

CUIRÁ   The small CERRADO alligator. [105, 106]

CUIATETÊ   A partridge; see PERDIZ. [63, 64]

CUMANAÚ   The fruit of the MUCANÃ liana. [27]

CUPATSIM   A lover, as well as a term of endearment, in Kamaiurá. [230]

CURICA   *Amazona*. Various species of parrot, some characterized by black heads and yellow markings on each side of the beak. [9]

CURIMATÁ   *Prochilodus*. This fish, also known as *corumbatá,* is very frequently found in Xingu waters. [6, 205]

CURURU   *Bufo marinus*. The marine toad, the most common toad in Brazil. [55, 56]

CURUTÁ   A small Pan flute or pipe which is both the voice of the spirit and the spirit itself; higher-pitched than the JAKUÍ flute but frequently played at the same time and particularly during rituals held around the men's house, or TAPÃIM. [119]

DESSINÍ   A wide strap made of the inner bark of liana vines, once worn by the Trumái women; it encircled the waist and passed between the legs. [27]

DIARRÚ   Also known as the *rei congo* or recongo, a species of fly-catcher. It is a weaverbird often kept as a pet so that the bright yellow feathers of the bird's tail may be plucked periodically and used in making a highly valued headdress worn during the JAKUÍ ritual. [91]

DUCÁ   A type of ONÇA (jaguar, puma, cougar, etc.), the father of the Juruna hero Sinaá. [232]

EMBIRA   Any of various trees yielding a bast fiber used for cordage and net making; the fiber itself. [57, 58, 72–4]

ENEMEÓP   A highly aromatic leaf which has a place in almost all Xingu rituals and is used in witchcraft, as bodily decoration and as a curative medicine. [58, 162]

GENIPAP   *Genipa americana.* The fruit-bearing tree, the fruit itself, and the blue-black juice of the fruit, which is employed as a body paint and used in ritual tattooing. [40, 95, 101, 124, 171, 205, 217, 218]

GRAXAIM   *Canis brasiliensis.* A type of wild dog, usually of a grayish-yellow color with some black markings on the face. [4, 9, 85]

GUARIBA   *Alouatta.* The howler monkey, which lives in bands of about a dozen and feeds on fruits, leaves, and plant shoots. There are five species of howler monkey in Brazil that are also known by the name *bugio.* [99, 101]

HORÍ-HORÍ   A bull-roarer carved from wood in the shape of a particular species of fish and swung above the head by a rope attached to a tall pole. The loud whining noise made by the spinning bull-roarer is the voice of the spirit that the bull-roarer itself represents. [119, 120, 158]

HUCA-HUCA   The Xingu wrestling which is held in the center of the village and is an important part of intertribal ritual and daily life in the dry season. Opponents paint their bodies and begin the match by circling each other uttering *"Huca, huca, huca."* They then drop to their knees and, after slapping hands, lunge forward in a test of strength in which each man tries to force his adversary off balance and down to the ground. When one contestant breaks the other's hold, they separate and begin again. [206]

HYLEAN   *Hiléia* was the name given by the explorer Humboldt to the great botanic region occupying the major part of the Amazon and bordering regions. [3]

IAIÁP   A triangular piece of dried gourd shell lined with fish teeth and used for bloodletting and scarification. The scraper is drawn along the skin in careful geometric patterns. [214]

IAPACANÍ   The name in Kamaiurá for a type of eagle. [179]

IAPÍ-ARUIÁP   A bird, a lesser variety of *rei congo* or flycatcher; see also -ARUIÁP. [91]

IAVURÊ-CUNHÃ   A dwarf spirit of the forest, a wood spirit. [59]

ICÚ   See PAU-DE-LEITE. [72]

IGAPÓ   Periodically inundated parts of riverine woodland; swampland. [8]

IGARANHÃ   A potentially malevolent spirit who has taken the form of a canoe and has the power both to assist and to do great harm to man. [135, 137]

IGARAPÉ   A rivulet or stream between narrow-set banks. [4, 10]

IMURÃ   The name for a type of wood in Kamaiurá. [114]

INHAME   *Colocasia antiquorum.* Any of the various yams and aroids. [27]

IRARA   *Tayra barbara.* A long-tailed, weasel-like animal with short black fur and a grayish head, whose diet is based on eggs, birds, and honey. [76]

IRRACUITÁP   The name given to a type of wood by the Kamaiurá. [114]

ITAPERUM   "Black water" in the language of the Kamaiurá. [202]

ITÓTO   The name given to a certain snake in the Karib language of the Kuikúru. [110]

IVACACAPÉ   The Milky Way. [148]

IVÁT   A mask representing a water spirit; the spirit itself. [158]

IVURAPAPUTÃ   The name of a type of tree in Kamaiurá. [114, 174]

JABIRU, JABURU   *Mycteria mycteria.* Various species of large, white-plumed, black-beaked storks which are notable for the enormous quantity of fish that they consume. [4, 8, 59, 60, 132, 148, 151, 234, 235]

JABUTI *Testudo tabulata*. A fruit-eating land turtle which lives chiefly in the forests. [6, 244]

JACAMIN *Psophia*. A "trumpeter" bird found only in the Mato Grosso and Amazon regions. The JACAMIN has a metallic, blackish-brown color and often forms flocks of over two hundred individuals. [4, 9, 34]

JACARÉ Various species of alligator or cayman. [195]

JACARETINGA *Caiman sclerops*. A small alligator with a white chest that is found in both Brazil and Paraguay. [6]

JACU *Penelope*. Various species of forest birds, also called guans, which are allied to the curassows and characterized by their feather-less throats. [9]

JACUBIM *Cumana, Pipile*. A bird closely allied to the guan and curassow. [4, 91, 92]

JACUNÂUM The fish which swallows the Moon; perhaps the large-mouthed fish (*Crenicichla*) sometimes called the *jacundá*. [161, 162]

JAGUA-TIRICA *Felis pardalis chibigouazou*. A spotted, yellow and black leopard cat which hunts birds, mammals, and small deer and swims extremely well. [104]

JAKUÍ Perhaps the most important spirit for the tribes of the Alto-Xingu; it lives at the bottom of rivers and lagoons and has a village at the Morená. The four-foot-long flutes played by the tribesmen are both the manifestation of JAKUÍ and the spirit itself. The tribes-women are forbidden to see these flutes, as they are a symbol of the malevolent supernatural and the human male sexuality. When the flutes are played and danced to in the village, always in groups of three, the women remain sealed inside their family houses; if they should see the flutes, they would be raped by the tribesmen, who are felt to become spirits themselves while playing the flutes. [111–21, 148, 151]

JAKUIAÉP A mask representing a spirit whose house is at the river bottom; the spirit itself. [158]

JAKUÍ-KATU A small mask carved from wood and regarded as a manifestation or child of JAKUÍ, the "chief" of the spirits. These masks are often carved as husband and wife pairs and are about one quarter the size of the JAKUÍ mask. [158]

JAÓ *Crypturus noctivagus.* A forest bird closely resembling the partridge and quail and known for the four notes of its song. [4, 9, 162]

JARAGUÍ, JARAQUÍ *Prochilodus.* A fish closely allied to others, like the CURIMATÁ, caught in abundance during Xingu dry-season months. [6, 203, 205]

JARARACA *Bothrops jararaca.* A venomous snake of varying shades of greenish coloring marked by dark triangles and arcs lined in yellow. [6]

JATOBÁ, JATOBAZEIRO *Hymenaea courbaril.* A large, straight-trunked tree, also called *jataí*, whose bark was used in the manufacture of canoes by the tribes of the Alto-Xingu until quite recently. Canoes are now carved from the trunks of trees in the fashion of the Juruna tribe. The JATOBÁ also yields a fruit, TERRETÉ, eaten by the Trumái. It is also the name of a river which flows into the Ronuro and then into the Xingu. [27, 106, 135–6, 158]

JAÚ *Páulicea lütkeni.* A catfish found in Xingu waters which frequently weighs as much as fifty pounds and provides a day's food for an entire tribe during the rainy season, when the flooded, murky rivers make it almost impossible to shoot the smaller fish with bow and arrow. [6]

JAVARIÁ *Picidas.* A woodpecker of one of the sixty-five species found in Brazil. [218, 219]

JEQUI A funnel-shaped basketry fish trap made from lianas and used primarily during the rainy season; the traps are secured on flooded forest land and visited every few days. [149]

JIBÓIA *Constrictor constrictor.* A snake found in dry forest regions; it rarely will attack a man, even when provoked, but catches mammals as large as the JAGUA-TIRICA. [6]

JIQUIÁ A type of liana. [58]

JURITI *Leptotila.* These birds combine various characteristics of other species that are commonly identified as both pigeons and doves. The JURITI lack the metallic-colored markings on their wings and are best known for their melancholy song. [232]

KUARÁIUMINHÃ A little cricket. [65]

KUARUP The funeral ritual of the Alto-Xingu; the tree trunks or posts erected in the center of the village which represent the individuals whose death is being commemorated. The funeral, or KUARUP, ritual can be held only when a person of chiefly birth dies. Various tribes are invited to attend the ceremony and take part in a wrestling tournament, which follows a night of mourning, dancing, and singing. The mourners provide food for the visitors, a part of which is presented by adolescent girls who have been in seclusion in their fathers' houses since their first menstrual period. These girls re-enter public tribal life following the KUARUP. [27, 55–8, 66, 208]

LAGARTO   *Lacertilia.* This term refers to various reptiles, but most often to one of the more than 120 species of lizard in Brazil. [6]

MAMAÉ   A spirit in Kamaiurá; spirits of dead individuals who visit various animal villages (birds, snakes, dogs), in a journey which follows physical death. [124, 128–32, 134, 209, 227]

MAMANGABA   Bumblebee. [85]

MANGABEIRA, MANGABA   *Harcornia speciosa.* A savanna tree about fifteen feet tall which is cultivated by the tribes of the Alto-Xingu usually in cleared areas of forest that are former village sites. The tree produces a spherical yellow fruit, the MANGABA, resembling an apricot, which has a soft white pulp and cherry-like flavor. [18, 58, 73]

MANGUARI, MAGUARI   *Enxenura Maguari.* The American stork which is most frequently called the *jabiru-moleque* in Brazil. [4]

MANIOC   *Manihot esculenta.* The staple root crop of the Xingu; most of the domesticated species cultivated contain a high concentration of cyanogenetic glucosides and must be processed to remove the poisonous juice before the tuber may be eaten. See BEIJU, CAUIM, MINGAU. [xi, 18, 24, 26, 33, 40, 41, 44, 47, 61, 62, 67–70, 79, 81, 84, 85, 89, 99, 105, 110, 116, 118, 140, 142, 147, 149, 167–70, 195, 197, 207–9, 228, 240, 243–5]

MANUCAIÁ   One of a group of hardwood trees, known for their height and straight trunks. Its bark and sap are made into drinks by the Indians and given to adolescents in confinement, to encourage them to take on the trees' characteristics. The liquid is vomited up immediately afterward. [207–10]

MARACÁ-ÊPS   Singers; song specialists who inherit or "purchase" the privilege and right to sing over the posts which represent the dead individuals at an Alto-Xingu funeral (KUARUP). The singers are said to become the voices of the dead and the songs serve both to narrate the ritual taking place and to remind the mourners of the possibility of the dead returning to life. [55]

MARACANÃ   A variety of macaw. [9]

MARAUCÁ   A woman's fiber belt in the language of the Kamaiurá. The belt is usually worn about five inches below the waist and is made from the BURITI palm. [207]

MARIMBONDOS   A common collective term for the wasps. Wherever the English word "wasp" appears in the myths, it is the translation of MARIMBONDO.

MARRECÃO   *Alopochen jubatus.* Sometimes called simply the "goose of the forest," it is also closely associated with the Orinoco goose and the rosy-billed duck. [4, 9]

MATRINXÃ   *Brycon brevicaudus.*   A fish renowned for its excellent taste; it is plentiful in Xingu waters during the dry season. [6, 161]

MAVU   A hardwood tree; see MANUCAIÁ. [58]

MAVURAUÁ   A festival song performed in exchange for food (usually MINGAU and boiled or grilled fish); a dance of spirit origin. [151, 185, 222]

MEARATSIM   A spirit associated with the flute spirit JAKUÍ whose village is found at the river bottom; a mask of the spirit. [158, 160]

MINATÁ   *Cocos nucifera,* etc. A coconut. [47]

MINGAU   A liquid made with MANIOC or PEQUI paste, generally the former. The word has been translated throughout as "manioc drink," except when PEQUIS are involved; see MANIOC. [198]

MOINRUCÚ A large snake in the Kamaiurá language. [201]

MOQUÉM   A framework or grill of sticks on which fish or meat is spread for broiling or smoking. The etymology of the word is Tupí (Kamaiurá). [150]

MORENAIÁT   The master, owner, or keeper of the Morená, where various rivers meet to form the Xingu and spirit villages are located. The indigenous concept of ownership or sponsorship closely parallels the Portuguese term *"dono."* Both terms rely on the context for definition and the indigenous term is frequently made ambiguous by the supernatural connotations. [117]

MOREREQUÁT   The term for the male chief in Kamaiurá. There are also female chiefs who traditionally have been tattooed with three small parallel lines on the wrists, shoulders, and thighs. Female chiefs may preside at trading ceremonies and be one of the three tribal chiefs who are given the honor of being seated in the village plaza of the host tribe during the KUARUP festival. [57, 123, 124, 222]

MORRÉT   MANIOC drink in the Tupí language of the Kamaiurá. [147, 195]

MUCANÃ   A liana producing a fruit called CUMANAÚ. [27]

MUÇURANA   *Pseudoboa claelia.* A large blue-black snake found near the water's edge and known for its immunity to the bites of poisonous snakes, which it subdues by constriction and swallows whole. [189]

MUTUCA, MOTUCA   Flies of more than two hundred species in Brazil and characterized as blood-sucking. [60, 77, 78, 193]

MUTUM   *Mitu mitu, Crax fasciolata,* etc. Various forest birds, but usually referring to a large black bird, the size of a turkey, the male of which has red wattles and a red bony crest. A smaller variety, also quite common in the Xingu region, has white wattles and a crest of feathers. The flesh of these birds is dark and is frequently eaten by women during menstruation, when the eating of fish is prohibited. Translated as "curassow" in the myths. [4, 167–9]

NAMIM   The anatomical term for the ear in Kamaiurá and the name of the ear-piercing festival at which adolescent boys have their ears pierced in the center of the village and are then carried into one of the village houses for a lengthy period of seclusion. The sons of chiefs in the Alto-Xingu have their ears pierced with jaguar bones, and the ceremony is performed by men who have been champion wrestlers. Other adolescents have their ears pierced with wood by less prestigious individuals. [98, 149, 150–2]

NHUMIATOTÓ   A flute made of bamboo in Kamaiurá. The Alto-Xingu tribesmen are also accomplished musicians and play flutes that look like Panpipes and are associated with the spirits. The longest flute made is between eight and ten feet long and is played at the funeral, or KUARUP, ceremony. Adolescent girls, recently emerged from house seclusion, dance behind the pairs of flutists, who move around the village circle, briefly entering each house to dance in front of the central hearth. [129, 131, 134, 187, 190]

OÁT   The Kamaiurá word for a dance to the music of flutes. [67]

OCARÍP   The Kamaiurá term for the center of the village; the cleared area of hardened earth around which the traditional circle of large, haystack-shaped, windowless, grass family houses are constructed. The house of the spirit JAKUÍ, where the flutes are stored and the tribesmen spend a large part of their day, is in the center of the village, and usually there are two well-cleared paths (one leading to the river and the other to the uncleared forest) emanating from the village circle. [115]

ONÇA   *Felis onsa.* This word has been translated throughout as "jaguar" and refers to various wildcats, pumas, and cougars that abound in Xingu forests and myth. The spotted jaguar is smaller than its relative the tiger and is considered a chief by the tribesmen. The Alto-Xingu chiefs often wear jaguar-skin crowns, armbands, and belts and, like the other adult male tribesmen, magnificent necklaces of jaguar claws. [4]

PACA   *Coelogenis paca.* A short-legged, tail-less rodent which has a fawn-colored hide and is primarily nocturnal. [4, 61, 63, 95]

PACU   *Prochilodus.* A snapper-like fish which resembles the piranha but is not carnivorous; it comprises nearly thirty species in Brazil. [6, 205]

PAJÉ   Witch doctor, medicine man, shaman. The word is used for a person with supernatural powers, both visionary and magical, and has been translated throughout the myths as "shaman." The presence of a PAJÉ is essential to the well-being of an Alto-Xingu tribe, as all illness and misfortune are due to a source (supernatural or natural) which must be discovered before health or the status quo may be restored. Tribesmen will frequently travel great distances to consult PAJÉS of other tribes who have won favorable reputations. [38]

PAPA-TERRA   *Geophagus, Acara, Astronotus, Cichlasoma,* etc. A fish also known as the ACARÁ. [68]

"PARECÓ PIÁ" "How are you, my son?" in Kamaiurá. The Alto-Xingu tribes do not have expressions equivalent to our "hello," "goodbye," "thank you," or "excuse me." This phrase is used in instances when "how are you" would be appropriate, but more literally means "you have arrived," or "it is you." [177]

PARIÁT A messenger who travels to other villages and invites the Alto-Xingu tribesmen to attend a ceremony or festival being held in the near future. Each PARIÁT is received by a chief of the village he visits and in turn serves as host for that chief (clearing a camp for his tribe, hanging his hammock, offering him food, placing a wooden zoömorphic stool for him in the center of the village) during the intertribal ritual. At the ceremony's completion the PARIÁT and chief exchange gifts of equal value, such as a shell belt for a large clay cooking pot or a toucan-feather headdress for a few gallons of PEQUI body oil. [67–9, 115–17, 178, 206]

PATACAT A round bean, once eaten by the Trumái. [27]

PAU-AMARELO *Euxylophora paraensis*. Yellowwood; the Brazilian boxwood or stinkwood sometimes called VATÁ. [72]

PAU-DE-LEITE A milkwood tree, also called ICÚ. [72, 211]

PECAÚ *Columba*. A type of pigeon. [67]

PEIXE-CACHORRO *Hydroscyon, Hyphorhamphus*. A fish noted for its large exposed teeth; frequently found in Xingu waters but among some of the tribes not eaten by women who are pregnant or nursing a small child. [67, 113, 158, 203]

PEQUEIATSIN A Kamaiurá festival song. [151]

PEQUI *Caryocar*. A tall tree (often fifty feet) cultivated by the Alto-Xingu tribes for the spherical fruits which replace MANIOC as the staple in the first months of the rainy season. Each fruit is about the size of a grapefruit, has a green skin, and contains one to four segments composed of a kidney-shaped seed covered with a yellowish oily pulp. The fruit is eaten both raw and cooked, and the seed and oil are extracted. The seeds are dried and later split, so that the kernels may be eaten at the funeral, or KUARUP, ritual, and the oil is used throughout the year as a body ointment and a base for body paints such as URUCU. [18, 26, 34, 61, 195, 198–200, 211]

PERDIZ *Rhinchotus rufescens*. Only vaguely resembling the European partridge, which is of a different family, this bird has always been regarded as the Brazilian partridge; it is found not in the tropical jungles but on the scrublands and gallery forest. See CUIATETÊ.

PERERECA   *Hyla, Hyella, Phylomedusa,* etc. Various toads frequently found in the trees and throughout the Brazilian forests; they are famous for their voices, which increase before a rain and seem to speak more or less the same number of syllables as their name. [42]

PIAU   *Leporinus.* A fish frequently shot with bow and arrow during the dry season and brought up in the large nets which are pulled across the shallow lagoons; also a man's name frequently inherited from the grandfather's generation—the source of all personal names. [6, 205]

PINDAÍBA   *Xylopia muricata.* A type of EMBIRA or palm-tree fiber used to make rope. [58, 73, 109]

PINTADO   *Pseudoplatystoma.* A large spotted fish, also known as the SURUBI, which reaches a great weight but makes little resistance when caught. [147, 151, 203, 205]

PIRAPUTSIÚ   *Brycon orbignyanus.* Perhaps the reddish fish, also known as *pirapitá,* which is similar to the MATRINXÃ. [203, 205]

PIRARARA   *Phractocephalus hemilopterus.* A large fish with brown and yellow coloring whose flesh is also yellow. [6, 205, 236]

PIRARRUCÚ, PIRARUCÚ   *Arapaima gigas.* Said to be the largest fresh-water fish in the world; it attains a length of fifteen feet and a weight of about five hundred pounds. This enormous fish takes its name from its reddish, URUCU-like coloring—thus *pirá-urucu.* [67]

PIRATINGA   *Brachyplatystoma filamentosum.* A large bronze-colored fish, sometimes called the *piraíba,* and known for its ability to leap so that its entire body is lifted out of the water. [6]

PITOARRÃ   Flycatcher; see BEM-TE-VI. [215]

PIUM   *Simulium.* A variety of gnat, sometimes known as the buffalo gnat, of which there are more than thirty species in Brazil. The bite of this gnat is marked by a tiny spot of blood which frequently remains visible for several days. The exposed bodies of the Alto-Xingu tribesmen are somewhat protected by their thick body paint, but the Indians say that sometimes they are forced to move their villages because of an unbearable number of PIUNS, mosquitoes, and ants. [6]

PORAQUÊ *Gymnoti.* The "electric eel" (*Electrophorus eletricus*), which is occasionally eaten in the Alto-Xingu but is also feared and avoided because of the painful electric shock it may transmit. The PORAQUÊ is particularly a threat during the late dry season when the tribesmen walk the lagoons pulling long fishnets. [6, 69, 158]

PORCO-DO-MATO *Dicotyles.* The two species of wild pig in Brazil, which are also called the *caitatu* and the *queixada* and are hated by the Indians for their destructive raids on MANIOC gardens. Dangerous when provoked and moving in large groups (sometimes as many as one hundred) through the forests, these wild pigs are never eaten or domesticated by the tribes of the Alto-Xingu. [4]

PÚA A fishnet. [111, 153, 158]

ROLINHA *Columbigallina.* Doves of various species characterized by their purplish coloring and blue-gray heads. They are frequently found in the MANIOC gardens which lie between the Alto-Xingu villages and the dense forest surrounding them. [162]

SALAMANTA *Epicrates.* A snake considered by many to be the same as, or very similar to, the reddish-colored JIBÓIA-VERMELHA as well as the rainbow or ringed boa. [96, 189]

SAPÉ *Imperata brasiliensis.* The tall grass (satintail or sape) used for thatching the large haystack-shaped Alto-Xingu houses. The houses are waterproof and last for several years, requiring only minor repairs. [129]

SAPEZAL An area overgrown with SAPÉ grass. [129]

SARACURA *Limnopardalus, Aramides.* A bird sometimes called the *frango-d'agua,* or "water hen," which is always found on river-banks and at the edge of swamplands. [106-8]

SERIEMA *Microdactylus cristatus.* A large, long-legged bird with a striking crest of erect feathers rising from the base of a curved beak which, like its legs, is red in color. A fast runner, rarely seen in flight, the SERIEMA is found on flatlands and feeds on insects, lizards, and snakes. [78]

SERINGUEIRO A rubber hunter, worker, or collector of wild rubber; the individual who extracts the latex from which rubber is made. [36]

SOCÓ *Ardea socoi.* A heron or bittern, also called *joão-grande* and MANGUARI, which spends most of the day hidden in the leaves of trees and becomes active during the night. [6, 148, 151, 158]

SUCURI *Eunectes murinus.* The South American anaconda or water boa, of which the Indians have no fear. It is frequently encountered in small streams or inlets and occasionally will be killed so that its tail may be cut off, dried, and then worn, hanging from the back of the head, by the young men who play and dance the long funeral flutes during the KUARUP ritual. [6, 243–5]

SURUBI *Pseudoplatystoma.* See PINTADO. [6]

TABATINGA A chalk-like powder used in body painting and also a sedimentary clay used in the manufacture of pottery. Alto-Xingu pottery is made exclusively by the Waurá tribesmen and traded to the other tribes in exchange primarily for shell belts and shell necklaces. [26]

TACAPE A club or cudgel once used as a weapon of war throughout the Xingu region but today seen only among the northern tribes such as the Suiá and Txukarramãe. [30]

TAIAÚ A variety of wild pig. [201]

TAMÃI A respectful term of address meaning "grandfather." [92, 174, 207, 216, 220, 221]

TAMEÓP A tree; the vaginal ornament made of its white inner bark, unique to the Alto-Xingu area, and more commonly called the ULURI. [27, 58, 207]

TAPÃIM The men's house or flute house (the home of the spirit JAKUÍ), located in the center of Alto-Xingu villages. Women are forbidden to enter because the flutes which they must never see are hung from the rafters inside. The tribesmen use the TAPÃIM during the day as a gathering place where they may sit talking while making new arrows or fish traps or spirit masks and costumes. Much of the daily body painting and ornamentation is done inside the men's house. [70, 103, 104, 114–16, 119, 148, 158, 160, 161, 190, 198]

TAPEMUCARÉP The term meaning parakeet in Kamaiurá. [100, 101]

TAPERÁ *Progne.* A field swallow of which there are three species in Brazil. The largest of the species is entirely blue and the other two are white-breasted. [161]

TAQUARA, TAQUARI *Panicum sanguinale.* A plant of the grass family; any bamboo, usually of the smaller species, used for making arrow shafts and also flutes. [44, 58, 66, 84, 114]

TASSIT A water root shaped something like an onion. After cooking, it has a yam-like taste. [27]

TATARUIÁP TATU + ARUIÁP—a spirit armadillo of monstrous proportions. [216]

TATORÍ The Kamaiurá term for a creel or wickerwork basket trap for fish. [148]

TATU-AÇU *Priodontes giganteus.* The giant armadillo, also called the *tatu-canastra,* which is now rare. Some of the Alto-Xingu tribes make head ornaments, associated with the JAKUÍ flute spirit, from its claws, but never eat its meat. [124]

TATUPEBA *Euphractus sexcinctus.* The hairy, banded armadillo. [76]

TATU-PEQUENO A small armadillo. [85]

TAUARAUANÃ Both a Kamaiurá festival song and a dance performed by the Trumái are known by this name. The dance, frequently seen in the Xingu, involves a number of men dressed in BURITI-fiber skirts, feather headdresses, and leafy branches which are tied to arms and shoulders. The leaves (see ENEMEÓP) are from a highly aromatic bush that is of great importance in the curing rituals of the tribal shamans. The center of the village plaza is the usual area for tribal dancing, and the music is provided by two men who sing while keeping the rhythm with a rattle and a percussive instrument made from a hollow bamboo tube beaten on the ground. [24, 151]

TAVARÍ The mask of a water spirit; the spirit itself, which is associated with the JAKUÍ flute. [160]

TAVARIRÍ The spirit which dwells within the tree; the name of the tree itself: its characteristics are that it is weak, burns easily, and topples with no difficulty. [207]

TEPARATÊ The coarse MANIOC dough which has been grated and squeezed in the first part of the process required to remove its high content of poisonous cyanogenetic glucosides. [195]

TERRETÉ The fruit of the JATOBÁ tree. [27]

TIMBÓ *Leguminosas.* The common name of a great number of plants and lianas with toxic properties that, when crushed and released in a small stream or pond, stun the fish, causing them to float upon the surface of the water, from which they may easily be collected in great numbers. [9, 41, 123, 149]

TIPITÍ   An elongated cylindrical basket made of palm-tree fiber in which MANIOC pulp is placed and squeezed to remove its poisonous juice. [40]

TIRIVA   *Pyrrhura*. The medium-sized, primarily green parrots which are noted for the scale-like design on their upper breasts. [9]

TRACAJÁ   *Podocnemis cayennensis*. A semi-aquatic, fresh-water turtle, one of six species in the Amazon region, whose eggs are dug out of the sandbars and beaches of the rivers, and boiled and eaten by the tribesmen. [9, 160]

TRAIRÃO   *Hoplias malabaricus*. A scaly fish, similar to the *tríara*, which is found in fast-moving rivers and is known for the excellent taste of its meat. [6]

TSITSICÁ   A type of black bird. [58]

TUAVÍ   The Kamaiurá term for the bast or palm-fiber mats which are used by the Alto-Xingu tribeswomen to squeeze and press out the poisonous juices from grated MANIOC pulp. The mats also act as sieves through which the juices run into large clay pots. The finest MANIOC flour is found in the residue at the bottom of the pots which held the poisonous juice. [128]

TUCANO REAL   *Rhamphastos*. The largest species of toucan, it has a large beak, black plumage, and a maw of white, yellow, or red. It eats mostly fruit and seems more to jump from tree to tree than to fly. The toucan sleeps with its head tucked under a wing and its tail lifted forward and up so that it appears to be sleeping on its back. [9]

TUCUMAIÁ   A drink made with PEQUI. [199]

TUCUNARÉ   *Cichla ocellaris, C. temensis*. A highly valued fish among the Xingu tribes and widely consumed during the dry season. The large black spot on the tail makes it easy to identify, and the flesh has a renowned trout-like taste and relatively few bones. [6, 67, 68, 113, 143, 161, 201, 203, 205]

TUIM   *Psittacula*. A small green parakeet or parrot with a short tail and blue markings. It flies in large flocks and when landing on a tree immediately separates into pairs. [9]

TÚIM   A white EMBIRA fiber; a term for the vaginal ornament or shield traditionally worn by Alto-Xingu women in the Karib language of the Kuikúru. [74]

TUPÃ   A Tupi-language term for thunder. [218–20]

TURUÁ   The manifestation of a forest spirit that lives at the top of the JATOBÁ tree. Hemorrhaging and serious illness are sometimes diagnosed by the Shamans as being caused by this spirit. [158]

UAIACAẼP   A hardwood tree; see MANUCAIÁ. [58]

UANDARÉ   In Juruna, "sun's cudgel," the ringed boa; see also SALAMANTA. [96]

UAPANÍ   A type of eagle in the terminology of the Kamaiurá. [179]

UARAIM   *Canis thous.* The "wild dog" which resembles both the fox and the wolf and lives in the forest in packs which feed on small birds and mammals. [227–31]

UÉGOVI   A tree. [72]

UERAVAPIRUM   *Enxenura maguari.* The Kamaiurá name for the JABIRU MOLEQUE, or American stork. [149]

UETSIMÓ   A fish of a species that can jump very high out of the water. [203]

UGÚVU-CUENGO   *Gypagus papa.* The term for the king vulture (*urubu-rei*) in the Karib language of the Kuikúru. This large, baldheaded bird can be seen circling alone in the skies and is treated with respect by the smaller vultures, who move out of his way if he wishes to eat their carrion and sit waiting until he has finished before continuing themselves. [108, 109]

UIRAPAREÁT   An archer in the Kamaiurá language. [183]

UIRAPẼ   *Thrasaetus harpyia.* The harpy or giant crested eagle which is kept as a pet, in large tepee-like cages, by the Alto-Xingu tribes. It is rare to find more than two in a village, as the eagle's owner must accept the added responsibility of hunting frequently to feed his pet. The tail and wing feathers of the eagle are removed periodically and distributed among the tribesmen to be used on arrows and in headdresses. [177]

ULURI   A small triangular vaginal ornament of whitish bark which is attached to a palm-fiber belt and worn just above the labia by the women of the Alto-Xingu; it is less commonly called the TAMEÓP. [27]

URUÁ   An important spirit dance of the Kamaiurá and other Xingu tribes; the flute played to accompany it. [69, 115, 207, 208]

URUÁGUI   *Catharista atratus brasiliensis.* The term for the common vulture among the Karib-speaking Kuikúru. [108]

URUBU   *Catharista atratus brasiliensis.* The bald, black Brazilian vulture which circles in flocks, high up in the sky, in search of carrion. The two species of a larger vulture, both known as the *urubu-caçador,* are distinguishable from each other by the yellow or red coloring of their heads. [9, 25]

URUBUTSIN   *Gypagus papa.* The term for the king vulture (*urubu-rei*) in the Kamaiurá language; see UGUVU-CUENGO. [89–93]

URUCU   *Bixa orellana.* A dye-yielding shrub which produces pods filled with seeds covered in a pasty red coating that the tribesmen separate from the seeds and repeatedly boil to make an orangish-red substance. This hardens and is used both as a body paint and in the decoration of pottery and spirit masks. Men cover their hair, chests, and backs in intricate geometric patterns, whereas women tend to paint a red stripe across the forehead and lightly cover the rest of their bodies in a shade of URUCU which is slightly more orange than that which the men use. URUCU is also known as *annatto* and is not italicized in the text. [26, 41, 43, 60, 93, 101, 109, 124, 205, 210, 229]

URUMACH   A large pot once made by the Trumái. [27]

VATÁ   See PAU-AMARELO. [72]

XEXEU   *Cassicus cela.* An oriole, frequently called the *japim;* it is a black bird with a brilliant yellow rump which gathers in groups in a single tree and has the ability to mimic other birds. The yellow feathers are used in Alto-Xingu headdresses and in the trading rituals usually held during the rainy season. [89, 91]